About

(David) John James was born in 1923 in Aberavon, Wales. He read philosophy at St David's University College, and after completing an MA in psychology at Cambridge, he joined the Ministry of Defence as a psychologist. As well as writing historical novels, James also worked as a teacher, and later joined the Scientific Civil Service, where he worked on aviation problems. As well as the eight historical novels he published in his lifetime, including the classics *Votan*, which Neil Gaiman calls, 'Probably the best book ever written about the Norse', and *Not for All the Gold in Ireland*, the further adventures of Photinus the Greek, he wrote one work of non-fiction, *The Paladins*, a social history of the RAF up to the outbreak of the Second World War.

James' skilful evocation of the life and myths of Dark Age Europe won him the admiration and friendship of Arthurian and Dark Age Britain scholars and authors John and Caitlín Matthews, who were the natural choice when the unfinished manuscript of *The Fourth Gwenevere* was unearthed after his death in 1993.

About the Editors

Caitlín and John Matthews are the co-authors of, amongst others, *The Encyclopedia of Celtic Wisdom* and *The Western Way: A Practical Guide to the Western Mystery Tradition*. Caitlín is acknowledged as a world authority on Celtic wisdom and the ancestral traditions of Britain, and John has produced nearly a hundred books on the Arthurian legend and related themes.

They live in Oxford.

The Fourth Gwenevere

John James

Jo Fletcher
BOOKS

First published in Great Britain in 2014 by Jo Fletcher Books
This edition published in 2015 by

Jo Fletcher Books
an imprint of
Quercus Publishing Ltd
Carmelite House
50 Victoria Embankment
London EC4Y 0DZ

An Hachette UK company

_____ catalogue record for this book is available
from the British Library

PB ISBN 978 1 84866 413 5
EBOOK ISBN 978 1 84866 414 2

10 9 8 7 6 5 4 3 2 1

Typeset by Ellipsis Digital Limited, Glasgow

Printed and bound in Great Britain by Clays Ltd, St Ives plc

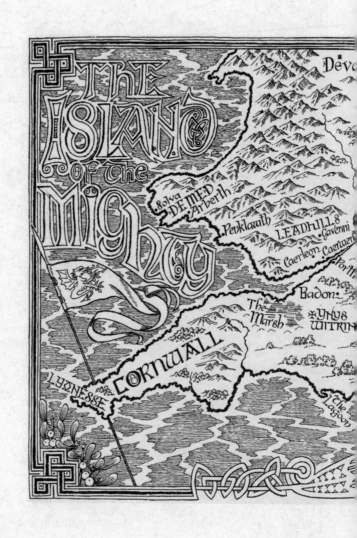

THE ISLAND of the MIGHTY

Dêva

Solva DE MED Arberth

Penklawth   LEADHILL8   Gavenni

Caerleon Caertwen

Porth

Badon

The Marsh   ⊹YNYS WITRIN

CORNWALL

LYONESSE

The Lagoon

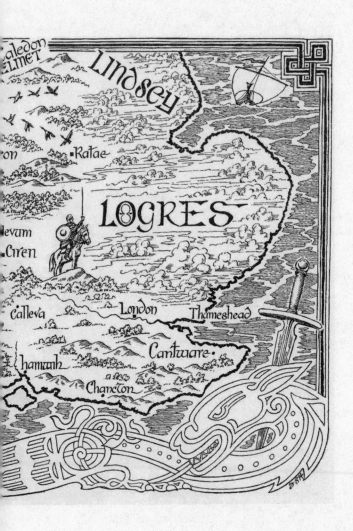

To the memory of John James, 'onlie begetter' of so many
extraordinary stories, including this last, best.

JM & CM

To Rachel, Katy, Penelope, William, Thomas, Lucas and Isabel.
When the two elder girls were little, they were fascinated
by the idea of Gramps writing books. He promised the next
one would be dedicated to them, but he died before it came out.
This is for all his grandchildren.

Helen Jones and David James

As promised.

Gramps

Finding The Fourth Gwenevere

The Dark-Age World of John James

The novels of John James have a deserved and fervent following. Few writers have so successfully re-envisioned the period of history known as 'the Dark Ages' (now called by historians 'the early middle ages') with such clarity. James' ability to plunge wholeheartedly into the myths that thread the Roman and Dark Age period for his material, as well as his sharp wit and undeviating irony, give his work a crisp definition and energy that has inspired the writing of many.

John James was born 30 November 1923 in Aberavon, Wales. After studying philosophy at St David's University, Lampeter, he took an MA in psychology at Selwyn College, Cambridge, becoming a psychologist at the Ministry of Defence. His work included the selection and training of aircrews at RAF Brampton.

He published eight novels, four of which were set in the seventeenth and eighteenth centuries, and the rest in the Roman and Dark-Age eras.

Votan (1966) reveals the travels of the Greek merchant Photinus among the Germanic peoples of Northern Europe, where his exploits cause him to become recognised as Odin.

Not For All the Gold in Ireland (1968) sees the return of Photinus the Greek, who this time travels into Britain and Ireland where he encounters Cú Cuchulainn and the Red Branch Warriors of Ulster.

Men Went to Cattræth (1969) is set in the late fifth century, during the youth of Arthur, and is based upon the earliest British epic poem,

Y Gododdin by Aneirin. This extraordinary novel is narrated by Aneirin himself.

In the *Bridge of Sand* (1976) Juvenal, the satirist, leads Roman troops to conquer Ireland over a magical bridge of sand with the help of Vergilius, the poet Virgil.

His first-person narratives are racily told, salted with wit and irony, capturing the laconic mode of North European understatement as well as the rhetoric of bards and druids. The figures of the wandering Shipman and the poet as carpenter of song and story recur throughout his work, revealing James' well-balanced alter egos.

James was a master of the oblique. He takes much for granted in his readers and makes no concessions to explain or gloss his material. One could say that reading a John James novel is a lot like reading an ancient text. When it was written it needed no glossing; now it does. So deeply is James embedded in the material that he writes as if from the period in which it is set.

For this reason we have provided brief notes, maps and glossaries. To make clear what James explicitly did not would be to denigrate his unique style, so we have refrained from adding anything to the text, except where it was required to make sense or when we felt James would have done so himself.

It can fairly be said that no other writer (with the possible exceptions of Peter Vansittart and Rosemary Sutcliff) has ever penetrated as deeply into the mind and heart – the very bones and sinews – of the Dark Ages. James quite literally works from *within* that world, as if he actually lived there – as, in a certain sense, he did.

We met John James through a mutual interest in the Matter of Britain, as the study of the Arthurian legends are known, at a performance of *The Birth of Merlin*, a play attributed to Willian Rowley and said to contain a few lines by Shakespeare, at the Theatre Clwyd in Wales. Here, as we sat on the grass drinking beer and discussing the Dark Ages, Arthurian literature and Celtic Magic, John revealed to us that he had another novel, nearly completed, called *The Fourth Gwenevere*. We were full of anticipation, but the years rolled on and when John died on 2 October 1993, the book had not appeared.

Fast-forward some nineteen years. We were discussing the merits of John James with our friend Penny Billington, who was as enthusiastic as we were about his work. When the subject of the unfinished novel came up, Penny got really excited and wanted to know what had happened to the manuscript. Unfortunately, we had lost touch with John's widow, and later learned that she had died. We had no way of knowing if he had a family, or if the remains of his work had survived.

But Penny was not to be put off. She set out on a personal quest, hunting though the Internet for any mention of John James' family. Eventually, she found a photograph of John's gravestone, and she called the cemetery to find out if members of his family were maintaining it. They were. From here she tracked down John's children and wrote to them. Did they know about the fate of the manuscript? After a few exchanges, John's children climbed up to the loft where several boxes of their father's effects were stored, and unearthed a collection of dusty 5¼-inch floppy disks – the kind that had been in use twenty years earlier. They were labelled *The Fourth Gwenevere*.

Wildly excited, Penny called us and together we persuaded the family to pack up the disks and take them – by hand – to a company in Cornwall that specialised in retrieving material from these outdated methods of storage. A few weeks later we received a collection of Word-friendly files – and found that what appeared to be more than two-thirds of the book were there.

But the chapters were not numbered, and at first glance there seemed neither rhyme nor reason to their intended sequence.

Determined not to be defeated, we settled down to studying the chapters, reading them over and over until, gradually, they began to make sense. We found that, as well as the main chapters, there were short interludes, written in a different voice to the main narrative. We realised that these were meant to fit between each chapter – but there were not enough of them.

The jigsaw of John James' final work took several months to sort out, but not only did we find ourselves reading one of his finest works, but also one that brought a surprisingly fresh eye to the well-trodden roads of the Arthurian Legends.

In the end we had a sequence that we both felt was what John had intended, and that in fact we had almost an entire manuscript. But we realised that there were some gaps, and with great trepidation, over the next few weeks, we set about filling in those gaps. In fact only a handful of the interludes needed writing, and as both of us had spent years reading and re-reading John's work, we felt we could do justice to the work as a whole.

Finally, we had a complete manuscript, which John's family approved. We prepared a glossary of unfamiliar or Welsh terms and places, as well as a map of the areas where the story takes place. There is also a cast list of characters (compiled by John himself).

Having gone as far as we could with the manuscript, we decided to get in touch with Neil Gaiman, whose championing of John James' earlier work is well known. On hearing that there was a lost final book, he became as excited as we were, and offered to help in any way that he could to promote it and to help find a publisher.

After a couple of publishers turned down the book, Jo Fletcher accepted it and the result is before you now. We hope that John would like what we have done with his last story, which is as close to his intention as we can make it, and that all his many fans will think so too. All of those fans, as well as the ones we hope will discover him for the first time, owe a huge debt, as do we, to Penny Billington, as well as to John's children, for sticking with the project, and to Neil for his inspired words and encouragement.

The Fourth Gwenevere may seem a strange title to anyone not familiar with the Arthurian legends, but the *Welsh Triads* write of Arthur having three previous wives, all called Gwenevere. In this book, the name is merely a title, and the fourth lady of that name becomes the dynastic cement between the British and the Saxons after the Battle of Badon, a marriage that will result, everyone hopes, in the birth of a ruler acceptable to both British and Saxon sides. The outrageousness of John James' suggestion of a Saxon wife for Arthur will certainly set the pigeons flying!

Readers will want to know where in John James' Classical and Dark Ages novels *The Fourth Gwenevere* comes. While there is no immediate relation between the published novels and this book, it stands chronologically after *Men Went to Catraeth* by some thirty-forty years, and it shares many common references with that book. Readers will be pleased to discover that Morvran, the narrator of *The Fourth Gwenevere*, is himself a descendant of Votan – Photinus – the hero of *Votan* and *Not For All the Gold in Ireland*. As James prophesied in *Votan*, 'Every one of these nations that is changed will be led by the sons of Votan ... and they will spread over the whole earth.'

The book is narrated by Morvran map Tegid, who is mentioned in the ancient *Trioedd Ynys Prydein* (*Triads of Britain*) as one of the three survivors of the Battle of Camlann. It is a case of the good, the bad and the ugly, for Morvran as the ugliest, Sandde Angel-Face as the most beautiful, and the saintly Cynwyl all escape unslain, we are told. John's Morvran is a seasoned campaigner, the King of Gwent, one who once ruled in Lindsey until the Heathen forces overran his realm and killed his kindred. Despite his limp and his ugliness, both tokens of that conflict, Morvran has more intelligence than the rest of the British kings put together and it is he who uncovers the truth behind the fall of Arthur, and he who is left to sort out the consequences of a secret plot so byzantine that only the Emperor of Byzantium himself could have set it in motion.

The humour and understatement of the novel juxtaposes the accustomed and sometimes isolationist ways of the British with the barbaric but determined incursions of the Heathen invaders; this theme is drawn out further when Britons meet Continentals on Morvran's quest into Gaul, where the British encounter foreign foodstuffs and very different modes of discourse. The fact that James, in his *dramatis personae*, lists Agaric, Count of Toulouse, and his sister Amanita, will give you some brief glimpse into his Dark-Age world which also sports fairies, ancestors and mythic beings who are as real as the other characters in this book. The conclusion of the novel is a fictional re-depiction of the tenth-century Welsh poem, *Armes Prydein* (*The Prophecy of Britain*) from the *Book of Taliesin*, in which the hopes of the British for the future envision a united, rather than a warring people, who will sweep the Anglo-Saxons from the land.

Reality is sometimes stranger than myth, as this book shows. John James rests in the Strata Florida Abbey cemetery in Ceredigion, Wales, itself a place of mythic moment. At the Reformation, goes the legend, monks fled into Wales with one of Glastonbury's most famous relics and settled at Strata Florida Abbey until the relic, the wooden bowl known as the Nanteos Cup, one of many Grail claimants, passed into the keeping of the Powell family. What John James would have made of that legend is anyone's guess, but we can be sure that his would have been a very down-to-earth exposition, with its own well-reasoned and intricately woven poesis.

Poesis is at the centre of myth, for it is nothing less than the act of transforming and continuing the world. As Diotima points out in Plato's *Symposium*, every bringing forth has its own innate beauty. As you read the last chapter of *The Fourth Gwenevere*, do not forget to add the name of John James to the list of the saints, gods and heroes. In the words of the *Armes Prydein*:

> In wood, in plain, on hill,
> A candle in the dark will go with them.

Caitlín & John Matthews
Oxford, August 2013

Prologue

Fulfilment

The men stood in the rain, under the edge of the wood. They looked down across the bare hillside to the little stream. On the far crest was another wood, perhaps a furrow's length away. They watched that. They looked into the face of the west wind that brought the rain, beating across to them as level as spears.

The men were silent. They stood in their blue cloaks, weather-washed and faded. Their long yellow plaits, uncut, hung down over their shoulders in front. Coloured rags were twisted into their plaits, and feathers, and small bones of birds, of animals, of men. Round their legs, beneath the knee, over their puttees, were bound the tails of oxen. Their faces under their beards were marked with scars, wide but not deep, made in childhood, rubbed with charcoal, that told their kindred.

Under their cloaks, their hands were on the hilts of their swords. For carrying the swords they were born, had lived until now. The men *were* the swords. They were nothing if they were not sword-bearers. They would live till the swords fell from their hands, in the dark rushing of their blood or in the palsy of age: though this last they feared, and were determined, each severally, not to see. The swords were more real than men, lasted longer, were harder to make, to find, to keep. And without the swords, the men were worthless.

The swords lived. Each was a being in itself, known by its powers, by its features, by the jewels in its hilt, by the bronze furniture of its limewood scabbard, by the healing powers of the stones bound above its hilt with charms and runes and the gift of blood, by the peculiar knotting of its own peace strings. Each was known by its name, which would be remembered when the men who for a short time had borne it were dead and rotted and forgotten: 'Jawbreaker', 'Skullcrusher', 'Bonegrinder', 'Crowfeaster', 'Widowmaker', 'Seascourer', 'Landwaster'.

Then there were the men on the opposite hill. They did not come, they were simply there. One moment they had not been, the next it was as if they had been there for ever, since the birth of time, as if the wood had never had any existence except as their shelter. They sat, slight men on great horses, huddled into their cloaks against the snow that would come from the east when the wind turned against them. But now it was the friendly west wind, the wind from the Island of the Blessed, from the place of the dead. Yet even now, as they settled their ironbound helmets more closely on their close-cropped hair, they were glad of the goose grease on their shaven chins, and the comfort of their long moustaches. Under their vermilion cloaks, some bright and new, others old and faded to russet with the weather, over the mail that let the world know they were the Iron Men, their hands were closed on the hilts of their swords.

For these men *were* the swords, they were nothing more than sword-bearers, for carrying the swords they had been born, had lived till now, and bearing the swords they would die, in the rushing of their own hot blood, for none of them could hope to die of old age. The swords were more real than the men who carried them, lasting longer, harder to find and to tame and to handle than even the great horses. And without the swords, without the horses, the men were worthless.

The swords lived. Each was a being in itself, with its man's face at each end of its cross hilts, the head of a sea beast in its pommel and ground deep into its blade. Each had its own name, given with incense and holy oil, that would live when the names of the men who bore it were long forgotten: 'Frost in the Morning', 'Dawn before Harvest', 'Mist Rises Early', 'Bees in the Summer Meadow', 'Butter in a Lordly Dish', and greatest of all, 'Hard is my Judgement', eight times quenched.

Now the men were here on both sides. They waited for noon. Grey cloud covered all the sky, yet they knew it was not yet noon. In the grass the spiders' webs still carried the dew. After a long silence and a stillness like the last frost, they knew that the webs were dry and it was indeed noon, that the years were accomplished and the Treaty fulfilled.

From the western hillside, four men came down the slope. One limped. They carried no swords, nor did they wear helmets, although they were belted as great lords. They were gay in new crimson tunics of southland wool, which shone beneath the worn russet of their cloaks, hanging knee length over their wide trousers of dark blue. It was by such splendour that they were known as heralds on this the day of fulfilment. They came down to the stream that lay between the two hosts, a mere rill that a little maid might step across. They bent forward and each laid his burden on the further bank.

The men on foot stood in the shelter of the eastern wood and counted what was brought. This was the price always paid: three bags of salt and three bags of meal, three jars of wine and three bags of iron nails. These four things, the elements that rule the world of affairs and of war, were laid down to be taken. Then as an extra, five men in working dress came down the slope and laid down a gift for the poor, the carcases of five boars, gutted and scalded hairless, each castrated before slaughter and each lacking the right thigh, the hero's portion.

The woman came out from the eastern wood. She walked smoothly and easily into the open ground, and waited there a moment, plain for all to see in her cloak striped in yellow and blue from collar to hem, her hair coiled about her head. Her eyes were no more blue than her dress, no more blue than the blue of the cornflower or the flax blossoms: her hair was no less yellow than the spun flax or the sea sand in the summer. The four men in new scarlet tunics saw her, through their violet eyes under the brown curls. They turned their backs on her and faced the west.

Now she walked down the slope without a backwards glance. All had been said that would be said. She scattered the webs in the grass, and woke the moles under it. She walked into the face of the west wind that brought with it the scent of the grave flowers and the murmur of ghosts, the west wind into whose teeth no living man would sail. She walked forward towards the line of the Iron Men, on their great horses, towards the line of painted shields, of undrawn swords.

She came at last barefooted on the grass to the little stream that clattered the pebbles before her. She looked down at the price paid for her, at the salt and the meal, at the wine and the iron: and at the extra, the meat. Then she slipped the cloak from her shoulders and, naked, entered the stream. She did not stretch out to step across it, she did not stoop to it, she did not wash her hands or face in it, she stepped into the stream as if it were not there. The water swirled about her ankles, and the pebbles bruised her soles, the ripples washed away the webs. She made two steps and came out on the other side. The messengers waited, their backs to her, and they held out between them a cloak of new crimson wool.

For this was the Treaty, that she herself should come as her own dowry, that she should bring neither clothes nor jewels nor gold nor silver. She brought nothing with her save her own body and her own mind and the skills she had sealed in them. The woman stood there all golden in the grey light: she turned her back towards the west and looked a long time towards the east. She drew the crimson cloak to her shoulders and wrapped it about her body.

Still she stood there, while from the east four men came down the slope. They wore new shirts, bright with the white of bleached flax, and by that they were known as heralds. They had laid aside their swords, but they carried their saxes, knives a cubit long, one edge honed sharp, 'the Cheek Opener', the other blunt and rounded, 'the Wrist Cracker'.

They tossed aside the carcasses and voided on them that no man might eat of the meat. They slit open the bags of meal and scattered it, so that the birds might live till there was man-flesh for them again. They smashed the jars of wine, that the worms might feed well, for in peace or war they were the corpse-eaters. They opened the bags of salt and poured it into the stream, that the boundary might be bitter. Only the iron would they accept, for that would make spears.

On the far western side, the four messengers walked up the slope, the new crimson cloak bright among their worn russet. They came to the line of the Iron Men. A horse was brought, and if the woman were frightened of this strange beast, she did not show it, but let herself be helped to mount. With the messengers, she rode towards the west and was lost.

The men to the east watched the line of the Iron Men fade from the slope. They did not turn to ride away, there was no swift movement. One moment they were there, in russet against the trees, in the red and yellow and sap-green and sea-colour and violet of their shields: then they were not there, the splendid paints of Empery melting into nothing as they had so often done in war. Now there was no reason to stay. The sword-bearers walked into the wood, and were seen no more.

Only the spiders rejoiced, and the moles were again hidden.

Interlude 1: Severn

The woman stood in the bows. She could see the blue hills of the Badon country. To the right were the blue shades of the Apple Land, and to the left the blue haze over the Lead Mountains. Between then lay the Marsh, and even from deck level she could see beyond it the white summit of the Glass Island, Ynys Witrin. The sky was flecked with white clouds hard against the blue, driven before the west wind, hurrying into the sun and the dry lands, where the wheat the colour of her hair would be yielding to the sickle.

She felt the wind on her, but she loosed the scarlet cloak, the robe of Empery. Her gown of yellow silk was the gift of the Bezant Emperor, brought to her and delivered with flowery speeches, first in the Latin she understood and then, more haltingly, in the common language of the people of the wide lands which had been hers at birth, by Theodore the foreign trader. The lace at the edges and the hems and in the girdle against her skin was also of silk, but of her own working. The wind blew the fine fabric hard against her body. She thrust her hands, as the sailors did, into her belt, a band of linen from the Irish sewn with plates, a palm square, of thin gold. Each plate showed a different picture, punched out with a needle point: the landing of Brutus and the Trojans in the Isle of the Mighty which now bore his name, the destruction of the Irish on the banks of the Archan, the treachery of the Heathen on the Night of the Long Knives, the stand of the Three Hundred in the Wood of Cattraeth, the rise of the House of Uther.

In such a ship, she knew, her ancestors had come to the Island, and had reached Vortigern's table where they had showed their strength and their hardness of mind. She stood as they had said her grandmother had stood, in the windy bows, looking ever forward to the long white cloud that always hovers over the land. But ahead now lay not the limitless waves of the story, but only the green lands of the Summer Country.

Then the long ships had come to an empty shore, to a land cleared of its people by the White Death. But around this ship were a host of leather boats to welcome it, like a swarm of so many huge gnats, paddled by as many as twenty men a side, their spear points gleaming where they were stowed upright in their buckets so as not to puncture the sides. The dragon standard of the Great Duke flew from the nearest boat, just ahead. And from the shaft of his pike there dangled also her golden net. There he sat, as a king might sit, ready to leap ashore and claim the land, if it were empty land or the enemy's land, as his. But this was not a king, could never be a king, although he might father kings if the peoples were to call his sons to be kings. If he could father any son. He never had fathered one yet, not even left a peasant girl with an unwelcome relic of his dukedom. And the woman here knew that he never would. Long before she was born, when the Great Race was new to the Island, and this man still a child in the north, Bladulf had gathered together his wives and his witchmen and his doctors and his gods, and they had tied the knot on the leader of the Iron Men, and there would be no king from that line. And she had learned other skills: she could make nets.

She turned. Forty feet astern, Theodore the Greek held his right hand to the steering oar. With scarcely the strength of a finger he controlled this mass of oak and elm and fir, held in rein the power of the flaxen sail drawing with the weight of a hundred bulls. This was a ship fit for a king-burying. And it was his, under his hands. He was a new man, of a kind she had not met before, with black hair and black eyes that both sparkled when he smiled, a man with skin the colour of kid-leather, who spoke to her in Latin with a strange new accent. He smelled of sweetness and of strength at the same time, like the scent of honey in a wolf's mouth.

The woman turned again to look forward, at the ring of boats, at the green hills, now so near. The bosun was there, at his mooring station, his bone whistle around his neck on a thong of walrus hide, his boat-hook ready to fend off, to grapple, to take the depth of the water, to feel the hardness of the rock, the softness of the silt. He looked her straight in the eye, in a way she had not found among the Iron Men in court or in camp or in bed. He murmured,

'Not long now, Lady. Not long now.'

He spoke in her own language, the common tongue, but in a strange dialect, evenly accented, the gutturals lost, the 'rrrs' pushed back into the throat. She looked close at him for the first time. The hair under the dirt and oil was as fair as hers, the eyes though blue were ice blue, not the violet of the Iron Men. His face was marked on the left cheek with four tiny triangles, cut lightly into a boy's skin as manhood taking, and then rubbed with charcoal. That, with the blue shirt, and the two light throwing axes in his belt, told her all.

'Not long now,' he repeated in that strange accent which told her who he was and where he came from, with no other word spoken. And then the forefoot struck sand, shaking her against him. The ship was grounded in the ebbing tide, would be there till the flood. The leather boats near a furlong ahead were motionless on the beach, and the tall men from Mona, in their shirts of yellow and green, were wading out with her chair upon their shoulders. So the woman left the ship and came into the Summer Country.

Chapter 1

Caerwent

I

'Oh, to have her for mine, naked under my hands, in my bed between me and the wall.'

Not wishing to see any disturbance start, there at dinner, I only answered him, 'Strict metre requires one to say, naked as a walrus' tooth. Ask any bard.'

That was what Theodore, son of Ariston the Greek, the Shipman, said in the Hall, in my Hall at Caerwent, under the torches at the end of summer feast. Gwion Lhygadgath, who was Porter to the Kingdom as well as my Huntsman at Court, had cried from the door to all the five corners of the world, that the knife was in the meat and the wine was in the cup, and if there were anyone who was pre-eminent in any art or craft or skill, let him come forward. But we hoped that too many of them would not come, because wine that year was scarce, and the new wine just brought out of the ship was not yet settled from the voyage. This night it was not only Theodore the bringer of wine who had sat down to dine in my Hall, in the Hall of Morvran, the ugliest of the Three Ugly Kings of Britain, an admitted bard, King of Gwent and Prefect of Caerwent, ruler of all men from Ross to Avan. As indeed I still am. I bear the great sword, Bees in the Summer Meadow. This night, Arthur, Great Duke of Peace and War, bearer of the sword Caliburn, Hard is my Judgement, had sat down to dine too.

This was to be the last time in that year that the Great Duke graced us with his presence. I had fed him, and his Great Duchess, and their household, and their grooms, and their craftsmen, and her spinners of flax and stuffers of lace cushions, and their horses and their dogs and their mules' widows' brothers-in-law, for thirty days of which ten were his due from the King of Gwent and twenty from the Prefect of Caerwent, the greatest port and the richest city of all the Island, now that London, the flower of cities, was so set about with the Heathen that its glory was almost gone. The Great Duke always came at this time of year to claim graciously what was his due and to eat our harvest before it was out of the fields, almost. But what I had, I gave freely.

Mind you, the Great Duke was willing to share with us what he had of his own production. He and his household had been hunting the day before in the woods beyond Usk, and they had killed (besides three wolves and a pole cat which even my own household would not eat unless under a vow to mortify the fat) two bears, seventeen hares, five stags and a tame boar, wild ones not being available and the owner not consulted. The Great Duchess herself had contributed four adders and three slow-worms, although how she had found them or killed them no one was able to say: eels, now, they would have been a different matter, although in spite of spending almost all her time crocheting nets she never caught any. Nor paid attention to the dogs, although she greatly objected to cats which do no harm but eat the mice and spiders and moles. And of all this Arthur was graciously pleased to receive the right thigh, the hero's portion, as it was commonly said he deserved.

Tomorrow he would begin to leave us, passing over the Severn into the City and Kingdom of Badon. Bedwyr was King and Prefect of Badon: he carried the sword Frost in the Morning. He was now Lord over the Apple Lands and the Leaden Hills, and the marshes around the Glass Island, all in Lawnslot's place. He had come here to see Arthur safe over the river into his own lands the next day. There were a gaggle of minor kings, like Gormant, one of the two Kings of the Cornish, and Kaw the senile, gnashing his tooth, as well as Melvas, King-Abbot of the Glass Island, all come to welcome him and to claim the due of friendship in a tangible, and even edible, form. Melvas was the only priest who would willingly come under the same roof as the

Great Duke, Protector of the Churches and Saviour of the Faithful to Christ. Even Tatharn our own parish saint, who had his Lhan beneath the east wall of our city and who would seldom miss a chance of increasing his sins and thus his opportunities for repentance by dining on forbidden fruits, would not have been there if Melvas had not persuaded him to come to say Grace.

The other kings sat at the head of the table with Arthur and Melvas. As Host, I sat at the furthest remove, at the foot of the lowest table, and Theodore with me. We had business to do, which the other kings and the duke did not need to know about. Theodore had brought in his ship the wine we drank that night. I had paid for it myself, in bronze taken from statue bases, or from the ties between stones in the old houses of the Romans. Theodore shivered in a draught from the opened door. Gwion leaned over me.

I told the Shipman, 'Be silent and hear how hardly Gwent is governed.'

Theodore was never entirely silent in any language. He talked often and to purpose, usually in Latin, as he did now, although he spoke our Language of the Angels from our youth together, and Gaulish, and also from his cradle the sacred tongue, Greek, in which Christ spoke his ten great commandments at the commencement of the world.

Gwion whispered over my shoulder in the language of this Island, 'They are coming closer. They seem to be casting about between wall and water to come at Camelot from the western side.'

'Take them,' I ordered. 'You will need ten men. Use nets. Esau will handle them.'

Esau Penpledren was my Cook of State, very good with snares and bald as a coot.

I turned back to Theodore. 'Do you remember when you were in the Island before? All that summer when your father went trading into Caledon?'

'I cannot forget. We were all younger then, you were not a king, and Arthur was just beginning to ride and fight.'

The first minstrel was standing up, an apprentice bard called Kian coming on for an opener with his prize piece, the story of how Macsen Wledig wore his crown at Segont, and called all the young men of the

Island to go with him into Gaul, to kill the Ravenn Emperor and reign in Eidal. This in one version or other was always Arthur's favourite song. Gildas the Pre-eminent Bard sat waiting for his own time, which he could choose himself, being careful to come on when men were not still too sober, nor yet too drunk. Gildas sat in a chair, and I also had a chair with back and arms, as we were the only admitted bards in the Hall: everyone else, even Arthur, sat on stools or benches, or some at the lowest table on bales of hay.

'No, I was not a king then, only a king's son out of the Eagle's Nest, and a beginning bard, persuaded to ride as a warrior in Uther's household. And after that the men of Lindsey called me to be their king, and when Lindsey fell and my knee was smashed and my face burnt, the men of Gwent called me to be King here in Caerwent. Let us not speak of that later time and that war. Let us only remember when you rode at my side, to see, you said, what the land was like. And we hunted the Irish raiders from Ross down to Merlin's Town, and destroyed them, and we put up a pillar there and carved on it in Latin "Here Theodore killed Irish". Why, in all the years since have you never come back yourself but only sent underlings?'

It was a long time indeed, but not so long as to account for those grey strands in his black hair, oil it as he might, or make him that had been a fat young warrior into a slender merchant, or a tenor so husky who had been a decent descant, or so pale a face that had once been ruddy.

'I did not keep tally of the years that passed. I always had other business beyond the Middle Sea, into Rome land, and into Ravenn, and even further into Bezant and Damask to talk with my brothers. But this year, I thought I would go into the misty Island, and see how the trade is going. How is it going?'

'Bad,' I told him. The minstrel was singing now how Maxen gave to the young men booty of gold and jewels and shining swords. Gwenki my Smith Royal in as loud a voice was telling Taberon my page the secrets of making a sword, and had just said, 'You must heat the billet to white in the charcoal, and on the bed of coals hammer it out into twice the length, and double itself on itself and twist it seven turns as a plait and hammer that flat and then quench it in the blood of birds, wrens preferred as the highest flier, to make the heavy iron as light as a bird.' Taberon at his age had no sword: he was my sister Creulon's youngest son, son also of Ceredig who came back alive from Cattraeth, and who wore his father's shirt of double gold hoops on black, not my black and red.

I went on, 'In most years we have finished the labour of breaking down the walls and gathering the bronze ties before the oats are ripe for cutting, but this year we were hardly ready for the ship.'

I beckoned for Taberon, that was fostered to me to learn the skills of a judge and a king, to pour us wine. Other men in the Hall had their wine poured by their wives, even their Queens, or by the wives of my High Officers of Court. Arthur waited for his wine till the Great Duchess saw fit to lend us her presence and pour the wine for her Lord. But Taberon could spare little time to pour wine for me, who had a Queen no longer, or time either for learning the craft of a smith or of any other decent craftsman, since he was always too busy carving a yew-wood spoon to be given as a love token to some girl he had not yet met, nor even heard of, and who might be anywhere in the Island, save in Logres.

'Work harder,' Theodore urged. 'Dig deep, break up the stone and find it. Bronze is not only in the buildings, the men of old came here to find it in the earth, and mostly in Cornwall. The island is full of the metal, here for the finding.'

'There is none left in all the Island of the Mighty,' I assured him. 'Even in Caerwent, this great city, there is scarcely a stone house left standing, except this Hall in which we sit where the High Rome-King sat for his crown-wearing. Very primitive were these Romans who had not learned the skills of civilised men to seek among the stones of the hillside the pieces left from the beginning of the world that will fit together neatly without the need of bronze ties or of mortar. For the Romans, lacking patience, would take stones of any old shape or size and carve them by force till they were square, they not understanding any other shape, and these they must therefore fasten together with clamps of bronze. Now we have broken down all these walls except for those around the cities, and given the bronze to you for wine and sword-blades.'

Mabon son of Modron, who was my eldest sister's son and was therefore my heir and held Caerwent for me when I was not there, whispered from behind my chair, 'They are gone down the wall. Gwion led them, and Leision, Bedwyr's huntsman, went also with Esau, Bedwyr's foster-brother.'

Theodore asked, 'Would you destroy this fine basilica, just to get drunk?'

'You want bronze, we want wine. Cider is the drink of men, and mead the drink of angels, but wine is the drink of heroes. Without wine, who can make war?'

'Or without sword-blades,' Mabon joined in.

'And when we pull this one down,' said Keinakh the son of Diweirdeb, a man from Kwmtwrkh Ukha, and therefore of taste and discernment, 'we will build a finer one, with timbers jointed true and filled in between with basket-work and cow dung well mixed with clay, properly thatched with reeds from Lhangors, and the cattle at one end and the men at the other to keep warm without all this nonsense of charcoal and braziers.' Keinakh was my Carpenter of State and professionally grudged the charcoal-burners every twig for their kilns.

'Who carries in the cow dung?' I asked. 'Hennin the son of Broga?'

And everybody laughed, because this Hennin was a man out of Cornwall, who ran here and there to do business for Gormant the King and for Gormant's sister's son Constant. Hennin carried Butter in a Lordly Dish, quenched the fourth time in serpents' blood to give subtlety, a sword that Tristam had given to his father: this possession gave him ideas above his station, which was one of gathering the wild berries of the woods and seething them in the cream of his half-fed cows. He had started life as a thief in a small way of business, a bywayman one might say, or a toepad. He constantly came to Court for some favour or other, or to ask Arthur to use his influence to get him a small post of profit under a king.

Hennin sat this night with the bosun out of Theodore's ship, one we had not seen before, but then we rarely saw any of Theodore's men twice, except for his skipper Lucan, who had not come on this voyage, his master being present. Theodore's men seemed always to be much concerned about the small hard cakes the skipper would dole out to them at the end of a day, and it seemed that Hennin was always trying to beg a taste, although they were denied to kings, and even to Arthur. I did not give much for his chances.

The particular man whom Hennin had chosen to sit by wore a light blue shirt, and blue clan scars on his face. We thought him to be a Frank. I had embraced him, and Gwion had watched him with care, and we knew that under the shirt he wore the bronze wristguards which are the fashion among the Kings of Armorig. There were five chains under his shirt, which might be of gold, otherwise why would he hide them, although they might be of bronze which is as costly as gold, commoner but more useful. And he wore a couple of brooches, the one now in view on his outer shirt being certainly of gold and showing the bees that are the sign of the King of the Franks. But he showed no other signs of wealth, and would not have been noticed in a crowd except for his scars and his habitual scowl. When he was in the ship, he wore two axes tucked into his belt, and with the blue shirt that told us much. Yet we ourselves were not inquisitive, only exchanging among ourselves such pieces of information as might be useful. And we forgot him and Hennin when Tatharn insisted,

'But first you must build a church for me as big as this Hall, as big as they have in Rome, a great Basilica to hold a vast throng at Easter First Mass, perhaps fifty or more beyond the Iconostasis.'

'Perhaps, perhaps,' I soothed him. Priests are always demanding something, and even Paradise cannot be worth the strain of satisfying them all the time. 'We will build you a church sometime, outside the walls of this town, in your Lhan, by the hands of good and virtuous men, craftsman like Keinakh, and a pity it is that he is himself without virtue, and will therefore be available only for building my Hall.'

'The Romans,' Tatharn told us, 'built only by the power and the skill of the evil magician Vergilius, who ruled their dead from his tomb, and not being able to come out of it, spanned the sea between death and life with a bridge of ice.'

Outside, beyond the wall, an owl hooted. That would be Gwion, who had already left us. I motioned to Taberon, who went out.

Tatharn went on with his tale, 'But when Vergilius met with the Blessed Paul' – and this was from a sermon that I had heard seventeen times before, one of Tatharn's better efforts, and one to make all hearers faint from its beauty, or at least to fall into a calm sleep – 'the Saint smote him with a sprig of broom, a plant that all wicked things detest. Then the Rome-King staggered on his throne, and died, and Vergilius was cast down for ever into his cave under the earth. Wherefore we always plant the broom on the right side of the house door, and the rowan on the left, depending of course—'

'Yes, yes, Tatharn,' I soothed him, 'we can hear these holy words on Sunday, but not now.' Outside an owl hooted, a tawny owl this time, not a barn owl as before. Then there was a confusion of other animal voices, some of the night, some of the day. By the directions, my gallant men, brave and sturdy as they were, were scattered and in confusion but dealing great strokes against the Heathen, or against each other, as was likely, because though courageous and strong they were also all utterly, utterly stupid. It was almost time to limp out and show them that I was not called Morvran the Ugly for nothing. Ugly in face, ugly in temper, I hoped they said.

Feeling me stir, Theodore mistook my intention and offered, 'Shall we drink? To peace?'

Across the table, a man asked, 'What is peace?'

This was Korlam son of Kroen, my Saddler of Ceremony. Keinakh answered, 'War is when kings call out their Households and ride out mailed against their enemies.'

'Peace,' Korlam answered his own question, 'is when enmities are made, are grown, are cherished. Peace is when no armies march on the border, and no kings ride out behind the duke. Peace is when the savages, in small bands, the feathers in their hair and the ox-tails tied beneath the knee, come through the morning mist to the lonely farm-house, and throw their spears through the man of the house, when he comes from the door in the first half-light to empty the pail and uncover the washtub and kindle the first fire. And then they come whooping and screaming to break through the unbarred door and cut down the young men with the sleep in their eyes and the ale in their heads and their sword hands empty. Then they carry off the women and the children and the cattle and the pigs and the iron tools and the grain back into their own country as they call it and I am sorry to hear you call it so too, a land they took from us, a land where neither the bell of the hermit or the words of the Mass are ever heard and our tongue of the angels is no more spoken. That is peace: all other time is war.'

Korlam and Tatharn wept together as was their frequent custom, mingling their tears with their suet pudding. But I stood and told Theodore, 'Come and see Peace.'

II

We went quietly from the Hall, so that nobody would take any notice, for men came and went frequently to visit the stables or to fight or for any other necessary purpose. But Korlam went to sit at the same table as Hennin. We walked under the walls of Caerwent to the house of thatch and timber where I slept when I was in the city. Here Taberon sat on my bed, holding across his knees Bees in the Summer Meadow, snug in her scabbard with her riding strings still tied but slackly. I sat down a moment on a high chair with arms, my right as a bard as well as a king. I rested a little because in the dampness of the seaside my knee ached which had been carved open by the Heathen when we lost Lindsey. It makes me less agile in fighting, not easily able to turn sharply, but otherwise I am well. Then I stripped off my shirt of state, hooped in black and red from neck to knee. Theodore was surprised to see that under it I already wore my mail. Keinakh brought me a helmet, a brow ring of beaten bronze and a crown cross of bronze over it, to strengthen the cap of boiled bulls' hide, padded with sheep's wool in the lining. Bards talk a lot of nonsense about mail. Armour is boiled leather, stiff as a board, to save bones from breaking and skin from bruising: metal is added only to make sure that the leather is not torn.

Taberon still held the sword. He was as near as we could find at short notice to a virgin to do the job, although he had come back from the summer at the havod in the hills tending the sheep with a great deal of respect for a lad who claimed that he had once, fleetingly, seen a girl all naked among the trees, not even her shoes on. I told Taberon,

'Once you have seen one, you've seen most of them. Just keep your eyes open, and learn to live as we all do, in the faint hopes of someday seeing something different.'

Taberon was silent as he held the sword. On the bed beside him lay the yew wood spoon he had been carving all last winter and this summer, now finished and polished to show the grain. I stood. The lad untied the riding strings of Bees in the Summer Meadow. He halfdrew the blade so that I could nick my finger on her and give her a taste of blood, lest too often disappointed she might turn in my hand and tear me. Kneeling, we honoured the blade. Then I settled her home, and hung the scabbard through my belt loop. So we went out and up the steps on to the wall.

The crowd were gathered on one of the wide platforms on the south wall, looking over to the water. On these platforms the Romans had placed their magic mirrors which could destroy ships a mile out at sea. If any of our magicians could make glass we could again have such mirrors. These mirrors were called, in Latin, catapults.

The riverside was dark. To the west were the lights of Camelot: everyone there was preparing to move out the next day and making a lot of noise doing it. Almost enough to drown the noise my lads were making out there in the marsh. It was only because Camelot was in such confusion and Arthur's Hall Ehangwen stripped down that the Great Duke had sunk so far as to dine in my Hall. But even when he dined in Ehangwen I sent the food.

Suddenly the noise in the marsh stopped. There was a long loud whistle, a human sound, not the noise of a strange beast out of place and out of season. We ran round on the wall-top to where a wooden ladder led down into Tatharn's Lhan. There was enough torchlight now to see that the lads going out had not done much good to his bean rows, although he was so fond of real food that his anger when it came would be more feigned than real. My men came back to me. Gwion was the last up. He held a net with two heads in it. Leision, son of Gwroldeb, Bedwyr's huntsman, brought a torch. Gwion rolled the heads out.

'Look at that,' I told Theodore. 'It is the fruit of peace. This one is the elder. Clan scars on his left cheek. Gamecock feathers in his pigtail, so I would say a Jute and on the warpath. Any ox-tails?'

Esau told us, 'Two below the left knee, five on the right.'

'They use them to count their kills,' I told the Greek. 'On the right calf for men, the left for women, or children.'

'This one was a warrior,' said Gwion. 'Red and blue face-paint, one gold ear-ring, Frankish work. Yes, I would say he was a Jute.'

'Thank you for the confirmation. What about the other one?' Gwion held up the net for me to look. I pointed out to Theodore,

'Much younger, red and yellow face paint, mostly yellow, two plaits with small eagles' feathers, one each side, clan marks on both cheeks, no ear-rings, silver nose-ring. So probably from Bamburgh, but not important, no experience, simply an escort, a learner. Any ox-tails?'

'One,' Leision told us, 'left knee.'

'The old one,' Gwion told me. 'I brought his mail in: the other didn't have any, only a helmet, rather shabby. But there are two swords out there somewhere. Look for them in the daylight, to be exorcised. I marked the place.'

I summed up, 'One green lad from the north, and one minor chieftain from among the Cantware. I wanted them alive.'

'There was no dealing with them,' Esau explained. 'They were fighting mad, as soon as they knew we were there. They preferred a fighting death to being captured. Our lads need more experience in hunting by night.'

'See to it,' I told Mabon.

Then to Theodore I explained, 'We have known for a fortnight that they were coming. They began from the savage settlement at Thameshead – nothing moves out of there we do not know about. At first they were making north and west. They slept by day, travelled by night. They thought they would not be noticed. But we tracked them night by night, by the mess they made when they slept, when they defecated and so on. By the direction we thought they might be going against Mordred, and we warned him.' Theodore raised his eyebrows, but made no comment. 'He sent Lawnslot with a batch of the cherry-and-whites, and he couldn't find them. They had turned west and south and crossed the Severn. But a passing Fairy had seen them swimming the river, and followed them – you know how inquisitive Fairies are, and not always reliable or very intelligent. He met a farmer, and let him know. We've tracked them ever since.'

'What were they doing?'

'Oh, coming to kill Arthur. We get two or three parties like this every year. At least.'

'You'll tell him now or wait till the morning?'

'Oh, no, we don't worry him with trifles like this. I'll tell Tatharn that he'll have to reconsecrate two swords at tomorrow's Mass. Nobody else need know. You'll have noticed that all those who went over were my lads, except Leision, and all the others on the wall were mine. We didn't let anyone know in Arthur's Household. It's getting chilly now. Let's go back to the Hall.'

We took Bees in the Summer Meadow back to my house, and hung her up with my mail shirt. I put on the red and black again. We went back to our seats in the Hall.

III

It seemed that no one had seen us go. The bard of the moment, another of Gildas' apprentices, was singing the story of the Flood and the rescue of Gwydhno Garanhir who steered the Ark in the hunt for the immortal whale which swallowed Jonah. And suddenly, he stopped.

For the first time that evening, the Great Duke's wife, the Gwenevere, was coming into the Hall, to pour wine for the Great Duke. With her came her bevy of handmaidens, good Cardi girls, each a great Lord's daughter in a silken blouse and at least five petticoats to walk around her to the head of the Hall. Their usual leader and mischief-maker was Tegai, Emlyn's daughter, a flighty piece if ever I saw one. The Lady did not always come in, and Arthur either went thirsty or begged wine from someone else's wife. Often she stayed in her own bower in Camelot, where she spent her days making lace and crocheting nets as was the custom among her people, and ate some strange dish of eggs poached in soup which was her favourite, mopping it with wheat bread when she could find it. Or so the Cardi girls told us. But tonight she came into the Hall, having robed in Mabon's house, by leave of Mabon's wife who of course sat in the Hall by her husband to pour him his wine and to quarrel with him over the better cuts of meat, for she was a hearty trencherwoman. It is a Heathen custom that the women do not eat with the men, and to be abhorred as unsocial.

This night she came and poured the wine for Arthur, and for Melvas, and for Bedwyr. She would not bother with us so far down the table. I was only Morvran the Ugly, whose food she ate here, the man with the scarred face that everyone forgot, that rode at Arthur's left hand and did the business of the army. If there was to be an attack by the savages, it was I who would know who was the nearest king to that place, and who else could be brought up in time, how many men they had, how soon they could be in the line, which way they could fall back if the attack was too strong, where we could find food for them, all the insignificant details of war that were not worth troubling a Great Duke with and with which he does not trouble himself.

Nor, really, did he trouble himself with who would pour the wine for him, being only concerned with how well it tasted that he should not be disgraced before his guests who would later serve the same wine to him, wine that I had bargained for with Theodore and shared out to the other kings, who could not be bothered with details like this. Arthur did not even look up to see her come, just went on talking, although everyone else was silent to look at her. Except for Taberon, who said, not softly, 'Oh, but she is beautiful. Is she not *so* beautiful?'

It was then that Theodore said, very softly, 'Oh, that she were mine to possess, naked under my hands, in my bed between me and the wall.' And being a man of poetic training, I did not rebuke him for fear of being overheard except to tell him the proper simile of the walrus' tooth.

Then it was Taberon who acted. As the Great Duchess poured the wine for the King-Abbot Melvas, the boy went forward and dropped on one knee before her. He reached forward and held out to her his greatest treasure, for he had put so much work into it. He gave to her his yew-wood spoon, his love spoon. And she accepted it.

The Gwenevere was dressed as always when we saw her in public, which was seldom, except at the great crown-wearings of Easter and Christmas. She wore a gown of one piece in white, with a coronet of gold, and a belt of gold lace, and shoes of gilded leather, and cloth of gold hemmed her robe. And over her shoulders as a shawl she wore a network of thread of gold wire mixed with linen she had crocheted herself, close-meshed enough to catch dragonflies and splendid in the torchlight.

Very few men had ever heard her speak, either in Latin or in the language of the Angels, which we commonly use, and it was uncertain whether she understood the latter: certainly she could not speak it, for the Heathen cannot, their tongues being too short. And like everything that is rare and beautiful and kept away from public gaze, she was looked at and lusted after and even loved by every man. Not because she was beautiful, but because she was guarded and forbidden to us. But no one, either from courtesy or from fear of the Great Duke, had ever dared to speak to her or to take notice of her in any personal way. Except, now, Taberon.

Upon this evening, looking into the Hall as if for the first time, with its walls painted by the Romans with strange beasts on the plaster, and the haze of smoke hanging a fathom above our heads, she turned from the Great Duke's seat, and walked down the way between the tables. She walked to us, to Theodore and myself, and poured us wine. And without a word she returned to her place by the Great Duke.

As is proper I did not look at her. I sat and felt that my face was flaming red with pleasure, and that all the scars would show that gave me the name of Morvran the Ugly, scars from the knife and the boot and the torch, scars that her relatives had given me that day in Lindsey, when I had rolled on the ground with my knee smashed, and Gwion had carried me out of the fight, while Arthur kept our backs.

But Theodore sat up in his tunic of silk and his short cloak, and looked at her: all in a royal scarlet as if he were a Ravenn man, and his black hair well oiled and more gold on him than I had ever seen on a man before unless he were a king bearing the whole kingdom's treasure on him for safety, and smelling of a sweet perfume. Theodore breathed in my ear, 'Oh, but she *is* beautiful. They did not tell us that she was *so* beautiful.'

'If you like that colouring,' I told him. 'But it is a matter of taste, and one not usually expressed, for that paleness is not seen as an asset: too many of her kinsmen show it. Yes, her hair is fair as where the branch was split in the spring and now it is August, and her eyes are the light blue of the thick ice hard enough to split a ship. We have seen those colours too often across the sparks of sword blows, over the linden shields. And her voice may well be beautiful, but who has heard it?'

'Not beautiful?' Theodore wondered.

'Oh, if it were beauty you wanted, then it was the Second Gwenevere you ought to have come to see. For her hair was the colour of polished gold in the firelight, and it had the feel of dancing sunshine off the west water. Her eyes were the colour of the sky at midday in summer when you look straight up to the zenith, or of fine woven lambs' wool dyed in woad when it moves on the loved one's sleeve, or of violets in the shady nooks of the wood after the April rain. And her voice was like the song of all the harps of the earth, and she spoke with the wisdom of the Saints, and she made verses that Ysbwriel map Lhwkh the first Pre-eminent Bard would have been proud of, if they had been more decent. She was made of the broom and the primrose and the meadowsweet, and she walked like the breezes over the fields of ripe oats, and she was the greatest beauty that any of us will ever see till we pass in the boats of the midnight from this Island of the Mighty past the Island of the Blessed to the far-off Islands of the Sanctified and to the end of time.'

'But surely when I was here before, the Great Duke had another wife?'

'He has had three before this one.'

'And all named Gwenevere?'

'Is there any name more fitting to a Great Duchess?'

'Sad that so great a man, so powerful and with so many faithful followers to do his bidding whatever they are told to do and to keep it secret, should be so often widowed.'

'Never has he been widowed, or mourned a wife as dead. But it is true, he is a great man and has many faithful followers who will do whatever he orders and will keep it secret, as secret as a grave. The First Gwenevere brought to us and the kingdoms wisdom. The Second Gwenevere brought to us beauty and gaiety that we might go merrily into battle. The Third Gwenevere brought to us all holiness and the knowledge of God. And this Fourth Gwenevere has brought to us reserve and dignity and distance and coldness: and above all she has brought us peace. It is not prudent to enquire further.'

Theodore took the hint, and turned to his dinner and asked no more. Only, as the feast ended and he left the Hall, with his bosun as guard begging for the little hard cake that was his due, Theodore murmured again so that none could hear, save only myself and the sailor, 'Oh, to have her for mine, naked under my hands, in my bed between me and the wall.'

Interlude 2: The Warming

The woman had stopped the singing in the Hall by her coming. The Iron Men's skalds made songs like the long north sea wave, though they lacked its rhythms. Makers everywhere wove words as runes whose magic would run before men, yet she had stopped this one.

In the smoke-filled Hall, no gaze strayed towards her, save one. Fearful of her eyes, the Iron Men would not meet hers and even their women looked quickly and then away. She could have been some strange beast brought home from foreign shores, a fearful beast whose manners were unknown. Here the Iron Men's women sat to dine beside their men, rather than decently in their own quarters. She did not pity their having to abide the drunken boasting, but nor did she herself raise their food to her mouth.

She had poured for the Great Duke, for Melvas, and for Bedwyr before the boy had given her his yew-wood spoon. Woven strands of the wood had been cunningly fashioned by his knife, made smooth by love-longing, she could feel. Among her people, no man knelt to a woman unless he was her slave.

The one man who did not guard his gaze, the Shipman dressed in royal red hung with chains of kingly gold, blazed among the British throng, though he sat in the despised place by the door. For him she poured, and for the cloven-faced man beside him whose ugliness kept his gaze downcast for shame of her beauty.

She also marked the Frankish bosun who very properly made no sign of kinship. She had swept silently past him, her face impassive. The Shipman's open admiration blazed after her, warming her passage, kindling her dreams. It was all that warmed her in her cold bed.

Chapter 2

The Apple Land

I

From Caerwent we prepared to travel to the Apple Land. This was Bedwyr's country, and yet not entirely his country. The men who lived in it might follow him to war when forced, and would take their cases, grudgingly, to his court, and not to mine. But they were not seagoers, and were nervous about disputing even the shallows with my men, fishermen who also hunted the crane and the duck in the marshes, who dug for cockles, and were bold to take what they had caught even to Badon and sell it under Bedwyr's nose, for cider and apple jelly.

I had given up my guardianship of the Great Duke as soon as he was on the water. Strictly speaking, Bedwyr was not responsible for him until he landed on the other side. Therefore we both had some obligation to plaster over the cracks. Each of us had afloat, beside the ceremonial crowd who were turning out whether they liked it or not if they wanted their rents to stay stable, a score of men in mail ready for action. My men were in red and black, although not more than two were actually Avan men: the rest were in Bedwyr's white, hooped alternately with black and a clear blue, conspicuous although not very serviceable if they fell in the mud.

True, there was no real thought of battle here so near to the Glass Island, not since ten years before we had caught the Pagans of Thameshead and their allies on the downs above Badon, and driven them from fold to fold and from ditch to ditch, till the last of them stood in a dingle where we cut them down. Bladulf himself died, even, at last. They died in their strength and asked nothing. And they came to sue for peace, and the Great Duchess was the token of that peace.

Even the Irish do not raid so near the Glass Island, for fear of the curses of the Holy Saints who live there, or are buried there. I would not like to face Melvas' tongue, either side of Jordan.

This land now was as safe to walk in as any. We could go easily, our helmets hooked at our belts, our shirts and scarves plain to see for anyone to tell our families and our lands. Wherefore the scarf I wore was the black, double-striped in gold, of the green hills of Cardigan where I was fostered and learned all I knew of value.

Once landed, the Great Duke went ahead with Bedwyr to where the Badon men held their great horses ready for use, and a horse-litter for the Duchess. She was, after three years among us, still nervous of horses and would not sit in a saddle if she could help it. Thus she showed her savage blood. The Heathen are afraid, all of them, of that wonderful animal sent by God to help us and named by Adam when he named all the beasts, including many who are seen no more. Therefore it is doubtful if the Pagans are of the race of Adam, if they are human at all, or if perhaps the Heathen were so named by the first man. I stood on the beach, ordering such things as needed ordering, and indeed there were many, and making a good impression on the men who would otherwise loiter even in the face of the enemy. My motto was always: if not now, then when, and if not by me, then by whom?

Theodore came to me. He wore his sailor's salt-stained dun-coloured shirt, and over it his cloak of state, worked in fine wool, white with a purple border. He asked, 'Where will you spend the night?'

'I go with the Great Duke.'

'Where will he sleep?'

'The Great Duke's travelling tent went on before, and is already pitched a few miles inland, with the fires burning and the carcases turning on the spit, and the wine cooling. As for tomorrow night – Camelot will be below the walls of Badon. I have my campaign tent, and then I will have it pitched next to the Great Duke's as is my right, but tonight I give that Honour to Bedwyr. I have to be in Badon at the

Great Duke's side, for the Table to decide on peace or war for the coming year. There are other kings coming to meet us there, and we will debate for days like a horde of clattering trees in a gale. But the real arguments will go on privately, in the evenings.'

'Tomorrow I sail for Bordigala. But I would like a last night ashore.'

'Have you a tent?'

'My bosun will rig one out of a spare sail, and come to pitch it. We often do that to make a shelter on deck. We will also bring our own wine, if you can find horses to carry it.'

'Offer it to Bedwyr. No, on second thoughts there is no point in making a ceremony of what is bound to be accepted. We will steal some horses to carry it. Nobody will notice. You can still ride?'

'Since we last rode together, I have ridden more miles than there are stars in the sky, all along the roads of Gaul and into Italy, as far as Bezant. I feel that this is the last time I will see the Island of the Mighty, and I would like to smell something other than the bitter sea.'

When he had ridden here before, he was young and so was I. That year we had offered his father so much in bronze that he had not enough wine and sword-blades to make up the price: he had left the youngest son, Theodore, as security while he sailed back for the rest. Theodore had ridden out with us that summer to clear Towy of the pirates.

We followed behind the Great Duke's party, along the forest rides where the little flowers sprang by our paths among the magic thorns. The sun was close above our right shoulders, and the August shadows were long. It was not far to where the duke and his wife would sleep that night, and dine in private first. Bedwyr himself had ridden on towards Badon, seeking its high walls and its roofs thatched with silver, and its gates studded with gold, they said, although both were so befouled with the smoke of the lead works that all was drab. He boasted that he had there a hundred statues of bronze, worth a dozen kingdoms in wine, and a hundred miles of pipes of the purest lead. This he would not sell for all the wine in Bezant: not yet. By now the barley harvest would be safe within the walls, and many of its farmers lived in the city all the year round, not merely in the winter as we did in Caerwent. Most of the rest would be coming in now for the end-of-harvest feast.

In an open space by a spring of pure water Arthur's people had pitched his tent. My own gentlemen had pitched mine already, but some way upstream. We had had enough experience of the habits of the Household. Supper was cooking under the sky. The weather was dreadful, bone-dry, and the sun full on us. I hoped that it would improve. Just after we sat down, the other King of the Cornishmen, Kador, came to us, weary after a fortnight's journey, but eager to find out what Gormant was up to. When he found that Gormant and Hennin were not eating with us he decided to stay, and contributed a dozen gallons of cider. So Arthur went to his own table, and I to mine.

I sat on the straw bales between Theodore and Kador and with us were the gentlemen of quality who had come with me from Gwent, Gwion and Esau and Korlam and Gwenki and Keinakh, and Branydh Crowstail, so called from the beauty and serenity of his countenance. Taberon poured the wine, not being able to persuade any of the Great Duchess' Cardi girls to join us. We each ate a few piglets roasted on a spit, and a couple of swans and some hares. Then we had a few bushels of last year's apples, carefully stored and now, just before the picking, wrinkled and sweet. But not as sweet as the cone of sugar that Theodore put out for us, the first that Taberon had seen, let alone tasted. We drank our way through Theodore's wine, and then began to work on the cider.

We told stories of forgotten fights and raids. Best of all was the tale they called on me to tell, of the fight that we had with the Pagans in a ruined church of the Romans, where Arthur found a silver dish a yard across, under some stones where the altar must have been. It was worked with the figure of the Virgin, immaculate and therefore naked as she rose from the waves with the little angels all around her, and her title on it in Greek, *Star of the Sea*. The Heathen came in through the west door as we left through the east, and they hunted us through the marshes for twelve days till we met some men of Elmet with spare horses. Then we could ring the savages against a river till some were killed by the sword, and the rest drowned. All that time, Arthur kept the dish like a buckler on his arm, and now he carried it mounted on leather as a Shield of State on feast days. This was the shield called Gwynebwrthukhel, Face against the Heights.

This was a hot night, as so often at the end of August. We lay under the stars, and drank the cider, and shifted around to keep cool or to talk to people we wished to confide in. I looked for Theodore to tell him that this was how we lived before we went to the wars, and this was how we would live again when once we had driven the Pagans out of the Island. And I knew now how I would argue in a week's time when all the kings had come. I would urge them to unite and go to war against the Heathen, as we had done years ago, Bedwyr and Kaw and Gawain and Mordred: and even Lawnslot. We had all been as brothers.

But I remembered I had not seen Theodore after the fourth flagon. I was afraid that he being a stranger might have wandered into the wood to relieve himself and have met the bears who would come to scavenge after our feast, or even the Summer Country men who have the same nasty habits. I left the fire and was no more noticed in going than Theodore had been. I walked round the sentries as an excuse, letting them see how energetic and conscientious I was, although it might have made a better impression if I had been able to remember the password I had myself given them.

And then as I wandered through the camp which was now, with all the Cornishmen who had come in with Kador, as large and noisy as a city, I came to an apple grove. The fruits gleamed golden in the moonlight, which the night before the cloud had hidden from view, but which this night of peace shone full. There, among the shining globes of the cider crop the Shipman and the Duchess walked alone, his hand upon her arm. So I came back to my fireside and drank the more and sang the louder till only I in the whole camp was sober and awake.

II

In the morning, we saddled and packed our belongings, or left them to the care of men we trusted to bring on after us in the sumpter train. This was no place to leave a thimble unattended. We were a large company now with the Cornishmen and those of Bedwyr's people who had come out with Bedwyr himself in the dawn to escort Arthur, and Arthur's Household who were from every corner of the Island. But Theodore left us. He said he was a foreigner and felt out of place,

and he would not come on to see the marvels of Badon, although
Kador tried hard to persuade him. So we embraced and I watched him
ride off alone towards the sea. I motioned a couple of my lads to ride a
little way behind to see he was not molested.

We left the rest of the camp followers hard at it striking the tents.
We expected to find them pitched again when we reached Badon, the
packhorses being more used to a hard gallop than were our mounts.
The Great Duke rode in the van at first, with a cluster of Badon Men
who wanted to tell their grandchildren that they had once been guides
to him, although who could be a better guide here than Arthur? After
a while he got bored and strayed here and there out of the column,
looking for familiar landmarks on the ground and unforgotten faces
among the followers.

I rode at the rear with Gormant, thinking that kings ought to stick
together if only out of mutual suspicion, and not wanting to show
undue favour to Kador. Gormant was a good man to have at your
back in a fight once you had convinced him that his life depended
on yours as much as yours on his. So I tended to stay close to him.
His sister's son Constant came behind, a well-grown man but never
yet in a pitched battle, although he talked to Taberon as if he had
conquered the Pagans himself and held all Logres as a dependency of
Cornwall.

In the middle of the column were the servants of the Great Duke's
household, around a cluster of horse-litters. They attended the Great
Duchess and the maids who travelled with her. Attended, not guarded
– these cooks and stewards could not have guarded a clutch of eggs
from magpies. She would have been better guarded if the Cardi girls
had been mounted, because they were all used to spending summers
up in the havod looking after the sheep and quelling the importunate
lads: like Taberon.

After we had ridden about an hour, we saw a farm house over on the
right. A gaggle of the men who followed the Households wandered off
towards it. They were men of no account, bards and beggars and
slaughtermen and physicians and the buriers of offal. We kings took
no notice of this, but Gwion, out of professional interest, trotted over
a little way, and then returned.

'There's a bit of a fuss,' he told us. 'Some of that crowd are trying to steal a piglet and the sow is putting up a better fight than the farmer.'

So Gormant and I slanted over a bit, not to ride to the farm but just to have a better view of it as we passed.

'Who gets the right thigh, the hero's portion?' Gormant was laughing. 'There's two beggars pulling on one end of the pig and three women on the other.'

'There's another woman come to break the rules,' I pointed out. 'She's brought a bucket of something to throw over the men. I hope it's nothing worse than dirty water, but from the careful way she's carrying it – they'll be lucky if it's only the bucket hits them.'

'There's worse than buckets,' laughed Esau, 'but if they get a bucket of night soil in the face those men may well turn nasty.'

'Look forward,' said Taberon in awe, 'the Great Duke himself is going in to stop them.'

'Stop them?' Gormant was bursting his gut with laughter. 'He's not stopping them, he's trying to get the pig for himself. Showing that he's just one of the lads.'

I could just hear Arthur's voice. I never heard it again. 'By God and his Mother, let the Great Duke be fed! I'll have that pig!'

'And by the devil and all his grandmothers,' said the farmer, coming from the house to help his wife and daughters, 'but you shall not have it, no matter who you say you are.'

I saw the sunlight gleaming on fork prongs and on the iron edges of spades, and then on long knives. There was a tumult and a pushing of bodies and howls of pain. A dozen men spilled out of the crowd, bleeding. Gormant and I trotted down to the riot. As we came up from one direction and Bedwyr from another, the noise stopped. The men all stood back. There on the ground lay the pig, half butchered. And Arthur was butchered too. There had been a mighty stroke to the base of the skull on the left, taking the ear half off, breaking the jaw and shearing the cheek almost away. There had been other strokes. The face was covered in blood. But there was no mistaking. This was Arthur.

I heard a voice say, 'This is no field to see a Great Duke die.'

It was one of the apprentice bards. I could approve the sentiment and admire the correctness of the meter, but it was a time to have things done.

Men looked at each other to see who had done this thing, and forks and spades and knives fell from hands till the ground looked like a smithy. And all eyes went to the one man who stood among the crowd with blood on his shirt and on his hands. This was indeed true of most men there, but he was not bleeding himself, and there was a bloody axe in his hand, and another axe in his belt. His shirt was blue. And worse for him, he was no man's cousin there.

It was as if God had struck us all dumb. The silence was only broken when Bedwyr came galloping up, a stupid way to make haste since it takes the horse so long to stop, shouting 'Peace! PEACE!' in a voice to rally armies or launch battalions to a bitter flight. As indeed I had heard him do so many times, listening to the orders, settling his helmet grimly on his head, and muttering as he always did, 'Here goes the last King of Badon,' while Arthur stood apart on some knoll to direct the battle, and I as was my task turned vague wishes into clear messages to named commanders. For under Arthur battles had changed, from shapeless attacks by whole armies, into an orderly movement by separate units, that division forward, that battalion back, that squadron to the flank. And even as I heard Bedwyr and looked at the body, one part of my mind was thinking, who will order our armies now?

We all looked to Bedwyr for orders, and the man in the blue shirt turned and ran from us into the wood. Kador had flung himself down on his half-brother's body, keening aloud the Cornish song of vengeance and mourning. Bedwyr went down on his knees, shouting at the top of his voice prayers to all the Saints by name, while Tatharn made the responses. I thought: as usual, if I do nothing neither will the rest. I shouted, 'After him! Into the wood!'

A fair number of the Badon men, whom one would have expected to know the countryside, ran equally at random in all directions, some even into the wood. I left my horse, which is not always an asset among the trees, and limped after them. My sword was still tied up in a bundle with my tent and mail, but I always carry a boar spear on principle. Taberon came close behind me with another spear, although he was still feeling a little green after last night's cider and the blood today. Gwion followed me and Branydh Crowstail too, with axes, and Esau with his biggest carving knife.

The Badon men were running every way they could think of, in and out of the brambles, but without seeing any track or smelling anybody. I caught sight of Leision who had only his bow and a skinning knife.

'Which way?' we shouted at each other at the same time. There was a cry from ahead, and we both ran towards it.

'He's in that briar tangle,' said a voice unknown. Leision called for beaters to form a line. No one seemed very eager.

I bawled, 'Alive! We want him alive!'

Some of the men who ought to have fallen back into a line of beaters were prodding into the bramble bush with spears and hayforks. They must have drawn blood, because the man in the blue shirt broke out and ran through them.

Leision called out, 'Stand clear! I want a shot!'

The man in the blue shirt turned and threw an axe at us. It went between my face and Leision's, so close that we both felt the wind of it. It bit into Branydh's side, but as he was carrying a large bag for unexpected trifles it only scratched him and his shirt stopped the bleeding. But when he changed that shirt at Christmas the wound opened again and turned green and he died: so I suppose some Saint had cursed him.

At the flash of the axe in the air, while I only thought that's one gone and one left, the beaters vanished, running to one side or the other or just lying down and persuading themselves that they had suffered many honourable wounds which excused them from further participation in the affair. As the man in the blue shirt turned to run, Leision loosed his arrow. He hit his target in the left buttock. This may sound a funny place to aim for, but a shaft deep there paralyses the leg: I know.

I shouted again, 'Alive! I want him alive!'

The beaters were all after him now, thinking him done for, which of course he was. I saw the spades and axes raised in front of me. I hobbled up as fast as I could. But I was too late. The body was hacked about, scarcely recognisable as a man's. I saw through the blood the scars on the cheeks. I shrugged. These were Badon men, not subject to my judgement. I would leave them to Bedwyr. Leision could bring in the carcase, since he had killed the quarry. But I motioned to Gwion to take from it any chains or armlets or other unconsidered pieces.

Back on the road, Kador was still weeping in a ceremonial way and cutting his own face with stones. But not deeply. Bedwyr had unlaced his shirt and unsheathed Frost in the Morning.

I honoured the blade, and told him, 'No. That will profit us nothing.'

'Oh, Morvran,' Bedwyr wept, 'my Lord is dead, my battle leader, my guest, my Great Duke. I swore to guard him in my lands, and now he is dead. I must die.'

'Nonsense. He fell in the midst of his own Household. How many of them can you see falling on their swords?'

'But there must be somebody's blood,' Bedwyr wailed on.

'Not yours, you must live for Badon, as he lived for the Unity of the Island.' Bedwyr needed another king to tell him that and he might have waited an hour before someone of sufficient rank came up to excuse him from suicide. 'Here, cut my finger.'

He reached out with Frost in the Morning and cut my left little finger, which is covered with scars from other peoples' blades over thirty years. When the sword was packed away and the riding strings tied very tight to prevent any hasty action, Bedwyr shouted again, 'How shall I live with my shame?'

'Very comfortably,' I said shortly. Bedwyr was now kneeling to weep with Kador. Brave men they were, to be given the hardest tasks in battle, but too easily bewildered to take decisions in emergencies. As always it was left to me, Morvran, too ugly for women, too old for ale, too lame to run from a lost field. I tried to think what Arthur would have done. I gave the orders.

III

It was dark now. I had had them bring the body of the Great Duke of War and Peace into my own tent, on to my own bed. The Duchess was no use, but one of her Cardi girls, Tegai, washed the body, and went away. I called a few men to me, Gwion of course and Taberon who in any case never left my side, being frightened to be fostered so far from home while great things went on around him, and my other great Officers of State. Bedwyr and Kador came in too, but when they realised what I was going to do they had no stomach to stay and watch. Kador only looked straight at me, and said, 'You were my brother's friend but not his kin. Do what must be done.'

There was no blood left to spill, I reminded him, but they did not wait to see that proved. I called for a smith out of Arthur's Household, and Sgilti came, who mended pots and pans for the Great Duke. I asked, knowing the answer, 'Can you work in bronze?'

'I have that skill, and I am pre-eminent in it.' He said this with a sideways glance at Gwenki whom he despised as a mere iron-basher, and a theoretician.

'Then find me a bronze pot, between a gallon and a gallon and a half. With a lid. And bring some of your tools and a brazier to seal the top. Now, Gwion, find me an axe and a sharp knife. Esau, I will need your butchering block!'

'Nevermore,' he swore, 'shall it be used for meat.'

I hoped that he meant it. Gwion brought Arthur's own axe, called Bells Beneath the Sea, from the noise it made on helmets. These few watched as I worked. Esau had searched the whole camp for salt and spices and for strong wine. The torches in their holders did not give steady light, but we did what we could. I asked the Virgin to help me. I reminded myself that I had butchered enough beasts in my time, and this was no bull's neck, and I was hard. When I had done, we set the head, all gashed and scarred but washed, wrapped in lambs' wool, in the bed of sweet savours in the pot, and then Esau poured in the strong wine. After that I had Sgilti seal the lid, and sent him away: Gwion had taught him a song to sing for purification, and when he sang it outside the camp a pack of wolves took him.

When he was gone, I sent for Arthur's Saddler, Saer, so old a man that Korlam was not offended. He brought with him sheets of oxhide as they use for shields or for mending Arthur's Hall, Ehangwen in Camelot. We laid the body on the leather and Saer sewed it all into a neat bundle with the spices, Korlam doing the duty of an apprentice. But that was not the end of his sewing that night. When he had finished, near dawn, and there was no one else there but myself, I had him case the bronze pot in leather. The case was thus fitted with loops for a carrying strap.

I told him, 'I have a last duty for you to do for the Great Duke. We three rode together for many years, saddle to saddle, knee to knee. We have borne shields together, we have scattered the Heathen time and again, have sewn our harness and our mail and our bodies. Now, Saer, do this. Take this pot, and go with it into Demed, past the Land of the Blue Stones, and as far as Solva. In the Place of the Nine Wells there lives a woman called Nonna. Take her this pot, give it into her own hands, and tell her what you have seen. But tell no one else.'

This he did. When Nonna heard his tale she called a young man named Keiswyn, who killed Saer for no other reason than that she told him to. Then Keiswyn, not knowing what was in the pot, carried it north along Helen's Road, and planted it in a crevice he had been shown years before, in a cave under the crest of a mountain. Though no one knows where, Arthur stays there for ever, looking out to the west and the north towards the Island of the Blessed, against the attacks of the Irish. The people there call it Arthur's Seat, as Nonna told them to, although he never went there or ever saw the place.

When Keiswyn had done this, he began to go back to Nonna. Outside Mydhvai he ate some oatcakes that she had given him. Soon after that he died, turning purple and green and yellow in several places of interest only to the physicians, of whom there are enough in that place to bury him but none learned enough to heal him. Thus we hid the Holy Head where no Christian will ever find it to worship, nor any Pagan to desecrate.

In a dawn, Gwion announced Melvas.

'Bless me, my father,' I asked him, 'and tell me that I have not sinned.'

'You have followed the customs of our fathers,' said King-Abbot Melvas, 'and in that there is nothing but virtue.'

'Have you done as I asked?'

'A pit is being dug, twelve feet each way and deep enough for three men to stand on each other's heads – which indeed I saw done and very indignant indeed it was that the bottom man was – and remain well hidden. Gravel has been brought by the cartload, and the lime, too.'

'And the men?'

'I have twenty young monks, strong enough to walk under any load you have for them for forty days and forty nights, and not tire.'

'Then let them take what they have come for. Keinakh my carpenter shall go back with you and come and go as he pleases between the shore and the Glass Island, for neither he nor I wish that he should become a Saint.'

Melvas blessed us all, and went away with Keinakh and all his tools. But Tatharn censed us with fumigation to cleanse us of the blessing of the Glass Island.

IV

Now morning was come, the first day without the Great Duke. We could give over the tent to the Cornishmen to guard, knowing they would not enter it as long as Tatharn sat at the door meditating. At noon they changed with the men of Badon. But we men of Gwent slept, most of us, by turns, having done the best that men can do and that there could be no improvement. We had only to wait now till it was time to move the body to Arthur's Hall, until Camelot was itself brought around the body.

And while we waited the kings came. They dribbled in one by one as the news reached them. The kings from far afield were already on the journey, coming to the Table to decide on peace and war, while the kings near at hand were leaving it till the last moment, and started only when the news reached them. So they came one by one, but over only a few days, riding and sailing to the Glass Island. We saw faces we had last seen a dozen years before, or first seen a dozen years before that, in the times of the wars against the Pagans. The hauberks of ceremony and the scarves were in the colours we remembered. My own people came first from Avan in black and red, singing like birds as is their wont. After that came Menevia in black all spangled with golden roses. Llwkhwr came in scarlet from heads to heels, and Sketti in shining white, until it rained, when they appeared in a drab mud colour. Keredigion were in green and red, and Deeside around the City in sombre grey. And the first men from over the sea, coming from Breze in silver scattered with black lilies.

At first the camps grew up around the travelling tent where we still kept the body till Camelot should stand again. The soldiers in the Kings' Households swept all the countryside clear of food and fathered children in every farm. Bedwyr ruled in dispute with the other kings that none of us should take more than one page and five grown men with us into Camelot, besides Saints, not only for the sake of peace but in consideration for our stomachs. The other followers were sent east in bands to form a screen between us and the savages at Thameshead.

Now, by the Mereside, Camelot rose for the last time, with its high towers and its spires. The tents stood against heaven like mountain peaks. But no mountains were ever painted or gilded by the morning sun as were the walls and peaks of these pavilions by the pre-eminent painters of Arthur's court. Nor did the caves of the dwarves far out under the seas ever hold such treasure, of gold and silver, of bronze and pewter, of ivory and of ebony, and most precious of all, of glass.

The tents rose first for the pioneers who pitched the camp, and then for the servants who did the work of the Court. Then came the tents for the soldiers of the Household and for the Principal Officers of State, the butler and the porter, the herald and the bards. Arthur was his own judge, and some pretty questionable judgements he made, too. The smith and the saddler needed no tents now in this world.

After that they set the tents for the Duchess and for her Cardi girls and for the Ladies who were to come. These were made so subtly that one might well ask what animal it was that had so fine a skin, since it was not possible to see the seams where the sewing was so careful and the threads fine as spiders' webs and the embroidered patterns and the painted colours so subtly placed.

Last of all they raised Ehangwen, the Hall of the Great Duke of Peace and War. This was no toy of subtlety, no artist's delight. There was here a showing of strength, a boasting of strength. It was whole pine trees from the forests of Skirrid above Gavenni that the posts were made from. It was not the leather of the fine skins of kids or calves nor even of pigs, that was sewn here, but the thick hides of oxen, fit for shields. It was with the sinews of horses that the seams were sewn, standing a finger proud of the surface, passed through holes hammered with awls like marlin-spikes.

And it was with gold that the surface of Ehangwen was covered, beaten thin and glued to the leather. The glue was what Merlin had made before he left the world of civilisation and went to live near Barri, trying to make glass. When this tent was raised for peace or for war, every man for twenty miles around knew it and hid his eyes from its brightness. There was no need to sound horns or make proclamations to call the Kings of Christendom for swords about the Cross. The glow of the gold-reflected sunlight on the clouds was a challenge to all the Saints in their glory, and to all the devils was their damnation.

In Ehangwen then was laid the body, all lapped in leather, on the bed of ceremony of the Great Duke. The kings came to bow before it, and honoured the body as if it were a sword. He was our creation, and he did not make us, although we obeyed him of our own free will. While he lay there dead we could not talk of what we were to do. But there was no burying till all the kings had come.

On the twelfth day since the death, the monks came from Bardsey. They had come to the Mere rowing their skin boats on the choppy seas and towing great logs of bog oak from the marsh of Tregaron, hard as iron, that will never rot. One log they brought to Camelot. Keinakh worked on it with axe and adze to shape and hollow it into a boat: not a coffin, for this was the Great Duchess' wish, that he should be buried in at least one way in the fashion of her kinsmen.

On the fourteenth day, all necessary things having been done, the First Gwenevere came, in a ship of the King of Menevia. For her a tent had been pitched and a guard set around it to keep the Saints away. This was the first that Arthur had to wife, and she was older than he was. Some said that she was in reality his mother or his sister. I knew both these ladies, and it was not true.

It did not matter. She had nursed him and made him not only into a man but into a warrior and a leader, and at last into the Great Duke of War and Peace over all the Island of Britain and beyond. He had called together the Christian Kings of the Island in life as he did now in death. It was he that was the first to bring all the Houses, of Uther and of the Gododdin, and at last even the remnant of the House of Vortigern the Proud, the Generous, the Unfortunate, to stand in shield-line against the Pagan, and to keep the Island, what we had by then left of it, pure against the Saxons and the Irish. But when Arthur became a man, he put away the First Gwenevere, because it was clear that he could have no child by her.

Now she lived in the furthest west, beyond Solva. Many said she was a witch. It is not unlikely. Certainly there were things she did that no one else could do, and there were things that she knew that no one else could imagine. She knew of men's deaths before they came: yet Arthur's death she could not foretell.

On the eighteenth day after the death, the men of Eiddin came. With them, riding in the midst of a great guard in dark blue crossed with silver, they brought the Third Gwenevere.

This Gwenevere was Dunwal's sister. She was vowed from her cradle to be a saint and a nun, to live on the Island of Saints which lies in the lake they call Leven as the Glass Island lies in the Mere. But after Arthur had beaten the savages in the Wood of Caledon, he heard of her. He ravaged the land more cruelly than any savage till he could bring the Lady out of that Island and into his bed in the south. He paid Dunwal a good bride-price out of the booty of Caledon, and after that the King of Eiddin and the Great Duke were good friends. But the priests and the Saints who had never been his friends before this, now became his enemies, all except Melvas and the Saints of the Glass Island, whom he had bribed well. Even the Saints of Bardsey had brought their coffin logs to the King of Gwent, and not to the House of Uther.

So we raised a tent for the Third Gwenevere, and made it as comfortable as we could to reward her virtue, with sacks of wool and pillows of down and cushions of silk on a bedstead of oak. But she had the sacks and the cushions and the pillows thrown out, and the bedstead too. She slept on the hard ground, as indeed she did in Eiddin after Arthur had put her away to take a fourth wife which the Treaty demanded. She spent every day and most of the nights on her knees, praying for the safety of the Kingdom of Eiddin and of the Island of Britain. And indeed she needed to pray too, for Dunwal, though I do not like to speak ill of my cousin, was not a man to follow and about as much use as a king as a wet haddock on Saint Potiphar's day. And for all I know, she prays there still.

On the twentieth day, we saw scarves of green, hatched some with silver, some with gold. My cousins had come, the house of Cunedda, that were kings in Mona and in the Eyrie and in Ardudwy. Their hair grew red and bristling down their backs, like the manes of horses, for witness that we were all descended from Buddug the Bitch, the Lady of Caledon, and her husband of one night, the Votadin himself. Now Gwion and I could sleep soundly, because we had always been one or other of us awake, lest our guard be forced in the night by some king or other who wanted to boast of being the Guardian of the grave of Arthur, or at least of some salient part of him.

Then, on the twenty-third day, about the middle of the afternoon, we heard the sound of a host marching to the northeast, with the sound of trumpets and what might well have been the singing of the cauldron hymn, which meant there were no Saints there. A little later, a small group came to the ridge inland of us. Three tents were pitched there, and we saw the flags fly and we knew the scarves. There was a sighting of the bright and midnight black, strident as a trumpet and clear as a drum, the colour of the House of Vortigern, the Proud, the Noble, the Unfortunate. Now we saw it was one tent for the four servants and one for Mordred, and one for the Second Gwenevere.

Oh, but she was lovely as a summer's day, and pleasant as honeysuckle in the moonlight. Nobody saw her who did not fall in love with her. She was a fit prize for Arthur, the pre-eminent in War, the Duke of Strife and Victory and the Emperor of Booty. And she was a whore.

After that first campaign when we had repulsed the Pagans before the walls of Glevum, and scattered them from crest to crest before Badon, and finally cornered them in the Dingle and killed them there, she was the only reward fit for him, the soldier's pay, the flower of the city on the Dee. Willing enough she was to marry him, but not for long. If a woman is loved of many men, indeed of every man, it is only natural that she should love more than one, even more than one at a time. And that brings tears: and not only the tears of women.

So she had loves many and lords many, kings and princes and prefects of cities, and never a word from any to the Great Duke, always so far away on one campaign after another. But this could not last. We all know how Arthur took her in the act with Lawnslot: and that great Prince, having more cunning than prudence, fled at once into the north, and after much wandering took refuge with Mordred. For Mordred, the Soul of Honour, against whom few at that time had hard words to say except for the sake of mischief, held that if a man has a choice between offending a great foe and a lesser, he should for his honour's sake offend the greater and so keep his virtue.

And she also escaped, although there is no telling how as long as there are any of Arthur's kin alive to visit it on us, and she made her own way to Mordred, since he was the only king in all the Island who had not slept with her, and the only one with courage to outface Arthur in his rage and remind him that he was no king but the chosen servant of all the kings, and not their Master. Which he could do as himself the last remaining descendant of Vortigern, the Wise, the Generous, the Unfortunate. There with Mordred, Lawnslot found her, and from that day on Arthur, Great Duke of Peace and War, and Mordred King of Radnor had not spoken face to face. But it was well known that Mordred, Soul of Honour, Patron of Bards and Saints, was more faithful to the Island of the Mighty, One and Indivisible, than any other man, whether priest or king, or duke even.

That afternoon, we saw the third tent between the two that each flew Mordred's standard, that also is the standard of the Valley of the Nest and flies upon the Knoll. This other tent flew a scarlet streamer, and we knew it must be her. And there was seen once or twice a flicker of the colours of Glevum, cherry on white, which could only mean Lawnslot.

So the count was complete and we could proceed to the burying of the Shield of the Island.

Interlude 3: The Veil

The woman sat in the silence. The bower was emptied of the Cardi girls who had gone to prepare the wake, but the smell of their close barley bread and sharp mead still lingered. The light chatter that had once filled the place to overflowing was changed to wailing now. She had suffered their clinging and lamentation for a time, until finally dragging their fingers off of her. Glad of their going, she considered the silence.

She kept apart from the other Gweneveres, biding her own place and minding her own counsel. Their part of the weaving had been done while she had been growing. Whatever power had been in it was nothing now. At her feet in a bowl of silver, the spawn of frogs peered like many eyes under the net-covering she had made. Salt-marsh and tide-lift marked the passing of the night as she netted the veil.

Her own people would know already of the Iron Men's disarray. The Frank's message would pass beyond the Apple Land, warning the Great Race to demand the fulfilment of the Treaty, to rejoice in the Great Duke's death that avenged the fall of Bladulf, her father, and those warriors who had fell on Badon field.

She cut a sliver of black pudding and finished a custard to keep up her strength, since none had come to feed her. Then she took up the netting hook once more and finished the black veil, trustful that the Treaty would be upheld by the men who had sworn and witnessed it.

Chapter 3

The Wake

I

That was the last night of the old world. We held a Wake that might
have drowned the firmament, and made the whole bowl of ocean spin
drunken on its pivot. The food was there already, because each of the
kings and prefects of cities had brought rations sufficient for his regi-
ment for a long campaign – I had taught them that much. The fresh
meat was sausaged into the tripes of pig and deer and ox, because the
time for salting was not yet come. This was probably the first great
funeral on record without ham. Or black puddings, for all those were
taken for the Fourth Gwenevere and her ladies. But it was the season
for the new loaves from the first barley and cakes from fresh cut oats,
to make plates and platters to soak up the gravy. There were onions
beyond count, although it was too early, or too late, for leeks – the
gardeners always have some excuse. There were radishes, and garlic
and lettuce and cabbage, both white and sweet, and red and pickled.
Although I have always considered that vegetables are things farmers
grow to hide how dirty their fields are.

There was fruit, too, although we regretted that the Great Duke
had been so ill-intentioned as to die after the end of the strawberry
season, although he was still in time for apples and pears and plums.
We had bowls of blackberries and dewberries and whinberries, and
cream and honey to pour over them.

And above all, there was cheese. There were cheeses to build a wall around Camelot, and around Badon after that. There were cheeses from every Kingdom in the Island, and from every city, and from every cheese market, and a cheese from every flock of cows and sheep and goats, and then double that number for luck and for seasons, that a man might have eaten his fill of cheese every day of the year, blue or yellow or white, firm or creamy, and still have new flavours to try. There were even, out of courtesy, cheeses from Breze and from Bro Erekh, and we praised them not to hurt the Bretons' feelings, but they were poor stuff and not worth counting into the list of real cheese. Gaul is not by nature a cheese country.

We ate the food that the regiments might have eaten that the kings had brought. They were now lying hard and eating worse in the hills above Thameshead, watching for our safety. But the host of Mordred was still undivided, lying over the crest, on firm ground and in ranks, always unseen.

That had always been Mordred's way, not to be seen. Men seldom saw him near Camelot, certainly not after the quarrel. Yet before and after, wherever the Great Duke's Army went, Mordred went first with his men, hidden in copses and woods and behind blades of grass and single mushrooms, nearer to the Pagans than either they or our own men ever guessed, and sending back to the Great Duke news of exactly where everybody was, both their men and ours. There were some of our kings who never knew exactly where they were themselves, and this gave Arthur a variety of interesting cases of trespass to judge.

As Arthur had his Great Strategic Insights, and as Kai led the Iron Men on their great horses in the charge which softened the Pagans up, and as Bedwyr was at the head of the peasantry on foot in the last great advance which over-ran everything, and as I laid out orders which roads to use and where to concentrate, and where to disperse to in case of accidents, and how to find food and where to store it, and who to trust to find it, and, especially, the drink – so Mordred always drifted like smoke in front of the army, and on either flank, and behind it. We could trust Mordred, the Soul of Honour; this night we felt we could ignore that host.

It was the night of the wine. Beer we always had in plenty. The beer of Camelot was brewed from the last of the barley from every field in Christendom, so that the spirit of the corn, fleeing from sheaf to sheaf as it was cut, was trapped in the last handful of ears by the final stroke of the sickle. Cider there was always enough of, pressed last year from the little apples of the Summer Land, and matured all the winter through. Some, which the women preferred, was sweetened in the cask by a few spoonfuls of honey, but most was strong and bitter and the better for that. Mead was made from the honey of the summer, and the best was made from the bees which were white as they had been at the beginning of the world in the Garden. But they were very rare. These were the usual drinks of the island, fit for everyday use, in steading or in court, or on the lesser feasts, Saint Enodoc's day or Saint Whitsun's. But tonight, in which the history of the world turned and the moon floated both horns down, we could ignore them.

The kings had each brought their best wine, in the big painted jars of baked clay that the traders used instead of the oaken casks which are preferred by civilised men. Each jar was poured, and every man had his fill. Yet there was not a jar there which had not passed through my hands in the way of trade, and all brought in by Theodore or his skippers, paid for in heavy bronze and dull gleaming lead. Any gold stayed in Gwent. Theodore also brought in the grey sword-blades, each worth more than five times its weight in bronze, although the price varied with the times it had been quenched.

Some wine was red and bitter, some was yellow and sweet, but all of it was stronger than cider or beer, and it was therefore easier to drink enough to do you good without your having to stagger out too often to increase the volume of the Mere. We all drank the kings' wine, we kings and our Households and all the Household of Arthur who were the thirstiest of the lot since it included the lesser servants of the Court, scullions and water-carriers and physicians and emptiers of chamber pots, priests (very few), admitted bards (quite a number), and bards' apprentices (very many, since there are few who in the end, after escaping from the plough, show enough aptitude at versifying to be called to a chair). The kings brought the wine, and the Households drank it all.

When the wine was flowing, the Harpists came in by squads, and when they had jangled enough, great masters brought in the Roman pipes. Some were blown by mouth, but many were of the more primitive kind which were pumped by bellows under the elbow, giving a sweeter tone but less force, and some very primitive ones which were mounted on wooden stands. The small drums were beat till their bells sang loud, and on the open space in front of Ehangwen we kings danced before Arthur, as we had so often done on the eve of battle. Swords were brought, not the battle-proud grey blades of Damask and Bezant, but poor rust-brown things, blunt Heathen knives fit only to be trampled on. These were so spiritless that they might be drawn without need to satisfy their thirst for blood. Over these the kings danced, two by two or four by four or eights about.

Friend danced with friend, enemy with enemy. What was stranger was that kinsmen danced together, brother with brother, father with son, with every appearance of amity. I, Morvran of Gwent in my fox-fur cape, danced with Leoline of Eryri in his shaggy goatskin. Gareth of Orkney stepped out with Lot of Norroway – at least, he claimed Norroway still though he lived as a poor farmer in Elmet. Gormant danced with Kador, the two Kings of the Cornish, born in the same hour to the same mother, but gossip said of different fathers, and indeed they were so unlike in looks and temperament that it may well have been true. Dunwal of Eiddin danced with Urien of Moray, and Gilmour of the Irish that are in Lheyn with Gilloman who brought the Irish into Menevia.

And between the dances we sang. We sang the new songs of Camelot, the Death songs of the Three Hundred at Cattraeth and the Wedding of Vortigern the Valiant, the Handsome, the Unwise, the Unfortunate, to the daughter of Hengist on the Night of the Long Knives. We sang 'The Roaming of Geraint', even as he laughed at it, and 'The Wedding Hunt of Khilwkh'. We sang the most obscene song in the world, which is 'The Lady of the Fountain', and I noticed Taberon sitting on a bale of hay with Tegai, head of the Cardi girls, and hiding her head in his chest so that she would not hear it. She said she was tired of spending every evening in the Gwenevere's tent as was her duty, since she had had enough of custards sweetened with honey and soft cheese and nothing solid except black pudding and even that made with a miserly attention to the oatmeal. So she had come out to have a fill of roast mutton like a good mountain girl. I had educated Taberon to be a gentleman and to accept gratefully what is offered. But most of all we sang the old songs again and again, some our grand-fathers sang from the time before the White Death and the coming of Hengist and the Pagans: 'Heads on the Gate', and 'Blood in the Marshes', and 'The Hunting of the Black Pig'. But not 'The Cauldron Song', because that was for a more solemn occasion.

When the choruses were all under way and the kings and their Principal Officers of State were too drunk to fight and too grief-stricken and maudlin to quarrel, Bedwyr beckoned to me. We were the only ones sober. We left the hot and stifling air of the open square, and sought the cool freshness of Ehangwen. We came before the body, lapped in lead over the leather, and laid inside the canoe of bog oak, brought from Bardsey to be hollowed and polished by Keinakh.

In and around the coffin lay the war gear of Majesty. Arthur's helmet had bronze moulded over the leather, polished so often and by so many hands that many swore it was gold. Before battle, we would all try to stroke it for luck. The Dragon crest was indeed of gold, and its eyes were rubied to shine in the blackest smoke. Leaning against the foot of the coffin was the Shield of State, Gwynebwrthukhel, Face against the Heights, solid silver. And over his breast lay the battle-shield, Pridwen, Costly is my Smile, six thicknesses of oxhide stitched with iron wire over a core of linden wood.

'These,' said Bedwyr, in Latin, which he spoke with difficulty, being brought up by bards with only little interference from priests, and he used the language now only to show the solemnity of the occasion, 'these defend only the man. But what of the weapons which defend the State?'

'No other man may use them,' I agreed. 'We must not let them lie here for the next boaster to pick up, or cast them into a cave for the Heathen to find.'

I took Rhon, Arthur's pike. It was seven foot in length, and a foot and a half of that was the head, hammered of steel of Damask by magicians in the light of the eclipse when the shadow of the sun falls across the moon, and this accounts for the rarity of these heads, a sixth time quenched in the blood of lions. The shaft was of broom wood, jointed and dovetailed to make a shaft to fly true: the ferrule was of heavy gold, the gift of the Bezant Emperor to the Duke of Britain, brought by the hand of Theodore, who had expected to be well-rewarded in bronze for his trouble.

Bedwyr picked up from beside the coffin Caliburn, Hard is my Judgement, eight times quenched. He loosed the riding strings and drew her. We honoured the grey blade, and wondered to see the snakes still run in the steel, though their lord was dead.

'Forgive us, Lady,' Bedwyr prayed. He was wearing his war gloves, seven thicknesses of pigskin, curved to protect his fingers about spear shaft or hilt. Thus protected, he took this sword by hilt and point, and shut his eyes to gather strength. Then with a convulsion of body and spirit he did what no Pagan could ever do: he snapped the blade across his knee. Nevermore would Caliburn strike till she was reforged: and that shall never be.

Bedwyr slid the two parts of the blade into the scabbard, and tied the riding strings with a seven-fold knot. I laid Rhon across my shoulders. We left the tent, moving silently among the shadows along the edge of the dance. No one saw us save only the bears and the wolves scavenging among the remains of our feast. They moved aside as we passed, but without haste, since they knew it was no harm that it was that we meant them. They have as much right in the Island as we have: clan and clan, they are our fathers and our brothers.

We came to the edge of the Mere. Across the waters on the Island of Glass we could see the torches of the men who worked on the pit, dug as I had directed, four fathoms square and four fathoms deep. But it was less deep than that now, although it had been finished two days ago. The singing of the Saints came from the Island, and the soft movements of the beasts from behind us: and other sounds, human sounds, and human smells, were very faint but near.

There was a little mound by the Mere side. We stood on it, ten feet above the water. In the winter the floods would rise above this mound, and wash away the earth, an inch or so every year, to spread the mud over the bottom of the Mere and cover what lay there. Here I used my strength, the strength I had to stand against a flood of water or of men. I leaned back like a bow, and sudden I sprang straight. Rhon rose above us, sheer into the night sky. He reached his height, and as he curved down we saw across the face of the moon, who rode him: Cernunnos, Saint of War, antlered like a stag, steered the spear downwards and westwards. They vanished. There was no splash. Where Rhon fell, no man knows, but it was further to the west than any of us can imagine. So David the Shepherd, that killed his thousands, went into Hell as herald to Jonathan who killed only his hundreds but was a king born.

Then Bedwyr took Caliburn, Hard is my Judgement, eight times quenched, by her hilt. He began to turn on his heels, to spin widder-shins, three times, six times, nine times. And as on the ninth turn he faced the moon, he let her go. Caliburn in her jewelled scabbard flew up on her own course, high into the air, arching over the Island of Glass and over the moon, and falling at last into the water. Where she fell, we do not know, but there she will lie year after year while the mud covers her. There will be no diving for the weapons, no finding them ever. They were safe. But the Defence of the Island was at an end.

As we breathed farewell, the third man on the mound spoke. This was the Scout of the Household, who moved softer than wolf or bear, invisible in his shirt of black with the silver cross above his heart. 'When swords are so needed, so rare, so hard to find, should even one be cast away?'

'There is an end to weapons,' I told him. 'And an end to honour and glory.'

'And a last duke,' said Bedwyr, 'and a last war.'

'It was well done,' agreed Mordred. And we saluted each other, and went our way.

II

The ceremonies of the funeral did not start till the next day, in the mid-afternoon. No one was fit to do anything earlier than that. I saw Gwion in the dim dawn, trying to find his bed and making a poor shot at it, for what benefit is it to have eyes like a hawk if each sees a different picture and both of them double? I got him inside a bundle of furs with Taberon as well to keep each other warm, and how a lad of that age could eat and drink so much I will never understand. Although I suppose Tegai the Cardi girl being a young woman of good appetite helped too before she went to get her own breakfast, a second breakfast, in the Gwenevere's tent. Taberon had got into bad company lately: my company.

But everyone slept off the wake in time, and even I could snatch a few moments rest for myself: while the rest snored, only Bedwyr and I were left, with Tatharn who was depressingly sober, to keep watch over the body.

We had the trumpets sounded an hour before dusk. We turned out all the kings and the prefects of cities and the lords of the Frontier Marches, and their retainers with them. It was not very light by the time we got them in order of seniority, and I had to stop several entertaining fights over precedence: regretfully. The summer mists that belong by rights to the dawn had gathered in sympathy over the lake.

While the kings were being marshalled, I called the pre-eminent Chief Bard of the Island, and he came with his apprentice bards and ovates. I asked him, 'Gildas, will you sing now a last song of the life and death of the Great Duke of War and Peace?'

The great bard bowed. 'I will sing no more. I will cut with iron the strings of my harp and break in the sound box, and I will snap my fiddle and tear the bag of my pipes. I will go to Saint Ilhtud in his Lhan in the Vale, and I will learn to write, which destroys all poetry in a man: as you indeed know, Morvran. I will become a Saint myself, and I will write the deeds of all the Kings of Britain, but *his* name I will never utter, that took me from the dust of the fairs and the market place, and made me what I am. I will keep my silence.'

So I bowed low to him that had been so great and our teacher, and I bade him go in peace. And he went out of Camelot, and all his apprentices and ovates with him, most to the fairs and the market places and some to the Halls of kings and lords, but a few went into the Glass Island. And that was the end of poetry among Christian men.

Then I ordered the trumpets to sound for the second time, as they had already sounded to call the kings into line. Now it was four kings who brought out the coffin on their shoulders. Four kings, that is, and all their retainers, for the coffin remember was of bog oak, solid, fine work to last a man a death time, not to speak of the weight of the lead. That lead alone was worth a couple of dozen jars of wine, but we spared no expense for Arthur, that drank more wine in an evening than most drunkards do in a lifetime. Yet Arthur was no drunkard: except in battle he had few virtues of sociability that I remember, nor any sense of humour either.

It was the kings from overseas that I had asked to do the carrying, to avoid disputes among the kings of the Island. I asked myself who Arthur would have appointed, and avoided them like the plague. I persuaded everybody that it was more dignified to stand still and mourn with torn garments and gashed faces, and to let the mere foreigners, Lot and Gareth and Howel of Armorig and Gilloman, do the sweaty work.

The lords and the kings and the Prefects of London and of York (although the last title was merely honorary since Bladulf took the place) stood in two lines by the waterside. Their retainers stood behind us, their pikes vertical to catch the last rays of the evening sun. The body came down slowly on all those shoulders, and stood at last on a little wharf I had had made from rough logs, just enough to stop the coffin from sinking by itself in the mud. It would never do to have a corpse bury itself, but Arthur would have been capable of it, for he never believed that anybody could do anything as well as he could. Although in truth all he ever did was to give orders and leave the work to somebody else: usually to me.

Then the trumpets sounded for the third time, at some length, and a lovely sound it was. It had been some trouble to have them brought. Silver they were, and gleaming and elegant, blown by all the youth of Gwaen-Kae-Gurwen, that vale of mystery and magic, where the dogs bark in tune, and all the centenarians live to be eighty. The music echoed off the face of the water, and the blast of sound made ripples in the mists as they gathered. There was a calling forth of the Great Ladies, Gwenevere after Gwenevere.

They were each of them dressed in black. Black to the head and black to the feet, and black between. There was never a sight of gold or silver, of glass or gems, or of any richness.

The First Gwenevere came down towards us, tall and straight still as an ash tree on Margam Mountain. She it was who had cast the ice into the sea, and the stars into the sky, to roll out the stone from the Mere, and the sword from the stone, and Arthur from the womb, so that we would have the courage to ride out, the White Death being over and the new generation ready for battle, to take again the Island from the Heathen. She walked as a standard raised to lead men to battle, and we forgot how old she was, and how bowed that frame from the height we remembered and how shrivelled was the skin on the bone: yet even now in her rack and eld she was worth ten times more in the seeing than any young lass of today in the intimacy of knowing.

She walked from Camelot, and came to stand by the head of the coffin, at the right hand.

Next from Camelot came the Third Gwenevere, slowly as a priest before the Mass, straight and true to the waterside. Her lips moved as she walked: she was unveiled and we saw but most did not hear. Those of us who stood in the front row could hear some of the words. She prayed for the soul of Arthur and for the soul of him who killed Arthur, and for the souls of those whom Arthur had killed, and for the souls of all those who have fallen by violence without a chance to regret their lives. I who am bound to fall by violence regret little about my life except missed chances at women or at wine, but what I regret, that I regret bitterly. Her fingers trembled on her beads, and her lips moved, and her bare feet went confidently: but she saw, we knew, nothing but the faces of the angels who will take us all into limbo to wait, saint and sinner, till the Judgement comes to take us by chance of colour, white or black, sheep or goat, predestinate before our births. Although which is doomed, black or white, sheep or goat, we do not know. As Pelagius taught us.

The Third Gwenevere stood at the foot of the coffin, at the left, nearest the water.

Then the Fourth Gwenevere came down from Camelot, all alone, her Cardi girls left behind. They at once went hell-for-leather straight back to the hills, riding astride like shepherds with their seven petticoats kilted to the knee, taking what they could easily carry and looked valuable. Tegai with her double-handful of fine gold chains was known ever after as Tegai Eurvron, the Gold-Breasted, and was the financial salvation of her father's kingdom

This Gwenevere was tall as no woman of the Island is tall, and the hair beneath her coif shone as if it were the rippling wheat at harvest. Her skin was indeed as white as a walrus' tooth against the black net she had worked herself for a veil. There was no man who could look at her and not lust after her as the unattainable dream. She looked at no one, yet she saw all, knew the prurience in all our eyes. She knew how each of us would do her will if only we too could have her naked under our hands, in our beds between us and the wall. She turned for no roughness of the ground under the shoes of black cordovan leather that Theodore had brought her, but ever went forward without looking down. For she was a Queen by birth among the Heathen, and she had always known that wherever she went there would be no obstacle, that all ways would be made smooth for her, that cloaks would be spread beneath her feet as indeed some of the kings did now, that all would be decided by custom within the truce. She came down past the kings and their retainers, past the hedge of raised pikes, dipped to salute her.

She stood at the head of the coffin at the left hand.

Now we waited while the sun dipped lower and lower, and passed beyond the mists and all that was visible was the evening in its blackness. As we waited we heard far on the water the splash of paddles and the fierce imprecations of the Saints, who not being in current practice in boat handling struck each other frequently in painful and interesting places. Not always by accident.

So Tatharn, being the only Saint on our side of the water, mustered a choir out of the retainers, and a reasonable choir it was too, only a little weak in counter-tenors. He called for a verse, any verse, of the great song of the pure of heart. And it was this song, louder than the rain on a holiday in August, sweeter than the yell of the rutting stags, that signalled the end of the afternoon.

Now it was that the Second Gwenevere came down to us.

She came not from Camelot but from Lawnslot's tent in Mordred's camp, where alone in the Island she felt safe. Black-veiled, in Mordred's black cloak with the eight-pointed silver cross over her heart, she walked as though she were going down through spring grass to meet her love on the edge of the primrose wood. From the edge of her veil the curls strayed out like beaten copper burnished with the palm of the hand and wandered where they willed as she herself had always done. Oh, in mourning she was as beautiful as a warrior in the battle-line, as brave as a bride on her wedding morning.

Lightly she came to the water, and stood at the foot of the coffin, at the right.

Now, when the First Gwenevere passed, all men lowered their heads and looked aside, for fear of her wisdom and her power and her spells and her threats and her malignity. When the Third Gwenevere passed, every man looked abashed at her holiness and we remembered our sins and it quite spoilt us for our dinners. When the Fourth Gwenevere passed, we looked aside, being quite put down by her icy dignity, that took no notice of anyone who stood in her way and would have brought her as calmly through the crowd of kings and hardened warriors had she been naked and not sheathed in black from head to foot.

But oh, when the Second Gwenevere passed, she who had been in the rye fields in the summer heat with so many of us, and jealous the rest were, but I name no names – when she passed by there was a remembering of the scent of the broom and the meadowsweet and the lily of the valley. We looked her in the face, and smiled back at her smile, loved back at her love. There are countless tales told of her beauty and of her hospitality and most of them true. Taciturnity is not a fault of our nation: mendacity, yes, but silence – never.

The Four Gweneveres stood together for the first time. The noise of the rowing was loud to our ears, and the raft loomed at us from the mists. The Saints of Bardsey, having some skill, paddled at the front and at the back, although they would have been grieved to hear these simple words applied to what they had built with such devotion and hard-won book learning, and so little manual dexterity.

The delay had been because there had been disputes among the crew about who were left- and who right-handed, and therefore who should row to port or to starboard. The mass of the rowers amidships were Saints from the Glass Island. Some were men and some were women, but there was no telling them apart for the sacking they wore; and it made no practical difference to them except in setting out the choir places, for their holiness shone in the lice in their hair and quite deflated lust. They paddled with the strength of the righteous, and brought the raft close in, till the prospect of rest prompted them to make one last mighty heave and ground their vessel. Many of the Saints then fell into the water and lost their sanctity with their lice. Indeed in the confusion many lost altogether their desire for holiness and mingled with the throng to slip away into the world at large.

Now the kings from overseas and their retainers and the Saints from Bardsey all pressed forward to lift the coffin on board, and there was a hope that they might come to blows.

But the First Gwenevere motioned them to be still. She touched the coffin with her left forefinger, stroking it gently till it lifted itself from the wharf by a hand's thickness. At her direction, with only the slightest touch for guidance, it floated on to the raft and laid itself down dead centre. And the Gweneveres stood around it.

The rowers bent again to their paddles, but with more labour since the raft was now heavier and their numbers fewer. Some of the retainers pushed it from the bank into the Mere with their pikes as boathooks, and it gathered way. Tatharn mustered his choir again, and gave them a note. At his un-priestlike bidding, they sang now for the first time the song of the old times, from before there were any Saints of Christ or priests or altars, the words only a few know, the song of the little cauldron which boils where no fire is. So by the sound of the most sacred hymn of the Island of the Mighty, a song never heard on a lost field, Arthur, Great Duke of Peace and War, passed from us into the dark.

III

It was night. I had asked myself what Arthur would have done, and I had given the orders. Kings and prefects, great officers of state and all the lords of the Island, we stood in a circle around Camelot. The huge tents rose into the mists like the peaks of Snowdon or the ridges of Plynlimmon. There was a little silence, while we considered what now had to be done and who should do it. Most of the kings held to the school of not doing anything today which can conveniently be left till next week. As usual, everything was left to me, which may be flattering, but is certainly inconvenient and entails much wear and tear on clothes, not to speak of all the guilt I incur.

While we waited, the rats began to leave, being wiser than the men who came out later. Many of the cooks and scullions who ran out of the gates were stuffing into their pouches here a cup or a bracelet, there a strip of good cloth. But seeing us there in our circle, silent and determined, these men faltered and stopped, and drifted back through the gate in the high fence. We might as well have let them through, because beyond our circle there were men who would have killed for a sip of wine, let alone for the cup.

Thus it was determined. I went alone into Camelot. I walked first to the Lady's tent, the sleeping place of the Gwenevere, where no man might set foot but Arthur. It was lit by torches set in iron frames, and hung with rich cloths. There were a few women there, and they shrank from me. I did not speak to them. I took down a torch and I fired the bed, that great mound of wool and down and the clean dry straw of the first wheat harvest, and thrown over it a bedspread of crochet work, an intricate pattern. The cloth took a moment to catch, and so did the straw, being close packed. The women screamed and fled before me into the night. The bedding flared high to the arras which ceiled the roof above the cobwebs, to the dry rafters and the tent poles, and kindled the pine of the bedstead.

If I had waited I would have gone the way of Camelot. I ran out of the door into the streets of the tented city, the fortress of one night within its fence of man-high pine logs, spreading fire wherever I passed. Soon I was sweating from the heat, retching from the stench of the burning hide and hemp. My jerkin was singed and my hair was frizzling. It was no time to stand still. The very grass burnt beneath my feet, the smoke curled around me and hid my way. But I knew without looking the way to Ehangwen, the great Hall where Arthur had feasted, although sometimes on campaign the feast was bread and water gladly accepted. I wandered a little here and there, finding my path barred sometimes, the tents in their new dresses of red and yellow flames and their necklaces of smoke hard to recognise. But I held fast till I saw the high pavilion stand whole and unsullied, repelling the flames of lesser tents as Arthur in battle, shielded in iron, had defied the death that struck mere men around him.

I myself set fire to Ehangwen. She was full of the gold and treasure of Empery, the Grand Duke's shields and armour and jewels, the clothes and ornaments of ceremony. Like all the Island, she could not be destroyed save by attack from within. I watched the fire grow till nothing could save her. And all that wealth for one who had started as a beggar boy stealing a sword someone had left by mistake in a stone.

I walked away as slow and as calm as a Gwenevere, along the wide log road to the main gate where our pine wood palisade flared from end to end. Those who had left before me were finished with. The cooks and scullions and chambermaids, those who ran from the flames, had been shot down like vermin by the kings and lords and prefects who stood around with bows, so that they might serve no lord but Arthur. That was the theory. Although if an arrow will hardly transfix a naked hare at fifty paces, it will not do much damage to a man clothed and running at a hundred.

I passed out through the gate, now merely a gap in the fence of flame, the fighting platforms fallen into a bonfire, and there I came face to face with Bedwyr. I knew that I must look like he did, my face black with soot, my clothes spotted with sparks and smouldering here and there. He grumbled, 'Thought you weren't coming out. Didn't want to have to carry you. Overfed you are.'

But nobody who entered now could live. We stood together and listened to the fire, to the falling of poles and the bursting of barrels. We smelled the burning of meat and of corn, of lard and wine and cloth and butter, all the harvest of the year, we smelled the melting of metals. But above all we smelled the burning leather as the tents themselves were consumed. And it is of that we will stink as long as we live, at least in our own nostrils.

Seek not now for Camelot, nor for the place where it stood. Camelot was no abiding city. A night here, a week there, raised in an hour to be a fortress, a guard house at some now-threatened point in a long frontier, a frontier in depth as well as in length, a frontier in the hearts of men as well as in land. A frontier where life and faith were alike in danger, and the worst danger the threat to hope.

What then did Camelot guard us from? It kept out darkness and dishonour, lies and deceit. It repelled intolerance and ignorance, despair and hopelessness, conceit and impatience. In Camelot shone learning when no learned men were left, and the love of scholarship of itself raised afresh the scholars and the priests to teach. There shone humour when there was nothing to laugh at, and the only reason for a smile was to make the unhappy smile in return. In Camelot was hospitality given without payment and gifts without price, friendship and love that asked for no return. In Camelot shone always the cauldron of our hope, the cup of Christendom, our Grail. Now Camelot is gone.

Look not now for Camelot. Do not ask where Camelot stood, for it stood nowhere and everywhere, might spring up in the twinkling of an eye where no man expected. Do not look at that blackened earth by the Mere, at the shreds of charred leather and the gobbets of melted metal as they pass into the earth. Rather look into the summer sun, look into the nests of the spring birds, look into bubbling wine and hot bread given in the name of friendship and of joy given freely among friends, look into your own hearts when you are flushed with success or happy in love, and say then, surely this place is Camelot. Dig not for Camelot in the earth of the past, seek it not in memories or in the midst of tears. Camelot never was: but Camelot always will be.

Interlude 4: The Glass Island

The woman left the raft as she was beckoned. Around her the monks and the nuns leaped and cavorted, danced as they chanted, capered as they screamed the hundred names of God, and the names of all the Saints and angels, spheres and stars and powers and principalities which come between God and His People. Not all here were Saints yet, but all aspired to be, if only they worshipped as they ought.

They leaped higher, gashed their flesh and rubbed charcoal into the cuts to make the scars blue. This was the first familiar sight the woman had seen for years. So danced her own priests, so they too gashed themselves for Odin and Freya, so too they wept from pain since being priests they were not men and therefore might show suffering without shame. Silent she asked the gods of her own place, if they still lived, if they still listened, for release.

The four Great Ladies walked at the four corners of the coffin. Monks carried it away from the Mere, between the fires which burnt blue and yellow as spices and salt were thrown into them to drive away the fiends of Hellfire, which is red only – the devils Ashtaroth and Beelzebub, Odin and Apollo. The monks carried the bier, all heavy with oak and lead and leather, from the edge of the marsh to the firm ground beneath the Hill of Glass. The Pit was dug there, twelve feet square, deep as twice the height of a man and a head over. The floor of it was beaten firm into gravel till it grated against a base of rock.

The Fourth Gwenevere walked to her place at the right hand of the Dead. Around her she heard singing. They had sung about her at the water's edge, and on the raft, on the beach of the Mere, from the waterside to the grave. Now they sang from above her on the hill. The monks were carrying torches and the flames leaped about her, as they would have done at a funeral of her own people. In answer, flames shone far away also, on the firm ground across the Mere, and were reflected from the low clouds above the place from which she had come. And as that light died to a whimpering glow, the moon came through the cloud and drained the colour from all their faces in her bleak light. And by that moonlight the woman knew that her gods still lived, still listened.

The coffin lay by the grave. It was on a bier made in the old style without iron, of seven woods, the Ash and the Rowan and the Larch, the Pine and the Spruce and the Holly, and pegged with stems of Elder.

The First Duchess, Gwenevere Ceridwen, she of the Cauldron, turned to the west, to which all souls must go at last, when the rower comes to the beach and calls for them. She held her arms bent at the elbow, the stance of the rower.

The Third Duchess, Gwenevere Mair, she of the Altar, the Weaver of the North, the stay of Dun Eiddin, knelt to face the east from which salvation comes. She passed her beads through her fingers.

The Second Duchess, Gwenevere Blodeuwen, the Flower Maiden that had been, Light of the Hosts, the singing heart of the Household of the Great Duke of War and Peace, Adulteress and Whore, faced the body where it lay. With a great sob, and then the scream of a tortured soul, she prostrated herself.

The Fourth Duchess, Gwenevere of the Flaxen Head, turned to the Moon. Her right arm was crossed on her breast, her left hand flung out to point into the silvery lunette.

The coffin swung on its ropes down into the dark hole, sliding close against the edge that was next to the dead man's right hand as he faced towards the east, towards the enemy. It grounded, grating on the gravel and the stone slabs beneath. Three Duchesses now stood face to face above the grave, looking down into the pit to see for the last time the box that held their bedmate, that held the shield of the Kingdom, the sword of the Island, the mail coat of civility as we knew it. But one Duchess did not stand but lay there where she had thrown herself face down on the grave-edge. She was still. The red curls showed beneath the cowl of her black cloak.

Nuns turned her over. Her hands still clutched the handle of the knife, driven well in with her own weight, to pierce the heart, the bosom that had once been Arthur's . . . and Lawnslot's . . . and Lot's . . . and Gareth's . . . and so many others' . . . yet always still Arthur's. The gay smile with which she faced her lovers was still on her lips.

Monks brought the other coffin, the oak brought by sea from Bardsey, shaped by Keinakh's adze. In this on a bed of bear fur and a pillow of wild goose down they laid her. Unwashed, for she had washed and adorned herself for this last briding. Nuns took from her Mordred's cloak with the eight-pointed cross: beneath it she was robed in white silk as for a wedding of a virgin, for she came to her first deathbed. Then this coffin they closed and lowered into the ground, at the left hand of the dead man; for she only had kept the faith.

A leaden cross was brought and thrown into the pit, so that any who came after might know that this was the burial of Arthur, Great Duke, that being a bastard might never be a king, but Lord over the Kings, laid to rest here in the Apple Land of his birth, and crowning the country with his Gwenevere. And the Three Great Ladies that still lived threw each into the grave the last precious thing she owned, her golden ring of union, marked with the head of the Bear.

And so the grave was filled in, and the ground smoothed down, and the hut of memory and prayer built above it.

Chapter 4

Cadbury Congress

I

All through the night the dying flames reared their questing heads in Camelot. They strived to live, as all sentient beings do. They sought new food, an unburnt piece of wood, a jar of oil or wine, a pot of butter. Then they leaped to reach the clouds: satisfied, they fell again to the earth. We stood guard about them while they still hungered. When the night was over, nothing was left of the greatest city of the Island except baked earth and twisted rubbish.

The sword was already deep in the Mere, and no one would ever find it. Something nameless had taken the pike and ridden it far into the west. The shields were burnt and melted. And Arthur was safe.

While Camelot was moved from Badon to the Mere, my men had also moved, and fast. They had taken the Great Duke's body, lapped in oxhide and in lead, and laid it in a light coffin of apple planks, sewn with willow withies, packed with the seven sacred herbs, with ivy and mistletoe, with green yew and pine needles, with gorse and broom and meadow-sweet, and it was laid in a horse wagon. With six horses, changed often, they could keep up a trot along the old paved ways that the Romans had laid by magic over all the Island so that every man at the last might come to the Mere. Now the greatest of all men was ferried to the holy ground.

When Camelot was raised at last above the Mere side, Arthur was already buried safe. His feet were towards the east to face the Heathen, faceless though he was, to keep the Island safe from the invader for ever.

On the Glass Island, he lay deep as the height of four men. Over the outer coffin of bog oak were poured gravel and lime by the wagon-load, to set hard as stone. Above that, the rocks which had been broken out to make the grave, slabs each the weight of a man, were fitted together again as God had laid them down to be the ribs of the earth at the beginning of time. The lime held them, and more lime and gravel were strewn over them to make a new floor.

If ever the Pagans find this grave, they will dig up a body, the first body they find, and expose it as a peepshow for their kings and louts to laugh at. But they will see the body of the tow-headed stranger who dealt that blow, and they are welcome to make what show they like of that body and that head. They will be satisfied, and will never dig deeper to find the body of the Great Duke himself, ruler of the kings. Arthur, the Glory of the Island, is safe on the Island within the Island.

When the fire was dead, what was there left of Camelot? The beggars that follow every Household scrabbled among the ashes and in the dirt. They found threads of melted gold or blackened bronze, ruined iron blades with shine and temper gone, shards of burnt ivory. Even of this, there was little. All was consumed.

It was the end. Camelot was over.

II

When it was clear that there was nothing left for us to take within our dignity, we kings and Great Ones of the Island rode away. There was not one of us, king or prefect, who could not call fifty men at least to follow him. A few were masters of vast hosts. Some claimed that they could muster a thousand men at need, but who had ever seen such an immense army in the Island? But this day each king rode, as he had walked to the Burial, attended by one man alone.

The weather was not good. The sky was blue with a few high clouds scudding. But the smell of the wind gave promise of improvement later. We rode to Cadbury, the great earth-walled fortress over against the Mere. From here I could see the silver streak of the sea, and the hills of Gwent beyond. We kings and lords climbed to the top within the walls, Taberon lent a hand to help me as I limped upwards; not easy, for like every other attendant he carried my saddle and my food and drink for the day. We sat, as we had so often sat, on our saddles, a circle of kings on the grass, and the space within was what Arthur had so often in laughter called his Table. The grooms left us. We ate and spilled our crumbs for the birds: we heeled depressions in the grass between us to take our beer jugs and our cider kegs. There was no more wine.

We had eaten. Now we looked at each other, and waited for someone to speak. Without Arthur, who knew who was to speak, or what to speak about? Some looked at me, but I could not think what Arthur's orders would have been. At last, it was Bors, tactless and ignorant and blundering as always, who said, 'The Great Duke of War and Peace is dead. Who will be the next duke?'

We were silent. Our followers were out of sight and hearing on the plain below. We sixty great kings, we who ruled the Island, and the prefects of the greatest cities in the world, whether we held them or not, London and Caerwent and Ebor and Lindum and Deva, sat wondering what we would say and who would listen to us and who would speak after us.

Then Mordred spoke. He was sitting, as always, with the kings on his right, the prefects on his left, the House of Cunedda and the Votadini next to him, the House of Uther ringed round to be opposite him. He asked, 'Need there be a duke?'

There was a ripple of laughter. Gormant of Cornwall asked, for he was Arthur's half-brother and thought himself entitled to the leadership on this day, 'What should we do without a duke? How should we then go to war?'

Mordred asked again, quietly, so that we all had to lean forward to catch his words, and somehow this prompted everybody to talk more quietly, 'What should we do with another duke? The last one was the Great Duke of War, and, I speak it advisedly, of Peace, but there was little use for him when it was peace. All he ever did was wage war. The great wars ended at Badon, and after that there was nothing for the great horses to do but to eat up forage, and nothing for the Iron Men to do but to scour rust from idle metal. After that, Arthur had to be content with the little wars, the small raids and the quarrels with Heathen who lived next door, and to each of these tiffs he would ride with us, myself to scout ahead and see what was really happening, and Bedwyr to raise the people to fight on foot, Kai to marshal the horse who were the Great Duke's Household, and Lawnslot to guard his back, and Morvran to forage and to remember what had been forgotten and to turn Arthur's vague wishes into orders which had sense in them and which we could obey. Arthur needed us, but did we need Arthur? When we had peace he wanted war again, and he stirred war up, in case we should ask him to his face what I ask you all now – do we need a duke? Peace was a name to him, but War was real. Just before he died, was he not planning a new War? For what else did he call the kings to meet him here? Did he not want to persuade us to come and make war with him? But what war was he going to make? Can anyone think of where any King of the Heathen is making war on us?'

'If there is no Great Duke, will there ever be peace again?' asked Lot. 'Will I ever see my kingdom again?' For the Kingdom of Norroway is a great realm consisting of fifteen islands each the size of Ireland, lying ten days' rowing beyond Orkney. The Pagans hold it now.

'There will be war, as soon as the Pagans learn that they have succeeded. The Pagans of Logres have killed Arthur, and when they know he is dead, that the shield of the Island is pierced, they will think they have us at their mercy.' Gormant was almost shouting.

'We do not *know* it was the Pagans from Logres who killed Arthur,' I pointed out. 'All we had was a body and a man who ran and was killed before we could make him speak. And he was not out of Logres but a man from the Franks, and no proof even then—'

But I was shouted down. They all *knew* in their hearts that it was the Pagans from Logres who ought to have killed Arthur, who always wanted to kill Arthur, and therefore it must have been the Heathen from Logres who had done the deed. They saw no point in discussion.

'They have opened war on us,' Gormant repeated, even louder. 'They have done the deed, and either they will come against us, or we will have to ride against them to pay our *Galanas*, our blood-price. We must have a duke to lead so many kings.'

'But if Arthur is dead, need there be a war?' The voice was soft, insinuating: we others had to strain to hear what he was saying at Gormant, we were left no energy for a reply. It was as it had always been, the House of Uther against the House of Vortigern. Mordred against at least forty kings, my family, the Votadini, leaning first to one side, then to the other, but for this moment more inclined to Uther than to Vortigern. Once it would not have been so simple. It would have been Mordred alone against Arthur alone, and that would have been a fair match. But sixty kings were no match for Mordred.

I had once seen Mordred face a maddened bull, unarmed. It was for a wager, when Arthur had pitched Camelot at Caerleon, and called a Table in the old ring work there that the Romans had built and called a Theatre, a convenient place for men to defend. The wager was only whether the bull would kill Mordred, but everyone came to see how Mordred would kill the bull with his bare hands. The only people not told about the wager were Mordred and the bull, and when they came face to face it was a surprise to both.

But Mordred did not kill the bull. He moved aside before it charged, not quickly, but quietly, softly, smoothly. He talked to the bull, telling it tales of summer meadows and wide fields, of cool waters and bags of barley and the warm milk of its mother, till the beast became quiet and he led it from the throng with his hand on the ring in its nose. It was Gormant who took the axe to it in the shambles after, and we ate it that night, not very good because it had not been properly hung. Mordred did not eat of it. Mordred talked the same way to the kings and the prefects, and I wondered who at the end would eat whom.

'The Kings of the Pagans are defeated,' he reminded us. 'The best of their men died at Badon, and Bladulf their Duke died among them. That was half a generation ago. We know they are dead, and who killed them. What does it matter if now and again one man comes alone, through fire and water by stealth and guile and deceit and by the wisdom of the devil to kill just one of us, and if by chance he lights on someone who looks important, duke or groom, it does not matter to him, it ought not to matter to us. A man's life is a man's life, no matter who he is. There will be no war from this unless we ride out and make it, as Arthur did so often. He would ride across a quiet frontier that no one had breached, shouting that we were invaded, and news it would be to all who lived either side of it. He would burn villages where the Pagans could not afford a knife between them, let alone a sea of spears.

'Hear me, I talk of what I know, of the Pagans. I ride across their lands, or walk, by night or by day, looking here and there for signs of war. I have even been in the last year to see the other sea, from the heights of Lindsey. The savages are people, like us, simple and decent: primitive, I grant you, and ignorant and poor as ship rats, but still only people. As long as we live in peace with them, we can hope to bring them to a civilised way of life. We may even bring them to the worship of Christ—'

'That is not possible,' put in Melvas. 'They are the product of the Devil, and incapable of salvation.' Mordred ignored him, and went on,

'Let us each rest from war, and do each what we do best. Let us grow our oats and graze our sheep up on the good lands, and hunt the deer and the hare, not men; and in the end the Heathen will stick to growing wheat in the foul river bottoms, and forget their own trouble-making – and Arthur's.'

'That is easy enough to say,' and this was Synager, who was the Prefect of London. 'You live secure in Radnor, rich in cattle and in bogs full of game. Sometimes, perhaps, you do ride out to Viricon on your frontier, and glance into the Pagan lands. We have not seen you in our city. But we huddle close to our walls and yearly watch the savages creep nearer. Clappa and Bala have built their homes across the river. Haccon has taken the island on the north side, and cuts us off from the food of the heights. Once let us drop our guard and they will be inside the walls with us. Then when London falls, surely the other cities and the kingdoms will fall, one by one, each in turn dragging its neighbours down with it.'

'Nowadays the Pagans are only twice as many as we are,' went on Mordred. 'If they wanted to attack us, they would have done so long ago, when they were stronger, and we weaker. Indeed they did so, but we held them at Badon, and forced the Treaty. Let us wait till we have regained our full strength and we are as many as we were three generations ago. Then we quite filled up the towns of the Island. That was before the White Death came. It destroyed the young men, and laid all the Island open to the Picts, and forced Vortigern the Proud, the Splendid, the Unfortunate, my ancestor, to call in Hengist and his three keels. They came to fill up the empty Island, without our permission, and many of the people of the fields being of the same blood welcomed them. But they did not live in our towns, which they could not take even when they were empty. Let us refill the towns, and in another generation we will outnumber the Pagans. Then if they will not submit and worship Christ, we can overcome them by force.'

'Mordred is right,' said Synager, and that he should say such a thing was in itself a great event in history. 'Our strength has always been in the cities. We ought to fill them up again and live in them all the year round, as many of us do in London. I cannot understand why so many of you only come into the cities in winter, or for the market days.'

'My people,' Bedwyr told us, 'will live next winter in Badon, as they have always done, and next spring they will stay there, and go out to keep their sheep and sow their oats. What is a city but a great hendre from which the lads go out to the havod?'

'My people,' Bors told us, 'have lived in Ciren in the summer for the last three years now, and only the shepherds have gone out to the flocks. We find there is enough good land close to the walls for our oats and barley.'

'That will be a start, if we can begin to get these towns back, and then we can elect a new duke. We shall need one by that time,' said Mordred. He was beginning to shift his ground. Arthur would have turned on him and made him justify his every inconsistency, but nobody there could understand what was ringing in their ears, that Mordred could be convinced by argument, and even in a pinch by hard facts, and made to look a second time at what he held to be truth. But it was Gareth who now went off on a quite different tack, the long voyage from Orkney having as usual turned his wits topsy-turvy.

'Yes, that will do very nicely for when Arthur gets back. We'll have the cities filled with people and nicely stocked for the war.'

'But Arthur's dead,' I reminded him. 'We've just buried the Great Duke. What do you think we were doing down there?' I pointed at where Camelot had stood, the ugly black scar on the grass. But my eyes strayed always to the north. I could see across the lowlands and the silver streak of the Severn to where the hills of Gwent stood up clear, and I fancied I caught for a moment the scent of the broom and the meadow-sweet. The weather was not yet good, it being dry and most of the sky blue with a few clouds scudding across it 'Do you think we burnt the tents for light to dig by?'

'Oh, but Arthur's done this before,' put in Bors. 'He's gone off playing the fool around the coasts of Gaul, like he did before when he went to steal horses, and you ought to remember, Morvran, because you went with him and so did I. That was never a funeral, not a proper funeral, who ever heard of a funeral with no ham? And he'll come back when the Pagans least expect it. I tell you, he's gone off to see the Bezant Emperor and bring a hundred thousand soldiers with swords of Damask to chase the Pagans out of the Island.'

'The Bezant Emperor we knew is dead,' I pointed out, 'and Dietrikh of Beron sits on the crystal throne.'

'Dietrikh is dead also,' Mordred corrected me. 'The Lord Almasunth strives with his brothers for Empery.'

'Well, whoever it is,' Gareth insisted, 'Arthur's gone off to deceive the Pagans and bring the Emperor back.'

'Or to see who'll stay true to his memory, and who will go over to Mordred,' suggested Gormant.

'But he's dead,' I assured Gareth. I looked round at the other kings who had not come till the funeral summons went out. 'I saw him killed. You all saw his body.'

'We saw a coffin, we saw a bundle in it,' retorted Bors. 'But who's to know what was in it? What was under lead and leather? What is underground?'

'Gormant saw him killed,' I reminded them.

'A killing it was I saw,' said Gormant. 'Who was killed, who killed him, I have no sure knowledge. I saw a dead face, smashed with the axe beyond recognition. I saw a head shattered. I saw clothes – anyone can wear clothes. I saw a man run. Who was Arthur, who was not? Who knows?'

'Are you calling me a liar?' I demanded.

'Oh, no, not exactly,' called Lot. 'Only, Morvran, sometimes you have been known to be careless with the details of the truth.'

'Not for profit,' Gormant put in, with the ingratiating smile of a peacemaker, which is the most untrustworthy creature in the world. 'Only that there is nothing that you would not say if only Arthur asked you to say it.'

I stared at him. I am Morvran the Ugly, and when I choose to look ugly, there is no one who will refuse me what I ask. The scent of the primrose and the honeysuckle was stronger. I knew what was coming on us. A moment more, and Gormant would have retracted.

But Mordred could never leave ill alone, and that was his weakness. He laughed. 'Never to flee, never attack, only hold still at Arthur's back. Morvran the sly, Morvran the lame, tell us all now, what is your game?'

'For that, Mordred of the House of Vortigern, I tell you straight, I will not follow you, nor will any of the House of the Votadini.'

There was a grumble of support from among my relations, and also from some of the minor kings who were not really related to us but who hoped to improve their social standing by being seen in our company. Then we all sat back, the scent strong in our nostrils, and nobody remarking that it was all out of season and there must be a Fairy about somewhere because it was more interesting to listen to Mordred argue with the others. However, it was hardly a fair contest with only forty-three to one. In a few minutes they were all shouting at once, and quarrelling with each other as to what each was entitled to say, as would never have happened had Arthur been there.

Then both Bors and Gormant woke up to this and both shouted together, 'Silence! Let there be a silence!'

And they were so loud and forceful that after a few repetitions, everyone else fell quiet, and left them to shout 'Silence! Silence!' at each other for quite a while. When they stopped, they were too embarrassed to say anything more, and left the kings looking at each other to see who would speak first. We would have been there to this day, if it had not been for Dunwal, a man of few words and those of unexampled and perfect futility.

He said, 'What about the woman? She's a Pagan. We can start by killing her. Then we can go for the rest of them. Kill the Nits!'

'We weren't talking about her yet,' Bedwyr pointed out, but nobody took any notice.

Mordred was shouting, 'She is a hostage! Keep her safe. While this Gwenevere lives, the Pagans will stay quite within their own borders. Kill her and they will come in force to seek out the treaty-breakers. Morvran, you made the Treaty – tell them the terms!'

But I kept silent as I had promised him. The argument continued over his head and mine as to what should be done with the woman.

'We could throw lots for her,' suggested Gareth. That was typical. Who would go to Orkney to start with, unless they'd been cheated into it, and then thought that being swindled was sufficient training for swindling others?

But Kaw the Senile, who held a poor little kingdom in the north called Leodis, and whose tastes were quite other than those of most men or he could not have stood it there, slavered, 'We could scrape her to death with oyster shells, as the Egyptians of Rome Land did to the Holy Saint Hypatia, who alone kept the faith against them'.

There was a shout of approval for this, and several minor kings began to argue as to who should have the honour of first scrape and how oyster shells could be come by now that the Pagans held Kent, and whether Penklawdh cockleshells would do as well. But at last they began to run out of breath and anticipation together, and Bedwyr who had plenty of breath left having been silent till now was able to shout them down. 'She is safe in the Glass Island. The Holy Saints have her safe. We have all sworn to keep her there, don't any of you remember the Treaty?'

Kai countered, 'That proves Arthur isn't dead. You're keeping that tasty morsel for him when he comes back from Hy Brasil or Bezant or wherever he's gone. And you and Morvran know exactly where, and when.'

'Of course he's dead,' Bedwyr insisted, so that Gormant was able to come in, back to his old point.

'Arthur's dead. We need a new duke. There's only one candidate possible. That's my foster son, Constant, Arthur's flesh and blood, brought up in Camelot and used to statecraft and treachery and all the other gifts so necessary to a duke. And not a king—'

'Because he's a bastard,' shouted my cousin Beli, King of Man, more truthfully than tactfully. 'Needs an estate for settlement, but no good in bed, I hear, and less good out of it. No, I'd rather follow Mordred.'

He thought he had settled the whole idea of having a new duke, if the only possible candidate was as bad as that, but several of the lesser and more stupid kings heard only the last words. They decided that the house of the Votadini were voting for Mordred, and all began to shout together,

'Mordred for duke! Down with Constant!'

This clashed with, 'Constant for duke! Down with Mordred! Constant, Constant!' from the other side of the table.

But then it came down, raining buckets, as I had been expecting from the clarity of the air, and nobody in his senses or out of them would have stayed on the top of a hill like Cadbury in that. Some kings like myself waved their scarves for their grooms to come up and help us down, and many of the less watertight picked up their saddles and began to make their way down the hillside unaided except by the cider they had hurriedly finished off. Some rolled down. And that was the end of the last Table at Cadbury Congress.

III

It was the last Table of all those which had brought the kings together in their splendour and wisdom, and a pity it was there was no Arthur there to laugh at it. He always laughed at a Table cut off by the weather, as usually happened, leaving him to make the decisions without much attention to what the kings had said. He knew they would all follow his lead, and put the blame for mistakes on each other, and not on him.

This day there were no conclusions. There were those who left thinking that Constant was now the Great Duke of War and Peace, and among them was Constant himself. And there were those who thought that Mordred was now the Great Duke, and among those Mordred was not. And there were some, like Mordred and Bedwyr and myself, who knew that there was no longer any Great Duke, and that the Unity of the Island of the Mighty was now ended, and that every king, however weak and humble, must shift for himself against the Heathen out of Logres, or against the Irish.

Only one thing in my eyes was definite. It was that no decision had been taken. The talk of this Table had gone every which way, and never come home at all. And that would never have happened if Arthur had been there.

So all the kings went home. The collected their hosts from the hills above Thameshead, and went by one way and another across the country of the Christians. Where they came to the borders of Logres, they would here and there, where it seemed convenient, ride across and find a village to take and sack, bringing home a few pieces of iron or even bronze, a spearhead or a ploughshare or a couple of knives, and perhaps a jar dug up from a Christian grave. It gave them enough pigs and wheatmeal to get home on, and stories they could tell which their bards could work up into great tales of valour and daring, of giants killed in single combat and maidens rescued from captivity. If the maidens wanted to be rescued, which even for real Christian captives was not always the case.

To the west, the people of the farms and hills were all Christians, and spoke the language of the angels. But to the east, even before the time of Vortigern, many of the people were not Christians and spoke the common tongue of the Heathen, since they were descended from the slaves and soldiers which the Romans had brought into the country from Germany in years past, so that the real nobles of our race were left only to hold the towns and give the laws and administer them and the markets and take the taxes. In the kingdom I had once in Lindsey nobody at all spoke the great tongue except myself and the warriors I had brought with me out of Avan to take back the lost lands. It had been the aim of Arthur to take back all the lost lands, and set up again kings in every city. But in that war both sides were exhausted and the Truce was welcome. Now the truce was over. Every king made war on the Heathen on his own account. So I went west, back to Gwent to hold it on my own account.

Interlude 5: Captivity

The woman lived in her hut on the Island of Glass. Three times a day, the strange people in their black shifts with their hair streaming behind but shaved across in front from ear to ear, brought her food. Six days in the week, they brought her oat porridge, and on the seventh they would bring her a little boiled fish and a radish. Twelve times a day they preached at her while she sat, silent, her needle busy on the lace cushion. Seven times a day they prayed together, kneeling before a little hut into which at dawn Melvas went alone, from which he came out with shining face. For there Melvas saw God, talked with God, made God, became God.

One Gwenevere had gone far to the west. There she would sit all the day in her cave, looking out to the west, to the golden hills of Wicklow, and the realms of the Red Kings of Leinster, the Ui Dunlaing and the Ui Gennselach. She prayed that the Irish should never come again into the Island of the Mighty and the Kingdom of Menevia. And she cursed the soul of Patrick the Evil One, who had taken the news of God into the Island of the Blessed, and saved the souls of all those sinful Heathen from Tara to Cashel, and twice as far and back again.

One Gwenevere had gone to the north. There she knelt all day on the Rock of Eiddin, and prayed to God for the salvation of the City. She prayed for the continuance of the kingdom that showed forth God's Glory in the North. Or would show it forth if only the King of Eiddin could take Dumbarton Rock again from the Irish.

One Gwenevere lay beneath the soil for ever. She lay marked with her name, far from her Lord and yet near to him.

Only the Fourth Gwenevere remained alive on the Glass Island. Here one day was like another, one Saint like another: there was no distinction here of male or female, old or young, only this, that the voice of a child was never heard there, nor was anyone below the age of decision allowed within the gate. The days became shorter, and the air colder. The rain fell, and at length sometimes the snow lay in the morning for an hour or two, but there was never a change in the daily pattern. Only her lace net grew.

Each day, all day, the Saints sang to God. Sometimes they sang in their own language which she had not yet mastered, and their song was a mystery to her. Sometimes they sang in Latin, and then it was easier and she could follow it. Always they sang most loudly of vengeance on her and on her people, and blessed those who should catch up her children and dash them against a stone. And this was the stone they had raised above the grave of Arthur. So she wept, although whether she wept that she had no children, or for the fate of the children she wished to have, she never knew. Only that tears were appropriate. And her tears fell on her lace cushion, which was the only familiar thing she had been allowed to send before her into this place. On her cushion she fashioned new nets, and into the nets she lured antlered stags and boars and hounds and birds and spiders and wheels and ships: and kings.

Chapter 5

Camlann

I

Mabon held Caerwent for me that winter, as indeed he had done for many winters in the past. I felt it rather weak-minded for a king to hide behind walls unless he were chased there, or for the necessities of entertainment. Here I disagreed with Bedwyr. I always went to a farm I had beyond Skirrid, on the fringes of Brecon, to do the work of the winter. So did all of my principal officers, each to his own farm. I had a good longhouse up there, and we were snug and dry, me and Taberon and three families of the people of the land at one end, and the cows at the other to keep us all warm.

We started work in October, bringing the sheep down from the hills and folding them in close to the house. At the end of this work we rested the horses and the dogs, and held as always our night of joy, with songs and dancing and the ale and the cider poured. The men clasped their wives in joy, and the boys of the farm looked with longing on those of the girls who were not their sisters, or they sat making their spoons with much carving for young girls from other farms they had met up at the havods in the summer where they kept the sheep. But I sat alone and drank in silence, toasting my toes for want of closer company, or I went out to hunt the bear and the wolves that came for the sheep, with as much hatred as if they had been the Pagans. For I thought then of a burnt house in Lindsey, and of three graves that no Christian cleaned on Palm Sunday.

II

After midwinter, the weather grew harsher, as it so often does, and there was snow on the hills and even in some valleys before lambing had begun. When that was over, and my skill and labour were no longer needed, I took my horse and necessary gear, and called Taberon, to go with me across the hills beyond Margam to where Gwion had his farm, under the walnut trees on the banks of the Avan. He was the greatest man in my kingdom, next to Mabon. Twelve families lived close to him, near enough for each to see his neighbour's smoke, and they had built a Hall fit for me to live in when I came, as was my custom and my right, to grace them with my presence for two weeks every year.

So each night, Gwion would call from the door of the Hall, as we had so often heard Kai call in Camelot, that the knife was in the meat and the ale was in the cup (for we were short of wine that winter) and that all were welcome who had tales to tell or precious things to sell. Nobody ever came, and we were glad of that, and it was just as well, since it meant the more for us to eat out of the meagre rations that would have to last us till the summer. However, since I would not now be called on to feed Arthur and his Household for the three weeks in August, we might have more to eat ourselves then. Nobody eats as much as a careless scullion, nor is as demanding and wasteful as a lackey.

The last night of that first week was a bad night. It was the night of the year when I had to remember Teleri and the two little girls, and the son who if he had been born would have been Mordred's heir, as his sister's son, as Mabon was my heir, and Mordred was Arthur's; if Arthur could have been expected to leave anything tangible, being himself a bastard of no estate. That night I always spent with men who knew me well enough not to cross me, out of their good will understanding well the reason why, and in the presence of Gwion's wife Iarwen, who poured the ale for him and me, and who would always persuade me to stop before the jar was dry. The ale she brewed, come to that, was bad enough to put a man off drinking for ever: her mead was worse.

Now that day we had had particularly heavy labour, in the sheep-fold, dunging out, and after that the night would have been a bad night anyway. I had not yet started on the serious drinking, or the hearing of petitions, if there were any, which is always a strain on a decent king, justice being usually quite impossible.

Gwion came back from the doorway muttering, 'Now all the other kings of the earth may eat, if they have any stomach for it.'

And another man came in after him, and this was a man I knew and did not want much to see, dressed as he was in grey with red stripes. He was wet to the waist and there were snowmen growing on the top of his ears. When he had made four good paces into the Hall, halfway up it, he felt my eye on him and stopped. He spoke in the ceremonial dialect of the Court, slowly and with great attention to grammar: 'All hail and greetings to you, Morvran the Lame, Great King of all the men of Gwent, and Lord of Glevissig, Pretender to Brecon, and Prefect of Caerwent, over all causes and over all persons within your dominions supreme.'

That had given me time to drain a pint, but I still thought it fitting to reply in the same dignified mode of speech: 'And greetings to you, too, journeying without my leave through my lands, Hennin son of Broga, warrior of Cornwall and farmer with little success of less than a hundred acres.'

'Master of the markets and owner of the cockling rights between Porthcawl and Kidweli,' he continued in the same style and without showing any emotion, 'I bring you also brotherly greeting from the Great Duke of Peace and War.'

That had given me time for another pint and I no longer had the patience to answer him in anything but my own dialect, speaking through the nose and sibilantly like my cousins in the North, but broadening my diphthongs in the cultured way of Avan. I told him straight, 'Arthur's dead. It was seeing him buried I was. Conveniently already dead as a roof tree. If you came from him, I'd say, sit down and have a drink. And a piglet.'

'I am sent by that most august personage, my Lord and my patron, the present Great Duke.'

'Look, Hennin,' I told him straight, 'you can stop all this elaborate talk and that high-class accent, and be yourself. And stop talking nonsense. What do you think you mean, Great Duke? You know very well, there's no Great Duke, not any more.' And I wept at the thought, and all the Avan men wept with me, the ale being well sunk.

By now Hennin was tired enough to take some notice of what I was telling him, and he came down into a more informal way of speaking, still a recognisable version of the Court dialect with all its noun-cases and dual numbers that most people don't bother with any more, but with a strong smell of the Cornish.

'Don't play games with me, Morvran,' he pleaded. 'I've walked fourteen flaming days to get here, seeing as how I was misinformed and went up to Bala first, and had to come back south by way of Cardigan to avoid Mordred, and not a drop of hospitality there in the west since Seithenin was drinking it all, and here I am dead beat and dry as a barrel of herrings it is that I am, seeing as how I only asked you civil for a drink and—'

'I do *not* see as how,' I told him firmly. 'But I'll give you a drink, and I'll let you sit down as well, if you come straight and tell me who it was that it was that sent you, because I'm dead sure that you didn't come here because you liked me.'

'That's true, because I never did like you very much,' he agreed, the fire having cheered him up, 'and I wouldn't be here only it is five days' service in the year I am owing to Constant of Cornwall that half the Island says is the Great Duke, and I think after going to Bala that it is cheating me that it is that he is, and I reckon that he's getting no more service out of me for the next five years—'

'It would have been only three days if you'd gone the proper way instead of gallivanting up to Bala,' I argued, 'and so you are still two days in debt.' After all, we kings and prefects and great lords of the Island must stick together, and if Hennin got away with his mistakes then anyone could play ducks and drakes with the basic elements of morality and the good of society. It is the business of the King sitting as Judge, which is after all what they keep him for, to decide these issues in accordance with the basic principles of virtue, like greed and selfishness. 'Anyway I'm letting you stay to supper because you were with us at Badon and a better horseholder we didn't have in the third rank.'

'I wasn't a horseholder,' he protested. 'I was an archer on the right flank.'

That, I reflected, was the flank that had folded on the first day. I let him off lightly. 'If you were a horseholder, you get dinner. If you were in that mob on the right, then you don't. And it's either go on ten miles to Ogmore, or back to Neath.'

'Oh, don't send me back to Neath,' he implored. 'Nobody who even looks human ought to have to go to Neath. For the sake of argument, then it was a horseholder that I was.'

I did not think it politic to tell him how much I agreed with his point of view, Neath men being what they are and several present. 'Sit you down there, and have a piglet.'

'You've pulled the right thigh off this one,' he grumbled.

I reminded him, 'Right thigh's the hero's portion, and a horseholder can't be a hero. What is it that it is you are after, then?'

'Well, Morvran, I've been all the winter with Constant. What in God's name did you want to make him the Great Duke for?'

'I didn't make him Great Duke.'

'Well, he keeps on telling people that you did, and if Constant doesn't say it then Gormant rubs it in. Keeps on telling people that Morvran was the first to vote for him.'

'Now, Hennin, you know I wouldn't do a thing like that, would I?'

'Tell the truth, Morvran, there isn't anything that we can say for certain you wouldn't never do.'

'Never mind that.' I was pleased at this reputation, I had worked hard for it. 'What's Constant up to? And if you came from the bottom end of Cornwall through Bala to here in only twelve days, than you didn't do so bad.'

'No, no, Constant is at Camlann and I started there.'

'Where?'

'Camlann.'

'Where on earth is that?'

'Oh, close to Glevum, in what used to be Lawnslot's country, just out of Gwent. Oh, I see what you mean. That's where Camlann is now. It's Constant's city, successor to Camelot. A Great Duke, you know, he has to move about in every comfort. He's had all the saddlers and tent-makers in Cornwall sewing it since Cadbury Congress. Not much gold leaf, and the painter was a botcher by trade and a bungler by training, but you can't have everything. Most of the time, you can't have anything, so take what you can get, I always say.'

'True. But why send you here?'

'How do I know? All I know is that he said to find you and tell you he was holding a Table at Camlann straight away. Well, he said I was to command you, but I've got too much sense to say that. So I'll say that he invited you to come to Camlann near to Glevum, but he sounded very insistent about it.'

'How insistent? Iarwen, be a good girl and pour this brave man some . . . no, not your best ale, but some of your flowery mead. Dandelion flavour, I think. Held horses in the rear like mad, he did, especially when we wanted them brought forward.'

'Very insistent. Said he'd cut my head off if I went back without you.'

'And if I don't go?'

'You haven't a little farm around here that you could let me have, Morvran, have you? Just about three cows' worth. I think you'd owe it to me one way or another.'

'I'll think about it. Have another pint. Elderflower and dandelion, this is. Good elderflower year it was last year, and we got those dande-lions from Brecon, summer raid, from round the church. Grow splendid on graves, dandelions do. I'll stay on the ale. Can you sing, Hennin?'

'Sing? No, Morvran, you know me, can't sing a note.'

'All right, we'll have a solo for you, you might spoil the harmonies if we let you sing in the choir. If you can't hit the note, here's another mug of the elderflower-and-dandelion.'

'No, no, I'll sing, but don't make me drink any more of that.'

So sing he did, and what's more we had him drink another three pints of the dandelion-and-elderflower, which saved on the beer, and helped us get through the mead which was not one of Iarwen's happier efforts. What we did not drink that winter visit we sealed down in pots for the road.

Because of course, I did go to Glevum, but not direct. I went first to Caerwent, the long way around to cross the Taff high up. Gwion came with me, and in Caerwent we hoped to find a few of our better young men, fine upstanding lads who could be trusted to carry home the news of Constant's defeat and destruction as was certain to happen if he were as mad as he seemed, a function often overlooked by those who are inexperienced in the raising of armies. I took Taberon who was getting a bit mischievous and restive, not having taken a head yet, and him sixteen, nearly or just over, give or take a year or two, counting being hard and Tatharn usually very uncertain with his figures and not always getting the date of Easter right.

I had Mabon, who had held the town all the winter, send out messengers to bring in all my principal officers of state, except for Gwenki who had a house near to the Usk, a Roman house once so it had a bath room. Romans were very dirty people. We got a night's lodging from him there, all of us, as part of my royal due.

III

Camlann wasn't up to much, not to those of us who'd seen Camelot, but it might improve with time and booty. It was a great deal better, though, than sleeping under a hedge, or in a house where people were so gross as to wash in hot water in a special closet instead of going down to the river every Michaelmas. I picked out a tent, and never saw who were in it, but I told Gwion that I wanted it and didn't care how I got it. I never did find out how, or who, but we were very comfortable in it all the time we were in Camlann. Delegation is the basis of all authority.

While Gwion looked after that, I myself went along to Constant's tent. Some fool of a sentry tried to argue with me. 'The Great Duke dines alone,' he told me. Stupid idea! Arthur never dined alone, that's when he did all his diplomatic work. 'He must not be disturbed.'

I motioned to Gwenki, who gave him a clout across the helm which left him moaning because he hadn't bothered to pad it properly. It didn't do Gwenki much good either, because he had forgotten he wasn't wearing his riding gloves, and I left the pair of them grizzling together. Taberon followed me.

Inside, Constant was sitting at table discussing half a pig. I pulled up a stool and joined him.

'Put that thigh down!' he screamed at me.

'Right thigh, the hero's portion,' I reminded him. He was speaking the Court dialect, but with a dreadful Cornish accent. I retaliated by using South Glamorgan, a mysterious argot. 'Where would you find a more heroic figure than mine, a bolder rider in peace, a more judicious planner in war?'

'On every flaming hedgerow,' he snarled. He was trying to copy Arthur's charming way of public speaking, but somehow he couldn't make it rough enough. I took his measure carefully. Constant in Cornwall might be a figure of fun, but Constant grown up, at large in the Island with half the kings thinking that he was the Great Duke and him acting as if he was, would take some careful handling. But after all he was only a Corn, and I was of the great house of the Votadini.

'So, what is it that you are wanting, boy?' I asked him.

'Finish your supper first. Or rather finish my supper.' He snapped his fingers, and his wife Igerna came in. 'Pour this great king some ale!'

She did the best she could at this ceremony, but it was obvious that she was finding it difficult to turn so quickly from wife of a bog-farmer to consort of the Great Duke: especially since she was Irish to start with. She managed to leave a great deal of froth on her beer – it was very black, a proper Irish recipe. An acquired taste. I bowed low to her in the fashionable manner, which took her aback, and announced in the High Court dialect, 'Most gracious lady, I have brought you the fairest produce of all Gwent, a beverage composed of the heather honey and the summer sunlight and the sweet dews of May and the flowers of the land, nurtured under the eyes of the most lovely and virtuous maidens of the kingdom, a drink such as the degenerate lords of the southwest have never tasted.'

Taberon bent his knee and presented to her six small casks of the dandelion-and-elderflower, handling them as if they were liquid garnets. I had laid down that Taberon was to be treated with all the consideration due to his birth, which at least made him cheap to feed.

After this exchange, Constant spoke. 'I have a grave problem. It concerns all the Kingdoms of the Island which I under the providence of God and the Virgin have been chosen to lead, unworthy though I am.'

'Unworthiness has nothing to do with it. You just weren't chosen.'

He bridled a bit at that, but he didn't wish to debate the matter further.

'I had it in mind to call a full Table, but seeing the urgency of the case and the expense to so many people I contented myself with sending for you and you have been long enough coming.'

'Only me? Not important, then, you thought.'

'I have also sent for His Grace the King-Abbot. He is taking even longer. The matter concerns a scandal against our late leader, the first Great Duke of Peace and War.'

'Against Arthur?' With Constant talking in the High Court way of speech, and Melvas coming too, it all seemed serious, at least in his eyes.

'Against Arthur, against his truth, against his honour, against his loyalty to the unity of the Island.'

I could not very well tell him, while I was eating his dinner, that he was showing his jealousy of a dead man. I informed him calmly, 'There can be no scandal. Arthur, as you say, was the soul of virtue and the Master of our hopes. If any man gave his soul and body for the unity of the island, it was Arthur. His every deed was open to the sky, and as well known to the meanest farmer as to his confessor – but there, Melvas talks so freely he might as well have had no confessor. If he had not been so open and honest himself, he would not have lost the second Gwenevere. He was incapable of deceit, and therefore he could not recognise deceit when it was practised on him. That is why Lawnslot sinned, and that is why Lawnslot still lives.'

'Yet there is an accusation of deceit, and it threatens the safety of all the kingdom. And above all it concerns you, Morvran.'

'I do not understand.'

'I will not explain, I will show you and you may then see what is happening, Morvran the Crafty.'

He led me and Taberon through the back flap of the tent, past Igerna at her cooking fire, and she gave me a filthy look: I supposed that she had tasted the elderflower-and-dandelion. Taberon snatched a meat pasty as we went by and got a clip round the ear, delivered with an Irish accent and the queenly words, 'Steal the dogs' dinner now, will you?'

Taberon dropped the pasty, believing it to be made of asses' meat, one having died recently as was clear from the skin and bones lying around. We passed on to the next tent, where there was a sentry leaning on his pike. He greeted me cheerfully, and I remembered that he had been a scullion, class three, in Camelot. Promotion strikes where it will, like lightning but less rationally. However, he peered suspiciously at Constant and dropped his pike to the royal navel.

'He's all right.' I jerked my head at the new Great Duke. 'He's with me.'

'Suppose you've got to mix with all sorts, if you're a king.' The pike returned to the vertical which is a convenient leaning angle. I remarked to Constant, 'I admire the close personal contact you keep with your troops.'

'It is a mighty host. And he is new.'

'New? He's as old as the hill. Couldn't guard a trout in a bucket. Who have you got in here? Three bards and a milkmaid?'

'This guard is for ceremony only. I have honoured guests.' Constant spoke loudly and in Latin. We went into the tent. I saw what he had there, and it really was serious.

They were sitting on the tent floor, their backs to the canvas wall, as savages always do. If you give them stools or benches, they only chop them up for firewood, and if you put down a bale of hay they either eat it or go to sleep on it. Their pikes leaned against the tent pole behind them, their swords showed under their cloaks. At least the riding strings were still tied. Beside the left hand of each there lay a brown and withered branch that had once been green. They had been eating their native bread made of wheatflour and yeast, and lumps of grilled something – I guessed it was not beef but donkey, whether they knew or not. And the smell—!

The nearer one was very old, at least forty, with his front teeth missing. He wore one pigtail, stiffened with tallow, and the fighting-cock feathers stuck into it showed that he was of high rank. He had tribal marks on the left cheek, three half-moons, themselves in a triangle. His necklace of small bones, including a cat's skull, told me that he was a witchman. He had three ox-tails around his right leg, four around his left. I was glad to see that he had paid for them: there was a long twisting scar from left wrist to elbow as if he had lost his sword and taken a slicing cut through his wrapped cloak.

The other was younger, and not a witchman of any order I could recognise. He wore two pigtails, elegantly hanging forward over his shoulders to his breast. There were eagle feathers in the right pigtail, osprey feathers in the left. He had no tribal marks. There was a gold ring in his left ear. Four ox-tails, all on the right leg. This was a big man, nineteen hands at least, the kind that has to be fed regularly, every other day at least, or he is no good at all, will flag on campaign and be easy to run down. One day, I thought, I will run this one down myself. If you do not make judgements like this in the first glance, then you will not live to learn.

I tried to make what I could of this. The older man, the witch, was a Saxon, perhaps from Thameshead and maybe a village chief, perhaps even born in the Island, although I could tell nothing from the strip of coloured rag that they wear knotted around their necks to show their social standing. The other – well, I couldn't tell until he started to speak, but he seemed to be a Jute from the wild country southeast of London, or a Friesian new come over, maybe even a Wend, since he wore a bit of yellow and blue as a scarf. But with hawks' feathers and gold on him he would be royal. The boughs showed that they were heralds, messengers of a sort, to a Great Duke who, the last time I heard him on the subject, was full of bloody threats and sacred oaths never to look on a Heathen and leave him living.

Constant and I sat on the bench opposite them and watched them eat. Nobody spoke. There was a silence long enough to recite the penitential Psalms. I know because I did recite the penitential Psalms, silently, which is always a strong charm in the face of witchcraft. I suspected that Constant was doing the same.

Finally he spoke first, which is always a mistake and showed that he was too impatient to be a statesman. 'This is the great king for whom we have been waiting.'

The two savages looked at me silently, without affection. I could feel my moustache go out of curl.

At last the witchman said, in Latin, but with the quantities wrong and some confusion between 'u' and 'v', 'Not great enough.'

Charming, I thought. I waited silent for a while, while I recited five
paternosters for the effect on my soul, which was not marked. Then
I shifted a little on my seat and let my cloak fall open. I brought my
sword round to where they could see her hilt uncovered but still tied
for riding.

My fingers played idly with the jewels in the strings. After an appropriate time, I observed, looking up at the roof of the tent, 'Here is Bees
in the Summer Meadow, six times quenched. We do not wear ox-tails.
I was at Badon. And at Linnuis. And in the wood of Caledon. And
elsewhere. In this Island, I have killed seventeen of your people. Irish I
do not bother to count. And many Franks and Goths when we went to
Gaul to fetch great horses.'

There was another silence. Then the witchman from Thameshead
spoke again, 'At Badon, you killed my uncle Bald. You wear his brooch
on your scabbard.'

Oho, I thought, I know you now, I know a great deal. I remembered
the uncle, a hard man to get the better of, not flashy or even very skilful
but unwilling to give up or retreat. Which is why he died. I heard that
he came from Scania, or at least that his brooch did. But any introduc-
tion was better than none. My credentials were established.

The older savage went on with the talk, still in his bad Latin. 'You
have killed many. This one' – and he jerked his head at Constant – 'has
never fought. Some day we will kill both of you. Where is the Great
Duke?'

'Arthur is dead. Many of our people accept this man as the Great
Duke.'

'But not all. Not you.'

'Let him prove himself.'

We discussed Constant not so much as if he were not present, but
more as if we were two teachers discussing a pupil there to learn from
us, and not a very bright pupil at that. The savages looked at each
other, silent. I wondered if it was true that the savages can talk without
sound.

The witchman told me, '*We* do not accept him.'

'It is not your business. Who cares if you accept him or not?'

'It is important. There is a treaty.'

'Arthur made that treaty. Arthur is dead.'

'Arthur swore to this treaty. Others made this treaty. Arthur only swore. Men who made the Treaty: they also swore.'

Where, I wondered, is Melvas? He and I and Arthur made the Treaty, and only we three swore. No one else knew the terms in full, although I suspected that Melvas had written them down.

I argued on, 'Arthur is dead.'

'Is Arthur dead? We have heard rumours before. If we paid gold to every man who came to say he had killed Arthur, then the Island would sink under the sea for the weight of gold and jewels. Some say he died last year, some a score of years ago, some in every year between. Before the Treaty some said he was dead. But he swore to the Treaty, living. Perhaps still he lives.'

'Arthur is dead. If he were not dead, would this man keep such state and claim to be Great Duke?'

'The Great Duke made the Treaty. We keep the Treaty if the Great Duke keeps the Treaty. There is a hostage.'

'There is, indeed.' This was from Constant, who had the look of a man who had been through all this before, and was getting tired of repetition. 'The hostage married the Great Duke. That Great Duke is dead. I am now the Great Duke.'

The witchman turned back to me as if ignoring the interruption while acknowledging that it saved a great deal of arguing. 'This man is duke? Where then is our sister? She is the duke's wife. That was the Treaty.'

'But' – and I was seeing the point – 'what if the duke's wife is not your sister? If there is a duke now, then this man may be the duke. That is his claim. The kings are not agreed. But this man has a wife.'

At this point, as if taking her cue, and indeed I would not have put it past her morally to listen outside but I doubted then if she had the wit or the Latin, Igerna entered the tent with several of her maids. I observed Taberon sit up and take notice. They brought us new cups fresh turned out of yew, and a bronze jug, probably the most valuable thing in all the Kingdom of Cornwall.

The elder savage asked, 'This? Wife for a Great Duke?'

For a moment I hoped that Igerna had not understood the words or the tone, but a glance at her face showed that she had indeed.

Nevertheless, she poured drinks for us all with every appearance of courtesy and then left us with a self-satisfied smirk. I raised my cup to my lips, but the smell warned me merely to go through the motions of swallowing. Constant and the others, too polite to demand that someone should taste before them, all took great gulps. The younger savage turned first green and then purple, and coughed violently. The older man was better controlled. He swallowed quickly and then closed his eyes as well as his lips as if savouring the after-taste.

When, as I suppose, he could trust himself to open his mouth without retching, he observed, 'A rare brew, indeed, and worthy of so great a duke.'

'A speciality of our hills.' Constant was in no condition to receive or pay compliments. I had to speak for him. 'It is much valued as it helps us to withstand the rigours of the winter.'

'I would advise you to brew more. Our sister is not married to your . . . Commander.' He was more subtle in his distinctions than I had expected. 'We would have peace with the Great Duke. Whoever is Great Duke. The Great Duke is married to our sister. If this man is not married to our sister then he is not the Great Duke. How can we have peace if our sister is not married to the Great Duke? If there is no peace, roofs will burn in winter. Men will go cold. Brew more of . . . this.'

I said to Constant in our civilised language,

'There's your problem, It's simple. They'll only deal with a Great Duke who is married to her, the Fourth Gwenevere.'

'You have worked all that out yourself?'

'I admit that it takes genius. Now, in practice, you are married to Igerna.'

'That is the least of our troubles. Hennin hates her like poison, and one dark night . . .'

'The moon is now full, and we are in a hurry, or at least you are. It seems a waste, too, of a good sharp tongue. Gwenki could do with a wife like that to call his own. For a consideration he might kidnap her.'

'Would the Church accept a few torn garments with blood as proof of being a widower?'

'No respectable Saint would, but I think that Melvas would rule that kidnapping leads naturally and necessarily to adultery. Divorce would be easier.'

'And cheaper?'

'I'm afraid that we would have to square Melvas as well as Gwenki. But if it's recognition as Great Duke it is that you want, then you must see that every step will cost you something. And it's your claim, not mine, so I'm not going to pay. And the wedding will be expensive – there'll be savage witnesses to fill with ale, for one thing, and every guest will expect a wedding present: I will, certainly. Where is Melvas, anyway? He helped to make the Treaty and he ought to share the blame.'

'I sent for him when I sent for you. Why did you both take so long to come? These ambassadors have been eating us out of house and home. Very finicky. Want ham and eggs for breakfast, won't touch oat porridge, and insist on barley beer instead of cider.'

I turned back to the savages. They had sat silent and motionless while we talked, looking straight ahead with glazed pale blue eyes.

'My brother and I will talk on this matter. We will bring you news tomorrow. A holy man has your sister in his keeping. We have sent for him.'

I turned to go, but the older savage said loudly, 'Stay! There is another matter.'

'What more?' I sat down again.

'For some years we have spoken with the Great Duke, by messenger. Sometimes they reach him. Sometimes you kill them, but not often. Some day we will eat the fox that kills the doves. Two went last autumn, to Camelot. At Caerwent. We think they are dead.'

'An old Jute, and a young tough from the north? Oh, yes, we killed them all right. We killed anybody who came to kill Arthur.'

'They came to talk our words to Arthur.'

'Why then did they come as thieves, lurking by night, armed, not as heralds bearing green boughs? Then we would have known that you were sending a message to Arthur.'

'Do you think Arthur wanted you to know all he did?'

'Arthur was our leader, our Great Duke. He planned for us. Why should he not want us to know what he was doing?'

But already I could understand why Constant was so worried. It was true, then, that Arthur had deceived us, and had new things to tell us at the Table he had called. If it had been known that Arthur was dealing in secret with the Heathen then there would have been the stormiest Table of all, called against Arthur and not for him, unless the Duke had something vital to say. I could press them.

'What was it Arthur meant to do? What was it you were talking to him about?'

'Not to, but with.' And this was the younger of the ambassadors. 'Is it really true that Arthur is dead?' This was the first time he had spoken, but whether it was out of politeness towards his older, but now I realised junior colleague, or simply that the damage the mead had caused to his vocal chords had taken this time to heal, I did not know. 'If Arthur is dead, then we must consult our friends and relations about the Treaty.'

'The Treaty goes on. We still hold your lady. She is safe and kept in honour. We will find a new husband to protect her.'

'No. That was the old Treaty. I speak of the new Treaty.'

'What new Treaty? The last treaty was between the Kings of the Island, all of us, and your Chieftains, all of them, and it took us a year to negotiate it.' Most of that time had been taken up with our own debates at the Table, and at last it had been left to me and Melvas and Arthur to deal with, just to save time and tempers.

'There is a new treaty between our kings, who are always all of one voice as you are not, and Arthur alone. That is why it is going through so quickly. Arthur alone made it. He said that he could see that your kinglets kept it.'

I could not believe that. Arthur would never have made a treaty without consulting me from the beginning, as it was I who would have to arrange how to carry it out, in detail and in practice.

I asked, puzzled, 'What was this treaty about? He never told me.'

'You swear that Arthur is dead? You swear by what you hold holy?'

I stood and pushed my cloak aside from my sword, laid my hand on her hilt. 'I swear by God and the Virgin, by Jesus and all the other Saints living and dead. I swear by the steel of the grey sword, and by the brooch on her scabbard' – I seized the witchman's right hand with my left and held it to the brooch to bind him with me in the oath. And then, for this was a grave occasion – 'I swear by three graves in Lindsey.'

The witchman knew of me, perhaps he had even been in the field against me. He knew what I would keep holy. He admitted, with a glance at his young leader, 'You speak true, King Morvran. Arthur is dead. There is no Great Duke. We will tell you. Arthur was planning war.'

'We had guessed that. He was calling us together, all us kings of the west and south together and the kings of the centre, as far as Ratae, the Legions' Castle on the Soar that Mordred holds, to fight against you.'

'Not against us. With us.'

I did not quite follow. 'Not against you? Then against whom?'

'We do not know. We only know that we agreed that we would not attack him or his little kings while he went to war.'

'And in exchange?'

'He would grant us the Vale of the Centre from the Humber to Luton, as we call what you called Coritan before we took it, and on the furthest edge the fortress of the Legions on the Soar, Ratae.'

Mordred's castle, that he held with so much difficulty against Lot? Would Arthur betray Mordred? And worse still, might not Mordred have known and sent the man who did the deed? But no, Mordred was the Soul of Honour, would not have done this deed by stealth. If he had known he would have outfaced Arthur in the Table.

'But now, what will happen?'

The younger savage answered, 'We must know what more will be ours. Is there to be a treaty? When are we to have the land of Coritan, and when shall we enter into the city of the Legions on the Soar?'

And more? If the Heathen were to hold these new frontiers, then Arthur had been granting them Lot's kingdom, and Kai's. And neither of these was a man of honour like Mordred. They might have done anything.

I heard shouting outside. I told the savages, 'That is a matter I must discuss with other kings and holy men.' I could see that Constant was trying to grasp what was meant, not being a man of genius but slower and clumsier at diplomacy even than his uncle Gormant.

'There is little time,' said the younger savage. I found it irritating not knowing their names, but they never do tell us those, for they think that if we know their names we will take them away and bewitch them. But we will not do anything of the sort; we will only baptise them and give them new, Christian names. 'We came to deal with Arthur, and if he is dead, then with those who made the first treaty and will also make the new treaty.'

'You shall do that,' I promised them, 'tomorrow morning. Meanwhile the Great Lady whom you have met will doubtless bring you more to drink.'

They shuddered. I shrugged. They were only Heathen, they deserved elderflower-and-dandelion. And I went out of the stench of wheat bread and barley beer into the purer air of Camlann, to meet Melvas as he entered on his mule.

Interlude 6: Release

The woman awoke. It was dark without a moon. She heard the whistle, she knew the note: it was a noise from her childhood. It brought her pictures from her past, the noises of men moving in the dark, men breathing in the night.

And these noises were real.

It brought her a shout, screams, the sound of iron on ash wood, sword edge on hard club, even sword edge on spade. There were smells around her, too, new smells for this life, but smells she knew as well as she knew the whistle. There was the smell of seawater and of tar grown old on salt-caked hemp. There was the well-dried fir for masting, and the elm smell of the deck. There was charcoal and wheat straw, and dried earth from a well-beaten floor, and all the smells of childhood. And there was also the sweat of men, and of oil on mail.

But there were other smells she recognised although she could give them no name. There were sweet smells of flowers, rendered down into scented oils. There were the smells of fruit, sour and bitter and acid and sharp, but mostly sweet. There was the smell of little cakes. There were the smells of garlic and of fresh wheat bread, and the smell of burnt hemp. And there was the smell of the blood of the Saints, so long desired.

Men struggled around her. She could hear the steel bite into the flesh, the indrawn breath of pain.

A hand grasped her elbow and a voice said, in her own language, 'The time has come, Lady, the time has come. This is the way.'

So the woman passed from the Island of the Saints. Her net she left behind, because this one had done its work. But her cushion and her bobbins and her bone hook she took with her.

Chapter 6

Melvas

I

Melvas was on his mule, an animal known throughout the Island for its evil temper and omnivorous habits, and reputed to be in private life a cheating merchant from London who had crossed false weights with one of the King-Abbot's relations. It is never wise to meddle with Saints since they have not, in my experience, any more of a sense of humour than Arthur had. But as there is scarcely anyone of any station in life without at least one cousin within five degrees who has attained Sainthood, this rumour may be said to have improved the standard of commercial morality throughout the Island.

As Melvas' slow progress continued towards the main square of Camlann, I returned to an earlier problem.

'Perhaps Melvas will take Igerna away and make a Saint of her. Or maybe he needs the skull of a Christian Martyr to start off a new monastery.'

'He may,' agreed Constant, 'but I'll try Hennin first.'

He went off to mingle unnoticed with the crowd. I watched while most of the people of the place knelt around the holy man asking for his blessing. He sat square on his mule yelling for someone to come and help him down, which the locals insisted on taking for some new liturgical rite. Many of Constant's clansmen took no notice but stayed as they were, milling about all hugger-bugger. This would never have happened had Arthur been there: he had many vices, but sexual tolerance was not one of them.

Constant returned. 'I have just made an offer to Hennin. I told him that he could have a farm in Powys, and that you'd arrange it with Mordred. But he's still very unwilling.'

'I don't blame him. Tell me, aren't you afraid of that mule?'

'Frankly, I am.'

'To tell the truth, so am I. But if nobody else will do it, I suppose I'd better.' I walked forward and helped Melvas down from his mule, which proceeded to breakfast on the walls of a tent. This was made of ponyskin, and I hoped that cannibalism would give it indigestion. Melvas' reputation for holiness was based on his wide learning and his travels rather than on any deeds of special sanctity. Even so I was surprised to see that he had washed his head and his feet, and even his hands, some time during the winter. I led him into the State Apartments, and settled him into a chair specially carved, rather badly and in a hurry, for important guests. Not that he was entitled to a chair, being no bard, but there was no harm in making him feel welcome.

There the Saint sat, panting with relief and gout, and blessing everyone in sight. Taberon got himself blessed seven times, which only led the lad to become more mischievous than before, arguing that he had been pardoned in advance for any sins he might commit in future. He was learning fast from Gwenki, that paragon of unscrupulosity.

Then I went to find Constant. He was standing outside his tent, trying to look Ducal, in the hope that at least a few of his followers would notice him and ask who the Hell he was. I thought of Arthur. Arthur never cared if you knew who he was or not. He just acted, and if action meant fetching you a good clout on the side of the head for getting in the way, then a clout you got.

Constant never had the Ducal look as we remembered it. His hair kept on falling into his eyes, and sometimes he'd trip over his own feet as if he couldn't remember where he'd left them. He was always in a hurry to be seen doing things. Arthur just used to say offhand that something particular ought to be done, and we'd fall over ourselves to run around and do it. Arthur never gave an order, he just made statements about what ought to be done. Pretty silly statements they were half the time, but we made them come true.

Before I reached Constant, I had a short consultation with my staff. I was able to tell Constant, flatly, 'Gwenki won't do it, either.'

'Won't do it? Doesn't he want a wife like that, fine-looking woman, good milker, and very acrobatic when the passion takes her? Tell him to have a look at her.'

'He was halfway willing till he did take a look at Igerna, and heard her.'

'Didn't we offer him enough?'

'I offered him the half of your kingdom.'

'But I haven't got a kingdom.'

'Well, half the reversion of Gormant's half of Cornwall when you come into it. But he still said no, he didn't want to live that far south, the sun gets on his nerves.'

'What about the other way?'

'He didn't want to try murder, too frightened of her hand-to-hand. He was afraid she might get it in first.'

'Aren't we all?' Constant was dispirited. 'Let's go and talk to Melvas.'

I made a reassessment of the priest-king's sanctity when I saw that he was well into his second pint of elderflower-and-dandelion. Constant bowed low to the splendour of holiness.

'Most Holy Father, was my messenger delayed in getting to you?'

'Messenger? Did you send me a messenger?'

'I sent Meirlys map Mokhyn to you, last month, with urgent news.'

'Oh, Meirlys, he did come to see me, but on landing in the Island of Glass he was so captivated with the sheer beauty of our singing and the clarity of our diction that he became a Saint on the instant and remains with us. I thought that was his main intention in coming.'

I reflected that it was unlikely that he ever got a word in. Constant, however, was more insistent and his voice was so grating and loud that he could not be ignored, whether he talked sense or not. Besides there was little likelihood that he would ever want to be a Saint, and less chance that any monastery would accept him.

'I sent Meirlys to bid you urgently to come here.'

Melvas, however, refused to be diverted from his train of thought. 'Meirlys is a man of piety and good lineage, and a bass-baritone who will be an asset to our society. Unlike some I could mention.'

Constant bridled. 'It is a deserter and a liar and an oathbreaker that he is, and one that forsakes his duty for the mere pleasures of sanctity and for the sybaritic delights of prayer and fasting. But your own holiness, great Melvas, shines forth the more for your coming without even knowing that I had sent to command your presence.'

Melvas came as near to indignation as he ever did, or at least to showing it, for he was well known for his dissembling.

Or it might have been indigestion, for it is very similar the symptoms of both are.

'You have no authority over me. No mere king, and certainly not anyone who merely claims the title of Great Duke, which is easy enough to say loudly, may command the elect of the Most High.'

'But if Arthur had sent for you, would you not have come for him?' I saw no reason not to stir the pot.

'But Arthur was Arthur, no matter what earthly title he might be crowned with or deprived of. And you, Constant, are no Arthur, no matter how many little kings and incipient Saintlets may say so. I came on my own behalf and at the bidding of God to acquaint the kings, beginning with you, Morvran, with my own news, and dreadful news it is that it is too.' He added, 'It was only stopping here out of politeness on my way to Caerwent that it is that I was, and out of fatigue and hunger and thirst.'

Melvas paused a moment to refresh himself with another deep draught of elderflower-and-dandelion. Then, 'Dreadful news it is that it is, too. O-O-O-O-Aw!'

And this was the dreadful wail that formed such an important part of his famous sermon on the Last Things, and men came from all over the Island, especially at midsummer, to hear it merely in the hope of having their blood chilled and curdled, although they had already done such evil things in my estimation, and in cold blood, as to make any further such contribution supererogatory.

'Five nights ago, evil men crossed the sea. Pirates came upon the Mere to the Island of Glass, perverts and sinners and whoremongers entered the Abbey and took from it the greatest of all the treasures in our safe-keeping.'

'You have treasure in the Abbey?' Constant was interested. 'Ready money?'

'Not treasure in your worldly sense, my son, although it is touched by your evident eagerness to take upon yourself the labour and worry and expense of guarding it that it is that I am. The marauders came as thieves in the night, in boats across the Mere, to take what was entrusted to our care by the Kings of all the Island. They came running ashore with swords and pikes and javelins and axes and clubs, they sent to their eternal rest so many of the Saints who came to resist them with sticks and choppers and kitchen knives. Now, oh blessed martyrs that they are, it is guarding in heaven the precious treasure that knows neither moth nor rust nor the webs of spiders nor any other corruption—'

I had heard this sermon so many times before that I had no compunction in interrupting. 'How many dead?'

'Five so far, but the gangrene is taking hold bountifully and promises us many more martyrs before long. Oh, are we not happy, that we have so replenished the heavenly choirs—'

'What did they take?' asked Constant. 'Not, surely, the Cauldron?'

'Well, now that is the problem, for it is nothing made by hands, and in fact the Cauldron is safer than it would be even in the Mere, but it is the one possession of our house that is irreplaceable without the substitution being evident. It is the earnest of our loyalty to the Unity of the Island, and the jewel in our crown, and the salvation of all the land of Britain—'

'What, Melvas? Tell us in a word!'

'You are in indecent haste, Constant, and you must learn patience, as we all do who are the faithful servants of the Lord and must endure all things for his sake even when we are given for drink the stale piss of mangy goats and the water of spavined cows and the urine of moth-eaten sheep. Now in a word, and to be brief and to be economical, for brevity of speech is the essence of spirituality and the saving of breath a sure passport into that celestial abode where the souls of the blessed never want for true wine or for breath to sing the praises of the Most High, a monarch not elected by mere mortal kings – they seized and stole and took from us, leaving her place empty and her hut vacant and her seat unfilled, that great lady, the Gwenevere.'

This was shocking news, even to me who have seen in my time the most shocking sights of the world. I looked to Constant and saw that our eager bridegroom was pale. It would, I reflected, be welcome news to Hennin, and even to Gwenki. Our new Great Duke of War and Peace, however, seemed too shocked to do anything practical, contenting himself with chewing on the edge of a table till his colour came back, so I asked, 'Who was it?'

But Constant was already back to his normal standard of rationality, and shouted, 'It was Mordred! Mordred!! I will kill him and bring her back. I will call the Kings of the Island against Mordred!'

'No, no, no, not by night,' Melvas corrected him. 'Whatever evil Mordred would have committed, and he is no more evil than any other man, he would have done it by day, unbridled conceit being his main if not his only vice, and then only in moderation. He would flaunt it in the face of all men, and take the utmost pleasure in being seen to do it. Besides he is my second cousin twice removed and it is heartily I am longing that he were further removed, to the utmost bounds of civilisation or even further, to Aberystwyth. Therefore if he had come to me, in the normal way of business, and asked for the lady as a loan against some appropriate security, say three hogs or a brood mare, to be repaid at some later date with a suitable rate of interest and a reasonable allowance to be made against natural increase, like Jacob dealt with Laban, as you well know, Morvran, being a king and therefore enlightened in the law as this oaf is not, it is not refusing him I would have been justified in doing either legally or morally. And I would certainly not have denied him in any case, the Lady being such a nuisance and so choosy about the way her gruel was cooked and wanting honey in it on Fridays and spurning any solid food like fish and insisting on washing her hands every week whether it was needed or not, a sure sign of evil intent. And while she was with us there were no flies within the ambit of her hut. I was always certain that her presence would bring a dreadful judgement upon us, as indeed it did, and has led several souls to a premature and closer contact with God.'

'If it was not Mordred,' shouted Constant, running from the tent, 'then it was the Heathen from Logres.'

I followed him, motioning to Melvas to come if he could find his feet with no better assistance than from Taberon, for this was no longer the Melvas who led the right wing at Badon, running lightly and swinging his iron-shod club. I was chasing Constant to make sure that he did not untie the riding strings of his sword which was Cherries in May, five times quenched, or pick up an axe or otherwise do himself mischief. I found him raving at the two Heathen ambassadors, who sat on the ground looking at him without any change in expression. He was shouting at them in the dialect of the Corns, scarcely to be distinguished from the corrupt jargon of the Armoricans and far removed from the musical speech of the Vale of Klydakh. It was therefore no wonder that our visitors could not understand him, because neither could I, hardly.

I spoke to them quietly, and in Latin, 'The Holy Father the King-Abbot says that wicked men have entered his sanctuary and have stolen your sister from where we had placed her, thinking her safe. Is it your doing?'

They looked at each other and at us, blankly. At least they knew what an Abbey was, they'd sacked enough. Then it was the younger man who spoke to me, quietly but with menace. Even in speaking he seemed to be the best bass I had heard for a long time. There was no longer any pretence about who was the more important of the two, or who made the decisions. 'The Treaty was that our sister would be kept safe and revered as a Queen. You swore to the Treaty, Morvran. And you, Melvas. You have broken the Treaty. All Britain will burn. Bring back our sister. Let us see her face. Or fire shall sweep from coast to coast to coast.'

'That I think likely if she is not found. If she is in your territory, then fire will indeed rage.' I agreed for Constant's hearing as much as for theirs. I tried not to sound less agitated than I felt: there are occasions when a royal training in equanimity is a disadvantage. And being revered as a Queen might be one thing, but having to live on what the Saints would give her in the Glass Island was another. 'Do you think that there are evil men within your own tribes who might have done this? What would they gain?'

Once more there was that strange interval of silence as if the Heathen were conversing without words, and indeed it may be that all of them share but one mind among them. Our nation count any moment of contact with no words heard as time sinfully squandered. It was the older man who spoke, as if it were his task to impart information, and the other's to make the decisions.

'That is possible. This is Bladulf's daughter. Bladulf we agreed should be Bretwalda, after the fight at Cattraeth. He was lord of the Island. Over all the kings. He went to Votan by way of Balday, the elder line, by the left-hand path. His wife was Corryn, last of the line of Scyld, the younger line, the right-hand path, the line of Freya. Bladulf's daughter is the last of the line of Scyld. Bladulf's daughter's son will be the Bretwalda. All will accept him. Therefore whoever fathers Bladulf's daughter's son will be Bretwalda before him. That too we agreed. If Arthur had given our sister a son, we would have agreed that Arthur was Bretwalda. He would have ruled the Island. And his son after him. It was easier that way. Otherwise our sister would have been a cause of war among our kings. Now she is a cause of war among your kings. Each wants the Unity of the Island. Under himself.'

'Would your kings go to war against each other?' I marvelled. 'Such a thing could not happen among us. We are the Kymry, the Comrades, the Brothers-Together. We may dispute but we obey the ancient law, the law of Brutus which Christ himself gave him: we do not fight among ourselves.'

'That is your strength,' the younger savage interposed. 'Your only strength.'

But the older man ignored him and continued, 'Therefore we all swore a solemn oath. No king from among ourselves might father her child. We sought an outsider. We sought the greatest man we could find. Not of our kings. Not of our families. Rome-King refused. Arthur was not of our families. He was the next greatest man we could find. He agreed. Therefore we agreed the Treaty with you when you were few and weak and we could have swept you aside. When the years were fulfilled we brought her to you, to Arthur. We fulfilled the Treaty. No king of ours would have her in his house. That would bring down the oath on him. It would blight his wheat and murrain his barley, it would spavin his cattle and thripple his hens. It would sour the ale in his casks. What we have drunk today tells us that you are great oathbreakers.'

'If it is not them, then it must be the Irish,' shouted Constant, who seemed incapable of understanding that you do not always have to shout at foreigners. Usually, but not always. 'They have already established themselves all along the Severn Sea. They are unscrupulous and determined, and being Christians they have the knowledge of good and evil to guide them in their deceits. And besides that they cannot cook, and you now know that as well as I do. And all mad.'

I ignored what he was saying, whether it made sense or not, and I said smoothly, 'She must be found. Otherwise we must be put to the trouble of silencing these honourable visitors who have shown themselves so civilised in their appreciation of the delights of our cuisine and our brewing. Oath breaking, even to ambassadors, holds no terrors for us, since we already have the blight and the murrain and the thripple and the spavin. If only we had a *truly* holy man to pray for us, perhaps we might be better off.'

'I am called Sebbald,' said the older ambassador, suddenly. This then was serious. The savages you will remember as a rule do not like to tell us their names, in case we bewitch them. Of course we do no such thing, we merely add their names to the general list in the Commination Services in Lent and so bring down the normal wrath of God on them. I could see that Melvas was making a note in the margin of his service book, using a silver point.

The savage went on, 'I am of the great House of the North, but I have lived for a long time at Thameshead. I go to Votan by way of Whitley.'

'I never heard of any of these places,' grumbled Constant.

Sebbald went on, 'And this good man' – I wondered for a moment who he could mean in this gathering, then saw he was pointing at the other ambassador – 'goes to Votan by way of Vecta. You may call him Oslaf.'

I bowed. Myself, I didn't care which way they went to Hell. But the younger man must be important if they still didn't tell us his real name, only told us what we might call him which is by no means the same thing. Especially at Commination time. Or which Royal House he belonged to, for it was obvious now that he was a king, or a king's heir.

Sebbald said, 'I swear this. I swear by all the Gods. I swear by your gods if you like—'

'I swear,' put in Oslaf, 'by my sword who is Landwaster seven times quenched, and by the hilt of my sword, and by the stones in the hilt, and I swear by the serpents that move in the steel—'

'I swear,' went on Sebbald, 'that none of our kings had a hand in this theft. If any evil man out of our people did this or helped in the doing of this theft of a woman, I will find him. I will hang him alive in a tree. I will carve the blood eagle on his back. And then I will torture him till he feels pain.'

'Why should we trust your oaths?' demanded Constant. 'You have already killed Arthur.'

'Why should we kill Arthur?' Sebbald was very calm. 'How would we benefit? Our law says this. Ask who benefits. From any crime. He is guilty. Two men benefited from the death of Arthur. The man who took his widow. And the man who took his crown. Are these one man? Or two?'

'In a way,' I pointed out before the argument got too personal, 'we all gained. Arthur was planning to go to war. Perhaps with you. Perhaps with the Irish. Perhaps into Gaul. He would not tell us. It was not his custom. Not till we were going.' I felt a little annoyed, I was catching this way of short sentences from the Savages who are an unpoetical race.

Constant was trying to work out what Sebbald was implying. I could see his ears twitching which was his way when trying to add two and two. Sebbald was right, there might have been as many as two men, and one of those could not care a snap of the fingers what became of the Unity of the Island. Constant had worked out something in his own dim consciousness where any mindreader had better take a candle.

'It *was* an Irishman! It is clear, for we know that there are Irish kings who want to take this island, and probably the woman is already at Tara, for no one but an Irishman would be so mad as to take to the seas at this time of the year, and they often do that, trusting in our belief that no one can sail before the end of March which in itself is a sign of their untrustworthiness and treachery. We must call all the Kings of Christendom for swords about the Cross.'

I did not point out to him that the Kings of Ireland were now all Christians, of a sort, being myself too occupied in holding his hand from undoing his riding strings. Once I had his hand still I had advice to give.

I turned first to Oslaf and Sebbald. 'Now, let us have a little calm, a commodity I have always found useful and cheap enough. You two must return to your own people and seek among them for the Gwenevere, or Mam Gwe as we do call her, the Mother of Gossamer, since she has brought to our own ladies the knowledge of the intricate making of lace and of nets.' It is never wrong to say something polite, however little you feel disposed to it. 'I will send two of my own great Officers of State with you to see you safe to the edge of London. Meanwhile, I will consult with others of my nation to decide what we may do to preserve the peace which Arthur and Melvas and I negotiated with you.'

I took Constant by the elbow and hurried him out into the open air. Melvas with some difficulty and much panting followed into the square of Camlann, where his mule was eating a bucket, iron rim and all. I spoke firmly to Constant. 'Look, you cannot go to war, not for a long time.'

'Whyever not? We must drive the Irish from Demed and then kill those in Tara. Is that not always a virtuous thing to do, and profitable as well?' Constant looked sulky, like a child who has been told he cannot have a ball he wants and argues on about how wonderful a toy it is. Arthur, even when a child, would have taken the ball anyway, as he took the sword.

'Be practical. First there are only a few kings who accept you as Great Duke, and those not of the best fighting quality or bringing the greatest armies, men like Kaw the Senile, and those who accept you are mostly your relations or they live in the southwest, or both. If you make war you will destroy the Unity of the Island. Secondly, the Heathen of Logres do not acknowledge you – and I have no idea what the Irish think, although I do admit there is some doubt as to whether the Irish can think – so you cannot depend on the Heathen to keep the Treaty and stay at peace if you go to war with the Irish. And thirdly, you cannot go to war without wine to pay those who fight, and we drank all the wine at Arthur's wake, as well as there not being enough sword-blades, so we will have to wait till Theodore the Shipman comes again from Gaul, unless someone goes there to ask him to come a little sooner.'

Melvas had now caught up with us, puffing, to say, 'There is no problem, Constant, you have no blame or culpability or responsibility in this matter. If any crime were committed, then it was committed in Bedwyr's territory, and it is himself that it is that you should call on to avenge it, being careful to make sure whether it is accepting you as Great Duke he is or not. Perhaps it would be more tactful if it were I who called on him to avenge this slight on the Glass Island and on the Holy Church and on the unity of the Kings of the Island at Table sitting. If you are the Great Duke, Constant, send for Bedwyr and command him, or let me go to him and ask him, to act for you and bring back by his own strength and cunning and force the lady who alone can establish you as Great Duke in the eyes of the nations of the earth.'

I realised that Melvas was even more subtle than I had thought, although I had to balance his wariness of offending Bedwyr against his apparently thoughtless offending of me.

But Constant replied, 'I will not talk to Bedwyr, nor implore him out of his charity to act for me. At the last Table, he was shouting for Mordred at the end.'

'That is true,' Melvas told him, 'but remember that if Bedwyr learns of this from anyone but you, from Hennin of the Speckled Skin for example, he will go to any lengths to stop you from finding the lady, and it seems to me that he has the greatest host at his call and the most wealth of all the Kings in the Island. You must act quickly and shame him into doing what he can, and that is much, to help you.'

'And you must consider the position of the Abbot,' I warned Constant. 'He may be a king in standing, but he has no army, and Bedwyr may take his not being consulted as a personal insult so that Melvas will lose all authority with him. Let us have supper and think.'

And there was one thing that I needed to think about. Constant and Melvas and the Savages had seen me as having standing as one of the Treatymakers: but Bedwyr was not a Treatymaker and it rankled in his heart. As a Treatymaker, it was my task to enforce the Treaty. As always, if nobody else, then it must be me.

II

'Now,' I told Constant and Melvas, with little hope that they would listen, or that if they listened would do what I told them, 'we cannot go to war without wine and without more sword-blades, because peace time is very expensive in wearing out of blades and in losing them down wells and in streams, and in breaking them up to make plough shares whatever use they may be. Now listen again. *I* will take care of getting the wine, and *I* will take care of getting sword-blades. Just don't you get in my way. Don't go to war till I come back with them. Promise me. And promise me something else: not a word to Bedwyr, either that the woman is gone, or that you hope to make war, or alternatively and on the other hand and as another case that you fear we may have war made on us.'

They promised. I didn't believe that they could keep things quiet, but it might give me a week or so if I hurried. We left Camlann the next morning, as soon as I could manage without being rude and attracting attention.

Keinakh and Gwenki rode off towards London. The two ambassadors trudged with them on foot, each clutching his withered branch of green leaves. In that wild country, who was protecting whom was anybody's guess. Gwion and Esau went off to the south and west. They said they would lie up for a day near Badon and then go on in the nights. They agreed that there was no reason why Bedwyr should know about them, and they would be quite comfortable. I noted that they now had two extra horses we had not brought with us, and on one of them they packed the tent we had all been sleeping in.

So that left only Taberon and me to go back into Gwent. Hennin, who had been hanging around watching what we did, got up in the dawn, a sight to which he was unaccustomed, and was torn three ways. At last he decided to follow me. He trailed us all the way down Severn side, piteously calling on us to wait for him, He wished to be saved from the wrath of Constant, who had promised to carve him into slivers unless he sent word of our progress, or regress. Constant was sure to need someone soon to take his spleen out on, or out of.

On the way, I began to consider. If I were going voyaging, I needed stock to trade with, and I had sent for that. I needed a ship, and I had sent to see to that. And I needed men enough to make a show. I needed good men, hard men, trustworthy men, who looked dignified and fierce enough to stand at my back or to plunge a knife into my enemy's. Men who were loyal, wise, full of initiative, original thinkers, hard, strong, ruthless, cunning, cruel . . . Well, I hadn't got much hope of finding anybody like that, had I? I would have to make do with my great Officers of State. And with Taberon.

'We're going a long way,' I told him, 'across the seas, to a land where men are so uncivilised that they have not yet learned to turn cups and bowls and plates out of beech and birch and yew. Instead, they form them out of clay which they first dry in the sun and cook in the fire. Horrible and insanitary, I call it, eating off pieces of scorched dirt, but it is time you learned that there are different ways of living. Gwion will be our lookout, and Keinakh will repair any damage to our ship and our weapons.'

'Where will we get a ship?' asked the impertinent lad.

'Contain your soul in patience and be still,' I warned him. 'All will be made known in time.'

'You always say that,' he grumbled.

True, I did. I went on, 'Esau must come. Not only is he a good cook, but he is also well versed in the ways of the deep and the treachery of the ocean, seeing that he lives on the shore above the cockle beds of the Llwkhwr River, and is said to have seen a whale alive, although it may only have been a dead porpoise.'

'I'm coming too,' insisted Hennin, who was always butting in between us.

'We're going a long way,' I warned him. 'Out of the Island, to where the people are so poor they have no cider to drink, but have to make do with wine they brew themselves out of grapes, and if you didn't like our elderflower-and-dandelion then you won't like theirs which is nothing like so good and nourishing.'

'Or,' he countered, being a man of imagination, 'I may make my fortune and find a fair bride and a fine farm to live, better than Cornwall where I can never be safe from Constant.'

Well, not much you could say to him after that, was there? I didn't like to hurt his feelings so I contented myself with making him feel not quite welcome by hitting him in the mouth every time he came in my way, and having him come with us first as far as Avan again, where Iestyn map Gwrgan of Ergyd Ukhav wanted me to judge a case he brought against Ianto map Dial of Ergyd Isav about sheep walk boundaries on Margam Mountain. The normal business of being a king. It was all good for his soul and for Taberon's education. But that put me in mind of something we were lacking.

So when we came back to Caerwent again, I went round the walls to where Tatharn was repairing his Lhan by rebuilding the clay and wattle fence we had broken down the last time with Arthur, and bringing his bean rows up to nine again. He was polishing his bell when I tapped him on the shoulder.

'You're coming with us!'

'To dinner?' He looked cheerful. 'Ask not what is in the pot, for where there is no knowledge there is no sin, as we are told in the first chapter of Holy Writ. By eating what is not recognised no sin is committed and no fast is broken.'

I knew that by this he meant that it was Lent and that he was hoping for a good beef stew or a game patty or a shoulder of nine-year-old mutton with mead as a change from his usual diet of vegetables and water. I ignored this.

'Come with us to the land of strange meats, to the country of the olive and the grape, where the country runs with wine and oil, whatever use that mixture may be, and outlandish dishes of peppers and spices tempt the holiest palate to an innocent self-abuse.'

'For a whole week?'

'For the whole summer, if we are not careful, and our expected companions are a very careless lot of craftsman. We are going towards Romeland and the country of the Ravenn Emperor, so there will be no difficulty for you in finding out when it is that it is Easter that it is going to be.'

'It is lucky that I have just recalculated and found that last Sunday was Easter.'

'Have you asked Melvas to confirm that? Last week he was keeping Mothering Sunday.'

'Melvas is a backslider and a concealer of wicked runaways. I go by my own count which is infallible considering that we have not seen the quarters of the moon for nine weeks. In all charity I will show these deluded and ignorant Romans for the salvation of their souls that their error it is in using that calendar which has no warrant in Scripture but is merely the figment of the imagination of a bush bishop and a hedge priest. Wait while I pack.'

He brought a bag from his hut. Into it he put his professional equipment: a chalice and a paten of lead tempered with tin, a book of the Mass and another of such parts of the Holy Scripture as he judged worthy of credence, and a small bronze bell set with precious glass and worth four jars of wine or half a sword-blade by Theodore's customary valuation.

Hennin trailed after us to my house within the walls, where we sat for a last square meal with all the good citizens – them and me and Taberon and Korlam, and Esau who had quietly come back in the night very satisfied with his work and leaving Gwion behind where he had gone. Tatharn sang a Grace which brought tears to the eyes of our many friends and clients who had come to the dinner just to make sure that we really went and therefore they could arrange their tax affairs by consulting with Mabon who would hold the kingdom while I was away.

Hennin crouched at the foot of my table, no special place being found for him, but he received an individual mention in Tatharn's Grace as an interloper and stranger within our gates, together with a call for his repentance and the restitution of expenses incurred.

III

It took a day to recover from the farewell feast, and therefore we found it necessary to hold a post-farewell-feast-farewell-feast. After that we were more or less ready to depart, in spite of a cluster of splendid headaches. Accompanied by a choir of boys and maidens, who had a limited repertoire and that religious and highly unsuitable for our purpose, we went in procession to the riverbank. Here a difficulty arose, for Tatharn refused to embark till we had a millstone stowed in his luggage.

'Look here,' I told him roundly, 'most Saints are content with an oak leaf.'

'I was taught on a millstone,' he replied, 'by the great Saint Twit, and therefore it is a millstone I must have. Oak leaves are just not safe.'

In the end, after he had threatened to curse us, and we remembered what a renowned curser he was, almost as skilled as Melvas, we agreed, and I spoke persuasively and in the end threateningly to the leading citizens of Caerwent. They agreed finally to present a millstone to their revered and much loved father in God, on condition that he bring it back unchipped or otherwise damaged, or one equal in weight and quality. Although where we would find another of such poor workmanship I could not imagine. But we got the thing loaded, and it was nearly as bulky as Esau's cook's bag with all its knives and choppers and his cauldron, which was all he had come back for. We set off across the water in a leather boat.

'Are we going all the way in this little boat?' asked Taberon. 'Because it was unsteady enough before we had the millstone, and now it is certain that I am that it is a little frail for the job.'

'Wise boy,' I approved, since it was not often he said anything so sensible. 'We'll go to the other coast opposite Gaul, and we'll pick up something there, moving by night so that Bedwyr doesn't find out. He might want to come with us, and that would be a disaster.'

'Will we have to walk?' Taberon asked, but I did not answer being too busy about the navigation. We went on the heading we took the last time, with the Great Duke, but having misjudged the tides, it took us a long time and we came ashore at the wrong place. We found a place to lie up until dusk, and Esau took Hennin to find us some horses, to ride and for packing. When dark came we pushed on to the edge of the Mere. Just after dawn, we came to the water's edge, in sight of the place where people wait for the Ferry from the Glass Island which they have to call from the Glass Island when they want to go off and be Saints. Here we wanted to spend the day. As the sun came up, Hennin was riding in front where I hoped someone would knock his block off. He reined in his horse.

'Look at that for luck,' he called to me. Beside the path was a little yellow frog, very pretty with its fine green stripes that shimmered in the early light.

'Now,' Hennin mused, 'if there were any justice in the Universe, I would kiss that frog and it would turn into a beautiful princess and I would marry her and we would live happily ever after.'

'Well, try it,' Esau advised him. Hennin shrugged. He got down from his horse and knelt to kiss the little frog, which was just sitting still and looking up at him in a particularly appealing and stupid manner. Hennin's lips touched the cold skin, and their tongues mingled; the light shook and the earth flashed and the two little frogs lolloped off hand in hand down into the Mere.

I shook my head at Tatharn. 'You naughty, naughty Saint.'

'Well, you were all appealing to him to leave us. Easy come, easy go, I always say.'

'Go like that?'

'God gives his servants gifts and talents to be used, and not hoarded. Now he will be happy throughout his life and next summer there will be a myriad little Hennins here to spoil our sleep. Although I do not think he is entirely up to his new consort's intellectual standard, he is quite safe, spiritually at least – he *has* been baptised.'

'Let that be a lesson to you, lad,' Esau told Taberon. 'Never be overcome by the contemplation of beauty. As they say, better the devil you don't know than the Saint next door.'

Tatharn gave Esau a frightful look, and I got ready to use my royal powers and dump that millstone in the mere. But our Saint only mused, 'I've always wondered what happened to their clothes, not having done it before. Pick them up, Taberon, and pack them on his horse. They may come in useful.'

IV

When we had hobbled our horses, Esau lit a fire and cooked us our supper, or breakfast. The others slept while the work was done to get up an appetite. But suddenly the cook shook me awake. 'We've got a visitor.'

'Never mind the visitor. Is the meal ready?'

'In a little while. But the question is, how many to cook for and what is the value of charity? It may be an ideal, but there are limits to our capacity. It's a Saint taking the easy way out, and you know Saints, pay one off and there's twenty more before you know it.'

We sat at the edge of the thicket, where we couldn't exactly be accused of hiding but where we weren't easy to spot either. There was a man, indeed, wading across from the Glass Island. Well, in some places he waded through the mud and in some places he swam through the pools and, all in all, he wasn't moving very fast. It was plain that he was a Saint, because he was wearing what was left of a gown of sacking, black where you could see it through the mud. He was now so wet that very little of personal holiness was left to him.

When he was wading the last few yards, Esau encouraged him by heaving a lump of mud at his head, grumbling the meanwhile that there were only four sausages and one egg and one rasher in the caul-dron so far. The mud so startled the man that he sat down on his bottom in the water. I shouted to him that he had better come out before he got piles, and told Esau to sing a bit louder to the pot.

The runaway was a young man, but older than Taberon, with a look of hard experience in his gaze. A Gower man, with brown curly hair and grey eyes. He squelched up to me, and I told him to sit by the fire and dry out.

'Fire and you go together, King Morvran.'

'How do you know my name?'

'I sang in your Hall at Caerwent that last night that the Great Duke sat there, and I was in Camelot at the end, over there, about a mile away. I was an apprentice bard and a second relief harpist, usually to go on when the others were drunk, or at least drunker than me. But that last night in Caerwent I was on early, to see you go out in the middle. For the Awen is terribly expensive in terms of hangovers, as you will know, King Morvran, that are an admitted bard, and I wonder where it is that your chair is, although perhaps you do not bring it on campaign. Oh, those were splendid and well-fed days. Nothing like that on the Glass Island. All the good times ended when you and Bedwyr went mad with your torches.'

'When kings and Great Dukes die, how are lesser mortals to hope to escape unharmed? As apparently you did. I trust you did well out of the looting. Many of you of the Household left too early for profit.'

'And others too late for prudence. They are still in the ashes. I got away, but I kept nothing, not even a harpstring. I had only what I carried in my head, the laws of a hundred and fifty bardic meters, a half-hundred tales of loves and wars, of meetings and of partings, of births and deaths and swift appearances—'

'Like yours just now?'

'Well, maybe. But, oh Magnanimous King, worthy successor to Vortigern the Proud, the Generous, the Unfortunate, that were once a bard yourself, have you anything to spare of your bounty for a man to eat? Or are you on the run, too? Nasty temper that Constant's got.'

'Bring out the meal,' I ordered Esau, 'for you have been singing long enough and there must now be plenty for all however little you started with. And wake up the others and tell them to refresh themselves by dipping their heads in the waters of the Mere, now made holier by the lice of this holy man.'

When we were seated, I gave the first manchet of oatcake and bacon and toasted cheese to the newcomer as polite custom demanded, and I asked him, 'Now that the knife is in the meat and the mead is in the cup, can you tell us whether you are pre-eminent in art or craft or skill of any kind?'

'Well, I suppose that I am pre-eminent in the skill of escaping. My name, by the way, since you have been so polite not to ask it, is Kian son of Gormodiaeth.' I had known his father, a splendid singer at feasts especially after success or victory. 'I escaped from the wrack of Camelot with my skin scarcely singed, and it seemed to me that not even a Saint could set the Mere on fire, nor would try, seeing that so many of them had been cattle thieves in their past lives and depending on the water for their survival. And it also occurred to me that Melvas kept the Monastery and he is a well-fleshed and peaceable man, belching often. (These are good sausages.) I reasoned that if I could reach the Island of Glass, then I could become as well-fleshed as Melvas is, and since I am as able and as devious and as cunning as anyone I have met in my station of life, I might in time become Abbot in succession to him. Or perhaps instead of him. So in hopes of spending my life in mortifying the fat in peace, I swam and walked and paddled my way across the Mere, and it is not at all difficult in spite of the enchantments, and so I came into the

Island of Glass. There I have been all the winter and I am sure that I am not going back. Melvas may be well-fed, but the others deserve their title of holiness through asceticism, not like so many of their former companions who once priested have wandered off to found each one his own Lhan, for a lazy and a shiftless lot they are.'

'Thank you very much,' said Tatharn, taking a third bannock of oatcake filled with bacon entwined with fried egg done up and over. 'I am sure that the wisdom of the Fathers has an appropriate word for you idle ballad singers of the streets and players in the markets.'

'I have never sung in a market in my life,' retorted Kian, taking a seventh sausage which was one up on Tatharn, 'and I would not know the low language needed. My place was always in court before the Great Duke and the kings.'

'Then it is learning that low talk you had better be starting to,' Tatharn told him, 'because a new phase of your life is about to begin.'

'It is well,' I put in to cool the talk down, 'that we have some scholarly and intellectual interest to add to our discussions. Continue, great poet.' For Kian was frequently changing from prose to a bardic metre, which meant that he sometimes had to vary the plain meaning of the words.

'Well, reckoning that the purgatory I knew might well be better than a Hell I do not know as well as some preachers seem to' – and I kicked Tatharn to stop him interrupting again – 'I stayed in the Island all the winter. But I felt that three bowls of gruel a day outside Lent and Friday nights might satisfy the innately sinful, but for a poet seized with immortal inspiration it was not adequate sustenance. Therefore I came tactfully away, not that it was easy since they counted us in and out for dinner. For the last few weeks I have established a reputation for regular fits of prayer through mealtimes at random. Nobody expects you to run away in broad daylight at supper time just when the summer is coming in.'

'That is most interesting. But' – and I looked at my own honest and upright followers, sincere and well behaved as they all were – 'it is not yet generally spoken of, but there is a rumour that the Lady the Gwenevere has been stolen and abducted and snatched away from her place of happy and secure and luxurious retirement. Can you give us any more information?'

'They chose their time carefully. They picked the dead hours between last and first prayers, when we were allowed to sleep for what the choirmaster considered a reasonable period.'

'Did you see them?'

'No, not see. It was pitch-dark. They stepped on my face where I slept against the wall of the lady's hut, close to the Grave.'

'So you didn't see them? What language did they speak? Irish?'

'Gibberish, with a horrible rolling of the "rs" and not a word we knew. Some of the Saints thought that they were dumb demons out of Hell, come for the Heathen in our midst, and would have been helpful in sending her off if only anyone had been polite enough to ask them. Others of us fought.'

'No known language. What did they smell like?'

'Is it fair to ask me about the smell of such people when I am eating the first real food I have tasted for months, and drinking the first good cider too? I congratulate you on your cook. Indeed the present pleasure so fills my mind—'

'And the pain of a good thrashing will soon fill your body. What did they smell of?'

'Smell?' He shut his eyes, held his nose, made a face and shuddered. 'Well . . . nasty is the first word. And salty. And sweaty. And . . . can you imagine what you would smell like if you had spent weeks at sea and eaten nothing but stale fish once fried in that horrible foreign plant oil with garlic? And their breath – horrible!'

'Breath? Close as that, were they?'

'Not difficult seeing the way they, and we, were running about in the dark. Now can I have some honey?'

'No!' I spoke sharply. It was the way he sat, crouching forward. 'Stand up! Now, take your shirt off!'

'But I've got nothing—'

'Take it off him, Esau!' It wasn't so much a shirt as a long tunic and it seemed that he had worn the same one all the winter, because between his careful hands and Esau's rough ones it came away in a series of rags. He stood there in a breech-clout which was in the end only a piece of fishnet twisted to tie but which looked ready to drift away in fragments if he sneezed.

'Turn round!' I ordered. The wound was there, at the back of his neck, angry and suppurating, running from the arm-root almost to the back-bone.

'The blunt side of a saxe,' was Esau's verdict, 'or the corner of an axe.'

'The axe,' Kian told him.

'Why are you still alive, that slept so close?' I demanded. And then thought, why so cruel? Bedwyr still lives.

'We had no weapons. I got one of them by the ankles. I was on the ground already. I pulled him over and went for his throat with my teeth. I saw the axe coming down. I rolled away as far as I could. Then all vanished. When I came back to the realms of men, she also had vanished, the glorious Gwenevere, the Golden Queen of all the world, Queen of all our hearts.'

'Lucky you were to see she was not there. You must have bled like a stuck pig.'

'A Saint sealed the wound with marsh mud, holy with his tears, which appear as maggots in the wounds of the holy. The others of our Household who had stayed with her, five of them, were all killed.'

'Then *you* must live!' I bade him. He looked past me to where Esau was throwing his rags into the fire, loincloth and all.

'You must not burn that. It is a net of her own weaving, all I could steal when she lived amongst us!'

'Sit still!' Korlam had his cobbler's apron on and was cleaning out the wound with mead. 'Another couple of days and you wouldn't have been walking anywhere, loincloth or none. Keep these stitches in for a fortnight and don't do anything with that arm till we have them out.'

'What will you do now?' I asked Kian.

'I have come to the edge of death, my lady is stolen, my comrades are dead and my oath is out. Whither shall I go in my shame?'

'Nowhere dressed like that. You'd better have some clothes. Lucky, aren't we – you're just about Hennin's size.'

Hennin was a very vain man, and a miser as well. We found in his bag two shirts and a pair of breeches, as well as a short mail coat and a pike which would not have been much use against a stork.

'Now, Kian, we have outfitted you lavishly, and since you are free as a wave you may as well travel with us on our ventures as our bard, which no great enterprise should be without. Thus did Maksen Wledig take with him a whole choir of bards when he set out to conquer the Ravenn Emperor. You must have heard that song often in the way of business.'

'And sung it often, for it was the only song Arthur would sit still and listen to. But where are we going?'

'Agree first. If you do not agree we will have the clothes back and throw you naked into the Mere to play with the gnats.'

'I agree. I will come.'

'Welcome. Now, gather round, all my true and loyal men' – for at such a moment I was surely allowed a little exaggeration – 'sit still and listen, and stop belching you in the back.' This was an opening to speeches to an army which I had found effective many times. 'We are bound on a great journey. Blood there may be before the end of it, and glory and triumph, bracelets of gold from landed lords, swords of grey steel from Emperors of renown—'

'If you will pardon my saying so,' put in Kian, 'or even if you do not, it is myself it is who is coming as bard. Fine language and alliteration are my affair. Please leave the lies to me.'

'I will speak no lies,' I protested, 'for anything I say may well come true and in any case I was an admitted bard before you were born. We are bound to a far land where we will bargain with the Emperor for swords and for wine, for great amounts of both ready for the war which is coming with the men of Logres. Many, therefore, are they that would like to stop us. We will have to sail the seas, and to ride far and fast, and fight great battles before we return to save the Island.'

'But this is like the old tales,' marvelled Taberon, 'where the hero seeks eternal life, or forgetfulness, or happiness, which may all be the same thing. Is it true, then, that in the olden-olden days the kings and great lords like yourself would ride out of Ehangwen at random to seek glory and excitement and booty and return again to Arthur?'

'Not in the olden-olden days, for then the Rome-King ruled the land with a rod of bronze and no man dared to own a sword even unless he allowed it. But in the merely once-olden days, when Gwion and I and even Arthur were young, we did all manner of strange things in the wars against the Heathen. Seven times Gwion and I harried the coasts of Gaul, and three times we sailed with Arthur south to

Bordigala and up the great river to where Theodore lived in splendour, and we brought back the great horses, and wine and sword-blades and whatever else we could pick up. We have no ships now, nor anyone who can build them. But we old men have the knowledge to sail them, although not always the strength.'

'And now the old days have returned again!' the lad exulted.

'If they have, then it is unlucky you will be, because then you will spend all your days out on the roads, sleeping under hedges out of the rain, not in a bed in your own house, and you will end your days as the barren king of a shattered kingdom with your house burnt and your wife and children slaughtered, while you were following a crazy delusion of an Island united and at peace in Christ the King. But the old times are perhaps not quite over, and for a short while we can show you how happy we were in the days of the youth of the world. I feel that this may be the last adventure of all and a time out of time and the end of time. Make the most of it now, Taberon. This may be the last exploit of the Iron Men.'

He still complained, 'But I am not yet one of the Iron Men. I have no mail, nor a sword either.'

'Then you must ride with us to get them. One must either take mail from a dying enemy, or receive it from a king. Stolen mail fits the best.'

'But you gave Hennin's mail and sword to Kian.'

'Kian paid for his mail in blood and fidelity, offering his life for the Unity of the Island and for the sanctity of the Abbey and for the honour of the Great Duchess.'

So we went on, riding by night along the secret hidden ways that no man had seen in the time since the Rome-King's wizards set the stones in place to the time we found them and rode, all mailed, against the Heathen. So often we came in arms when we were not expected.

V

At the fifth daybreak we were on the edge of the great heath, and I encouraged my people. 'We will ride into the heath as far as that ridge, and lie up for the day in the scrub. And before the moon is set tomorrow night we will smell the salt and see the lagoon.'

We left the shelter of the last woods and rode out into the open land. And when we were too far out to be hidden, there came up on the crest of the ridge, from horizon to horizon, the helmets of an immense army, a mighty host, forty or fifty horsemen at the least. I could see who it was that led them. And the sight was not welcome.

Interlude 7: The Wanderer

The oars plied their way over the surging tide. Under a crooked moon, the woman drew in the cleansing spray. Free from the confines of the Saints' island, she settled under the canopy, her hands idle, as the ship's bows keenly sought the open seas. Behind, the Island of the Mighty lay in utter darkness, while ahead an unknown bourne waited. The stars aloft were map enough for the Shipman who steered her, his brown hand navigating as his keen eye gave witness.

She knew that for him she was but a treasure among the many riches he had garnered, yet one pearl was all she sought in return. With but one pearl her weird could run.

The oar creak ceased as the mariners felt the channel change, their blades rested. The great sail billowed, big with wind, as the whole ship raised itself upon the waves, man upon woman over the serpentine beds of lost Lyonesse.

Beneath the sea-surge, the pallid shuttling crabs, the grasp and release of pale anemones in the shifting tides. The salt song sang in her veins, the very same that once lured her people from their low marshes, to seek out the fat lands with their fertile meadows fit for wheat. The hunger for betterment had primed her people, been the calling of her life. From the east and north her own people had sailed, settling the Lindsey coast as far north as Northumberland and down by Thameside, as far south as the Cantish cape.

Towards dawn, the Wanderer showed bright upon the eastern horizon. One voice rose to greet it, followed by another and another, raw with longing, in a thread of acclamation. The sailors who had known the Middle Sea and the jagged coasts of Lusitania, still sang the known features of the trackless wave as men greet home.

She who had no sword to mark landfall nor to clear farmsteads where she might make home, set her face south, taking up her needle, thread and cushion to weave a new net.

Chapter 7

The Lagoon

I

If blood were to be spilled then it were better that it should be mine alone. I halted my party and rode forward. Taberon held Kian back. The other king rode from out of his household alone. I had under my hand Bees in the Summer Meadow, her riding strings untied.

'You ride in my lands,' said Bedwyr.

'It does you no harm.'

'True. But it was not polite not to ask my leave. And you are riding my horses.'

'Oh. Are we? I thought that they were merely strays badly looked after and un-groomed, that someone had turned out to be rid of.'

'They all have my brand. The fourth in line, which is named Dancer, looks a little unwell.'

'Overloaded she thinks she is. Carrying Tatharn's millstone, and objecting that it is not her turn.'

'Tatharn has just fallen off.'

'Again? Suffering is good for his soul.'

'True. But what are half a dozen horses between us if they provide such occasions for self-improvement for him, and for amusement for you?' Bedwyr had, I was glad to see, stopped fiddling with the riding strings of Frost in the Morning.

'We have never kept count of these little things between us, Bedwyr, not since we were foster brothers together.'

'Oh, the horses are yours, while you need them.'

'When you ride in my marches, Bedwyr, help yourself to ponies.'

'That has always been my custom, Morvran.'

'I know. It always seemed impolite to mention it. And mean. But if it is only the horses you are worried about, then let us go on caring for them as if they were our children, while you go hunting and we to wash our feet in the sea, which Tatharn assures us is a sovereign cure for the rheumatics and other ailments which we are subject to at our age.'

But rheumatics or not, this was the first time I had seen a king go hunting with such a mighty host, seventy or eighty horsemen now he had called in his flankers. I hoped he was wondering where my flankers were, since there were faces well known to him missing on my side. And it was after his breakfast and before my supper. I did not feel inclined to brawl on an empty stomach, and he never did either.

'I am worried about other things, Morvran. I hear a rumour that you were gone on an errand for Constant.'

'There are strange things to be heard if you listen carelessly.'

'What did you do to Hennin? We picked him up on the edge of the Mere, stark naked.'

'Tatharn wonders what becomes of the clothes. He can wonder on.'

'He kept on talking about being king of all the frogs and feasting for a thousand generations. On flies.' Bedwyr tried to look disgusted, being a man of varied and coarse appetites, but his sense of humour spoilt his expression. I could see him smile now he had removed his helmet, which was one he had taken from an Angle in battle and had two bronze cheek pieces to hide his face.

'We ate worse in the wood of Caledon, before you bullied the Elmet men into coming back up with you to get us out. Hennin left us of his own accord, and because he had no common sense nor ever will have.'

'Not on a diet of flies. But he did convey to us, by croaks, that you were going on an errand for Constant, perhaps to Tara, or even into Armorica.'

'I was going across the sea, but not for Constant. I am going for my own health and pleasure. I am going where it is that it is that I am going because of something I heard somebody else say while Constant was present, but that is an irrelevance.'

'Apart from your pleasure, what is it that it is that you are going for?'

'I pass out of the Island of the Mighty for the sake of the Unity of the Island. It may be, Bedwyr, that I shall never return but that will be the will of God, and not my present intention.'

'You are going to look for that woman, that gilded gorgon as beautiful as the buttercup that poisons our pastures.'

A pity that Kian cannot hear you alliterate, I thought. And that Taberon cannot hear from his horse our long conversation in the High Language of the kings. It would do his grammar a power of good.

'I am going to find the salvation of the Island. We cannot fight, Bedwyr, without swords, and our men will not fight unless we can strengthen them with wine. I am going to look for both, and if I cannot compel the traders to bring them then I will take them. Even Constant must see that we will have to fight sometime, whether we want to or not, and we cannot fight unsupplied.'

'Constant is going into Ireland to find the woman.'

'Constant will only ride into Demed and riot a little with the Wexford men who have settled around Denby of the Fishes.'

'But he will have our men killed because of her. War against the Heathen or war against the Irish, it may go one way, it may go the other. Not much harm done, except for the dead. But if that woman comes back to us, she will destroy us utterly. Because of this woman, Arthur died. How many more?'

'Arthur died because of a pig. I was there.'

'Whatever he died for at that instant, he is dead now. We must look after ourselves. You must not go out of the Island, Morvran: you are too valuable.'

'I must go. It is my gesa.'

Bedwyr stiffened at the sound of that ancient word hardly ever spoken in these days, only half understood by those who hear it. The word had not itself come into my mind before. But now by the speaking of the word, by the mere thought, I was sworn to myself to do it. I was consecrated to the quest, whether my aim was clear in my mind or not.

And Bedwyr, having heard me swear and knowing the ancient ways, could not in love or honour even attempt to persuade me to turn from it, any more than I could myself refuse the task and hope that my soul could be saved.

Yet the King of Badon still asked, 'If I refused to let you go? Would your gesa demand that you should fight with me?'

I had my hand on Bees in the Summer Meadow, and I felt her tremble under my palm as her snakes writhed in the steel like a quickening child in the womb.

'Would you then fight with me, Bedwyr?'

'You know very well that I would not fight with you, not after all we have done. But my young men might brawl with yours, and there are more of mine. Would you go on your journey alone, Morvran?'

'At the end we each go alone, Bedwyr.'

He sat his horse and considered. In that silence, for the last time we felt unity. He asked, 'How many are you?'

'I have with me, or coming with me, well, with Taberon and Tatharn, with Esau my cook of state, with Keinakh and with Korlam and with Gwion and with Gwenki, with Kian my new bard and with another I may not yet name . . . we are, or will be, ten.'

'And one of you a very young man, and one a boy. What kind of number is that to cross the seas with? I know that the kings of the Heathen that are in Logres go always in companies of eleven and their Households are dressed in stripes from neck to heel to show that their way is down to Hell. The civilised kings from Elmet and the north go out in companies of thirteen, and wear mostly plain colours, or quartered. And there are Christian kings from the Antipodes beyond Jerusalem who go out in companies of seventeen and wear no sleeves to their shirts and dangle their trophies from the brims of their helmets. But we Kings of the Unity of the Island wear our shirts coloured in hoops, and go out always in companies of fifteen to do all things in dignity and good order, and in sobriety and in quietness, and to seek the unknown. You are five short.'

'I came away in something of a hurry, Bedwyr. My sister's son Mabon holds Caerwent for me, and I did not dare take from him any other man whom he might find useful in a crisis.'

'I will make up your numbers on the same principle. I have a huntsman, one Leision, and he is a little given to boasting.'

'Is that not true of all of us?'

'That is his defect. But as is well known, his virtue is in this, that he will never catch cold or sneeze, even though he be wetted all over with fresh water. Now, Leision, find four of the men to go with King Morvran.'

'Right, King Bedwyr, find four men and send them with King Morvran.'

'No. Find four men and *take* them with King Morvran. You are going too.'

'No, I can't.'

'Yes, you can. And shall.'

'My mam will kill me. She doesn't even know I'm out with you now, she thinks I've gone on a drinking party. I said I'd be back on Wednesday, when I'm sober.'

'If I tell you you're going, then you go, Leision.'

'Well, you go and ask her, then, and I hope she doesn't kill you.'

'I'm not asking her. I'll just tell her I sent you.'

'Then it *is* killing you she will be, but I don't suppose anybody will notice, not in this kingdom that gets on very well without you, so I suppose it'll have to get on without me either. If you do get killed when you tell her, don't blame me when I get back. I'll find four fools.'

'Four other fools,' Bedwyr corrected him, waving for cider and cups.

I asked, 'Typical of your household?'

'One of my best men. I grudge you nothing. His virtue you have heard, and it is useful it will be if you go over the seas; his defect is this: that he is too eager to express himself in hyperbole. But the rest, they're a shower of ungrateful lechers who do little but loaf around and eat my pork and drink my cider and wear their hair long and their breeches tight in the crotch and they got no reverence for their elders and—'

'Careful. You're going red in the face. You'll have apoplexy.'

'Can't. I've had apoplexy once. Stands to reason, can't have it twice. Like measles.'

'My Aunty Flossy had measles twice.'

'Your Aunty Flossy was a short-tempered sluttish bad-minded shrew.'

'True. But a *lovable* short-tempered sluttish bad-minded shrew.'

'As you say. Leision! Where are they?'

But Leision did not answer, being engaged in collecting, by means of blows and curses, mostly reciprocated, four volunteers from among Bedwyr's happy Household. When he got back he had somehow collected Lhyswen the Eel from Ratae, Gleisiad the Salmon from Karliol, Kimokh the Lobster from Glevum, and Krank the Crab from Calleva, all therefore obviously well fitted for a career on the sea.

'Not too bad,' I told him, 'for general and unskilled labour. With Gwion as hooker and me as stand-off we have the makings of a decent second-rate pack.'

'Under these conditions of mutual satisfaction,' said Bedwyr, resuming the cultured language of the Court, 'perhaps you will excuse me from turning out myself this season. You can all ride straight down to the lagoon and start training.'

'Not today. My men have been on the move all day, and I hope to lie up here as planned and go on at dusk.'

'You want to ride at night?' Leision objected. 'You can't do that, the horses won't know the way.'

'You can have the day off,' I comforted him. 'Go away and hunt us something for our dinner.'

'In the thicket,' Bedwyr told me, 'there is a fire and over the fire there is a spit and on the spit there is turning a stag. I am riding back to Badon to talk sweetly to some mothers. I do not know whether to wish you success, Morvran, because success for you may mean disaster for us all. But I will pray for your safe return. May God and the Virgin go with you in spite of all that Tatharn can do.'

His butler poured us now the precious wine, in silver cups, and we drank.

'To Freedom,' Bedwyr toasted me, in Latin.

I echoed him in the old language, 'Dros rhydhid.'

We embraced from horse to horse, an action most impressive to the beholder and quite terrifying to the performer, since the horses don't like it and tend to bolt, depositing their riders in the steaming heaps they so thoughtfully prepare beforehand. But on this occasion we stayed in the saddle.

Bedwyr waved to his people to join him as he rode north.

I called on my own men and led them to the stag. 'We have unexpected allies,' I told them, 'and now we are almost complete. We will not, as I feared, have to accept help from wanderers on the Heath or drifters along the coast or even from unemployed kings in Armorica or other places beyond the seas, in the great realms of Cornuaille or Lyonesse, of Migraine or Accidie or Faiblesse.'

'Are we going to Gaul, then?' Leision asked.

I ignored him. How in God's name could I tell now where we were going? The strain of acting as the all-knowing leader sure of himself and of his goals was almost insufferable, since from one moment to the next I had no idea what to do. But I called all my followers to unsaddle and to indulge in mutual conversation and introductions of the stag and the oatcakes and a few casks of cider that Bedwyr had left for us. Mead would have been better, but that king had little imagination.

We lay up there on the edge of the heath for another night and a day, drinking all the cider to save the trouble of carrying it. This allowed the horses to rest before their last journey over the sandy wastes, where the serpents gambolled in the sun without fear of entrapment by a Great Duchess.

It also allowed our new comrades a chance to settle in. Esau had them out for most of the daylight exercising at arms. After everybody had felt the edge of his wit, they were all united in hatred of the cook: but they still had no idea of what drill would be like once Gwion began to teach them the great new secret manoeuvre, Arthur's last tactical invention, known only by the slogan of up-and-under. But this hatred lasted only till the meat was served and for three swallows of mead thereafter.

II

When we at last came, facing the evening, down the hill to the edge of the lagoon, we found there two stout houses, warm and dry, as well as a few fishermen's huts. Some Corns were already in one of the houses, where the outside walls were adorned with the picture of a sea beast coloured green and jumping out of the water while spouting foam from the top of its head.

'A whale!' said Taberon, but Esau insisted that this was only a dolphin. We told the Corns that Constant was coming, and rather than stay to meet him they ran off across Purbeck back towards the creek where they had been hunting swans. Esau took possession of the house and what had been brought there out of Cornwall, bags of twice baked bread and salted meat and dried apple rings, and sausages by the mile, and flagon after flagon of cider. The Badon boys elected to stay here with him.

I took Taberon and Kian further on, to the other house which had painted on its outside wall the head of my great-great five times great-grandfather Votadinus, who married for one night the Lady of Eiddin, Buddug the Bitch. From this union spring all the great princes of the north. He was easily recognised by his long red locks, from which we his sons all have the ridge of red hair down our spines from neck to fork, and by his one eye. There was plenty of food here too, although it needed more immediate attention, being mostly on the hoof or claw. And Gwion was there, sound asleep and guarding it well.

We let the Badon boys rest up there for couple of days to get their feet back after riding so long. Then Esau told them, as a change from having them kill cattle and set out meat to dry in the sun, because it was a very bad time for weather that year, 'We're off to work now, lads. We're going to get a boat.'

He and Gwion had their own methods, I supposed, although it was not politic to enquire too closely into them. That night, the seven of them all left quietly, on foot, with their faces blackened with charcoal.

Taberon asked, 'Why must they go off like that to get a boat? We could all ride in that big leather boat they took with them on their shoulders to get out of the lagoon over the headland into the open sea.'

'They were going to use that only to slip quietly along the coast and creep further east into a river,' I told him, and added, 'Although the boat they took is big enough to carry us all if we go out fishing, it cannot hold everything we will have to take, like food for several days, and other things.'

'What other things?' he demanded.

'Wait and see,' I told him. Then I relented and showed him how each of the Badon boys had brought not only his own gear on one horse, which was bulky enough as it was, but also another packhorse with a couple of bags of assorted bronze letters from statue bases, and other pieces of the metal which made up a sizable fortune as a gift to our enterprise. A generous gesture by Bedwyr, and unlike him: he had refused for some time to throw any of the wealth of Badon, letters or wall bolts or jugs or statues of which he had plenty, into the common stock to buy wine or sword-blades for the kings' soldiers.

We sat there for several days doing very little but listen to the man of the place grumble about losing his best boat just when it was good fishing weather. He had a couple of smaller ones, and we took those out into the lagoon and brought back a great deal of fish to dry for ourselves, or even to eat fresh, a desperate measure. I hoped that we could get the seasickness out of Taberon before we sailed.

Then, when the Badon boys had been gone for five full days, Korlam came down to us from where he had been keeping his watch, that is from the top of what the people of the place called the Evening Hill, for no good reason. First he asked for his dinner which was not yet ready, and then while waiting for it he mentioned idly that a large party of men was approaching from the northeast, across the heath. I reached down Bees in the Summer Meadow, and began to untie the riding strings, but Korlam stopped me, saying, 'No need, they are horsemen and not savages.'

I went up the hill, to greet Keinakh and Gwenki, and with them was Synager, the Prefect of London. He had brought a column of forty men, and a score of packhorses, all laden with leather sacks full of bits of bronze. A hungry-looking mob, who grudged us the few sacks of oatmeal and cheeses and dried fruit they had also brought us.

I motioned Korlam to hide the food and drink we had gathered for ourselves. I asked, 'Was the journey peaceable?'

'Moderately so, as far as Calleva,' said Synager. My own men kept silent, they would tell me the truth later. 'After that, we were followed. Always there were Heathen in sight, never very close, but always going our way. At night they camped so close we could smell their fires and their yeasty bread.'

'And Bedwyr?'

'After the Standing Stones, we saw horsemen away to the north. We knew that it was Bedwyr, because I had sent to him and he had promised. The savages stayed close to us, but we felt safer.'

The savages are still terrified of horses. One of the great secrets of the Iron Men, by which we lived, was that there is really no need to be frightened of a horse in battle, only of its rider. For the first thing you must do when breaking in a horse is to teach it that it must never, never trample on a man. Therefore there is no need to fear that even in battle the horse will tread you down: it will throw its rider before it does that. When it turns aside from you, it is then that the rider has a chance to throw his javelin. The savages had not yet learned that you should not fear the horse but stand fast and strike at the rider. So Bedwyr merely by hovering a mile or so from the London men could protect them.

Once Synager had unloaded his packs of bronze and his men had found that there was nothing much around for them to to drink, he took them all and the light horses away again towards London. He reckoned he could make twice the speed without his cargo.

III

Next morning, we saw the ship was in the lagoon. She had come in across the bar in the dawn mists, towing the leather boat behind her. The Badon boys were already out of her, cooking breakfast on the beach over a fire of driftwood, never bothering to invite us. I went out to see when the smell of frying bacon woke me up. Invited or not, I ate some of it.

'Heathen bacon,' said Leision, when I came back for a second plateful, 'and Pagan eggs. Hope there's no spell on it.'

'What a time to tell me,' I protested. 'Next time, get Tatharn on it first thing.'

'Oh, we've had him round already, really early, exorcising like mad, or we'd never have tried it ourselves. Not till after you'd had some. It was our first hot meal for, oh a week, isn't it?'

I took a good look at the ship where they had run her up on the sands, and paced her out. She was not what you'd call a thing of beauty or an ornament to the seascape, but she'd do. About eight fathoms long and two fathoms and a bit wide, shaped like a porridge bowl underwater, so she'd roll unless she were properly ballasted and trimmed to a fine pitch.

'Went into Hamwih in the dusk,' Gwion told me. 'They were all asleep on shore. Four men in her, and a cargo of hides, probably all rustled along our borders and ready to go to the Franks the other side.'

I could smell the cargo. 'Get it out,' I ordered, 'and stack it under cover. Bedwyr will be back for it at the end of the week, coming to make sure we've gone. Then clean her up and get to work, before we push her back into the water and load the cargo.'

Taberon, at last awake, came and wondered, for such a great ship was never seen in these waters, except when Theodore or his captain came once a year or so. 'Is this the kind of ship the Heathen build?'

'No. This is one of ours, from the olden-olden days. See, it's carvel-built, smooth as a baby's bottom, while the Heathen cannot build elegant ships this size and use lap-strake, all rough and ridged. She was built, oh, many years ago, up in Cardigan or somewhere like that. Our first fathers used such ships to fight against the Rome-King. Not many left now. But she's been altered a lot in that time, and now Keinakh will have to alter her back.'

'I wonder what her name is. What was Arthur's ship called?'

'Oh, Arthur never had *a* ship.' I almost laughed at the boy. 'He took what came to hand. We started off in a different ship each time, and not always the same ship all the voyage. One trip we used four, one after another. We'd run one aground awkward so that she split up at high tide. Seeing one with a better cargo, among all kinds of reasons for changing. We never knew what their original owners called them. Arthur called them the first thing he'd thought of, *Gwyvyn a Rhwd* if the day's office was about moth and rust, or *Mokhyn Du* if he'd eaten a black piglet the night before, and that was only two of the many.'

I looked at the prow post. It had been sawn off short and still showed fresh.

Gwion shook his head. 'Nasty that one was. You wouldn't want to look at it, let alone sail with it. Nor the name that went with it, neither.'

'You've got your tools,' I told Taberon. 'Get Keinakh to let you have a block of lime wood, and carve a figurehead for him to mortise back into place. And make the eyeholes big, we'll need them. Otherwise please yourself.'

Korlam came for breakfast. He had taken his pick of the hides, and was already sewing a new mainsail. He munched at the bacon between two slabs of oatmeal, and said, off hand, 'Saw a funny thing from the hill before I came down. There's been a small fire burning all night. Out there in the scrub, to the east, small but quite bright as if there was somebody awake to feed it.'

'That'll be Arthur,' said the householder, a surly man named Sarrug. 'He used to come here a lot, and then go out on the heath when he saw a fire burning.'

'Arthur's dead,' I reminded him.

'So they say. But I think it's Arthur. Used to come and talk with the Heathen.'

'Don't believe that. But Arthur's dead, I tell you, I saw him killed.'

'You've told me that before. It wasn't true then and I don't suppose it's true now.'

I didn't argue, just clipped him around the earhole. I asked Korlam, 'Didn't you go to look?'

'By myself, and at night? Don't be silly. But there might be somebody there. At dawn I could still see it burning, hard and dry, no smoke. Then it began to smoke very hard, as if somebody had piled straw on it.'

'Anything else?'

'Something tall stuck in the ground, standing up straight. Looks like a rag tied to a pole. Wasn't there yesterday. Shall I tell Gwion to have a look?'

'No, Gwion's a bit busy. Let it be till tomorrow.'

But I thought about it all day, while we got the ship higher out on the beach and gave it a good going over with hot water and brushes, and burnt some incense Tatharn had spare to get rid of the smell.

That night, Korlam persuaded Gwion to come up the hill with him to stand watch. He saw the smoke die away with the sunlight, and then a bright clear flame take its place. He came back to tell me that it hadn't gone away, but met me coming up. Before dawn, I went out, careful not to tell Taberon because I wasn't going anywhere he could be of help. Not if he was looking for an adventure. I wore my mail coat, I carried a pike two fathoms long, with a good damask head, and hung

Bees in the Summer Meadow around my shoulder. I pondered a little, then I stacked the pike again, and took three javelins. Leision saddled a horse for me, and gave me some hot oatcake and honey and mulled mead for breakfast. I went to the top of Evening Hill, and stood with Korlam to watch the sun come up, the fire die down, and the smoke rise from the straw. Against the early light there did seem to be a pole there, and perhaps something fluttering from the top. Gwion came up, but against the sun he could see little more than I could.

At last he stiffened and said, 'There's someone there. I saw him move. I think he's sitting under a bush most of the time. But he has to come out now and again to put wood on the fire.'

'I'm going down.'

'Well, if you get killed don't come back and complain to me,' said Gwion.

I had a last swallow of cider, settled my helmet well down, got up on my horse and rode to the east.

After I had recited nearly all of Psalm One Hundred and Nineteen, I was in clear view of the fire. I stopped and watched it for a while, standing in clear sight of the man sitting by the fire, under the bush. At last when I guessed I might have outlasted his patience, I dismounted and untied the riding strings of my sword. I looped my reins over my arm and walked forward very softly.

It was, of course, Oslaf. He sat cross-legged on the ground, and did not rise. His sword, in its scabbard with the riding strings tied, was ten feet from his hand. His pike was stuck into the ground, point down: what that did to the edge I didn't like to think. Otherwise he was dressed as a herald, with his shirt on inside out, all the seams standing proud. He had turned his mail shirt inside out, too, the fleece showing; it was lying on the ground, and picking up all the end-of-winter scraps of dead leaves. There was a piece of white cloth tied to the butt of his pike. And in his hand he held a green branch – holly, I think.

I threw my horse's reins to the ground and told it to stand. It did, not for my telling it but for my selecting a good clump of lush grass on the dry scrub. I was dressed normally. I did not find a green branch. Oslaf was the suppliant, not me, and I left him to stew in it. I did not wish him peace, as he wished me. I simply stood there, my fingers fidgeting on my sword hilt as if it resented unemployment. I had him at my mercy, and he was not absolutely sure that I would respect him as a herald. If Tatharn had been there he would have argued that there was no duty of respect to one unbaptised, even if he carried a whole holly tree.

I asked him in Latin, 'What do you want?'

'To speak to Arthur. We usually speak here.'

'Arthur is dead.'

'If you say so.' He spoke as if he knew better but was willing to humour me.

I replied at length, being very careful with my Latin grammar, but stern and gruff at the same time. I was pleased to see that Oslaf's knuckles whitened where he held his branch.

When I had finished he answered in Latin with a foul accent and not such good grammar. 'Till Arthur comes, I will go with you.'

'Am I to understand that you are asking for permission, please, to come with us?'

'I seek my sister. You are going to find her. Wherever it is Arthur has sent her. I know it is you who knows where she is. If you did not know, would you be leaving the country?'

'You cannot come. I cannot guarantee your safety, and where would my honour be if my men ran a herald through the body while he slept, which I am sure they want to do.'

'It did not happen. Not in Constant's tent.'

'True. But this is not Constant's territory.'

'Is it your territory?'

'For the present.'

'For the present? This is my territory. For ever. I have been five days walking from London. I guarded your horses and your bronze. All that time we were not out of earshot of the Londoners. Most of the time we smelled them. At the drop of my hand, my people could have killed all of yours. They would be far gone before the horsemen in the north even heard of it. We knew Bedwyr was out on his border. The men at Thameshead have been in arms. Now, wherever Bedwyr has gone, they follow him. This show of an army is not in the Treaty.'

'That goes for both sides. But now we have the bronze.'

'And we have you. How many are you? Twenty? No more. If we wish we can take the treasure you guard. And take your lives.'

'But you cannot go where we are going, because you do not know where that is. We will there be beyond any help you can rely on.'

'You mean that when you are clear to sea you will cut off my head?'

'Quite possibly.'

'If necessary, that too I will suffer. It is my oath. It is my oath that I will find my sister the mother of the Bretwalda, or die. I swore on the Holy Stallion, and the Mare, Hengist and Horsa, that are both my ancestors.'

I thought about that. There was room to bargain. What he was telling me was that if I let him go back to his people to say that I refused him, then they would come about us in the night, masses of them, and kill us before we could sail. He was telling me that I would not get very far without him, but he had not told me that I would get very far with him either.

I asked, 'Will you swear to me that with you aboard your people will not attack us?'

He considered that. Then he said, 'In the names of the Kingships of the Jutes and the Angles and the Saxons and the Wicca and the Wends …' He went on with the names of a dozen Heathen royal houses which I had, mostly, never heard of before '… that you will be allowed to depart from the land and return to it without scathe or scrape or scot or harm or hurt, and that you may voyage the seas into the lands of our brothers the Goths and the Franks and the Lombards and the Vandals and that you will be let to go and return, you and your ship and your crew and your cargo whether you take it from hence or bring it back into the Island, all this for a year from this day or as long as I am with you in your ship at sea or in your company on land whichever is the shorter time.'

He swore all that in Latin, and very impressive he made it sound too while I memorised it, it being a skill common to bards that whatever we hear spoken that we can remember and repeat. Then he stood up and brought out from under his mail shirt a bag of good soft calf leather. He loosed the drawstrings, and from it he drew out first an adder tangled in a net, and he cut off its head. Then he opened it a little more and he brought out a hare, alive and kicking, and he cut its throat and he sprinkled the blood on the ground around us both in a circle. Last, he brought out the eggs of a pigeon, six of them, and he smashed them on the grounds, all the while mumbling to himself so quietly in his own language, which he did not believe I could understand, that I could not really follow. Then very loudly in his own language he swore, as far as I could follow it, to the gods of the earth and of the air and of the realms beneath that he would behave himself as long as I did. He did not ask me to swear.

Then I told him to come with me, to see what would happen. He put on his mail shirt inside out, to save the bother of carrying it in his hands, and hung his sword from a sling, hilt down. Last of all he shouldered his pike, butt up and point down, and the point looked blunted enough to reassure me. I mounted and he trudged alongside at my stirrup. After four hundred paces, Gwion and Leision appeared, mounted, as if out of nowhere: I suppose they had been hidden in some fold in the ground and come out when they were hidden from Oslaf by my horse's body. Whether any of the Pagans had been watching us from cover I did not know.

When we came in sight of the houses, the Badon boys all came out, and saw him, and there was a rush for swords and axes. I called out loudly that Oslaf was a herald and therefore sacred, that is that they should not kill him till I gave them leave, or at least not where I could see them, my honour being more valuable than theirs. And they, grudging, gave their word.

IV

Oslaf didn't like the look of the ship much, even though we had been at some pains to wash off the new stains in the waist. However, since he had known the owner and didn't care for him, there wasn't too great a fuss about that. But he was less pleased with the work we had done on her in the three days since the Badon boys had brought her in.

In the first place we had built a new tabernacle for the mast, and that, he said, was placed wrong, much too far aft. And we had brought the yard down, and hoisted it up again in a way he had never seen in a ship, with the mast before the yard, and the yard itself slung by lashing it a third of the way along its breadth. A mast, he told us, ought to be a third of the way from the bow to the stern, and a yard should be balanced exactly in the middle and slung in front of the mast, otherwise the gods would be angry and not send winds dead astern, for winds even a fraction away from the dead fore and aft would make sailing impossible, and there were not enough of us to row the ship in the open sea. As if we would ever think of exerting ourselves beyond necessity. We simply put Oslaf down as a simpleton who had never seen a dipping lug, and therefore had no understanding of the principles of voyaging. Later, when Gwion was exercising Taberon as a helmsman, as one of the skills necessary for a king, that precious pair took us so close to the wind that Oslaf was very frightened indeed at the angle of heel, to the point of being seasick. Which did not increase his dignity or his careful air of confident authority.

When we had the ship back into the water, we began to load. The bronze was packed very tidily in the bottom of the ship, and we sailed her several times across the lagoon, partly to exercise those who had not been at sea before, but mainly to adjust the trim by moving bags of bronze about the vessel. On top of that we stowed the cheeses and the meat and the oatcakes and the nuts and fruit, and more cheeses after that. The casks of mead and cider were all low down at the bow and the stern. Everything had to be repacked several times, not only because of the effect the food, uneaten, had on the trim, but because of the way in which the trim would change when it was eaten, or drunk.

Taberon said plaintively, being tired of carrying cheeses about, 'I never realised that there was so much planning and preparation to an adventure.'

'No,' I told him, 'nor do most people, which is why so many adventures begun with such high hopes and such great intentions fail miserably. And for a war this is twice as true, which is something I could never really persuade Arthur of. So carry your cheeses manfully and never forget how many, or how few, you have left.'

Last of all we stowed Tatharn's millstone, high up where he could get at it easily in case of emergency and also where we could move it about quickly and easily to change the trim. We also stowed his staff, a branch of oak a man and two heads tall, struck by lightning from the trunk and showing the mistletoe scar, thus being doubly holy. It had a ferrule of bronze, sharp as a serpent's tooth. Then he agreed to carry out the last important and sacred rites of preparation.

Taberon had carved a very artistic figurehead which Keinakh mortised firmly into the top of the prow post. It showed the head of a boar, life-size, very realistic, with tusks and all, and deep eye sockets. It took a coat of black tar very well. Tatharn produced from the bottom of his bag, all mixed up with chalice and paten and bell, a piece of alder wood. With this, Taberon was able to make two white eyes and glue them firmly into place. For alder is a holy wood, and eyes of that wood will make sure that a ship will never go astray but always come, in her own good time, safely into the harbour she seeks.

That last loading took all day, and in the night the ship lay safely alongside the wharf. In the morning, Tatharn made all safe. He said Mass, for the safety of the journey and the sanctity of the ship, three times. I suspected that if he had not been coming himself he would have thought once enough. The first Mass he said standing on the shore above the high-water mark. Then he said Mass standing on the wharf. The third time he said Mass standing on his millstone in the waist of the ship. We fourteen stood and sang the responses, a different setting each time, all word perfect luckily because Tatharn was tetchy enough to insist on saying another Mass if there were one mistake. But Oslaf, the unbaptised Heathen, stood all the time above high water, with his back to us, fearful that he might be bewitched.

So after Mass, we had our breakfast, enough to last us to supper-time. We ate the most of three little pigs and a calf that we found unwarily loitering around the back of the houses. Sarrug was a little vexed at this, and wanted something to compensate him for his vast expense in hospitality. I told him that we were leaving behind a score of horses, all fine beasts except for the sway-backed Dancer. I did not think it politic to let him know that Bedwyr would be along before the end of the week to reclaim them and to take compensation for theft or for receiving of stolen goods.

High tide was about noon. Therefore we pushed off from the wharf in time to take advantage of the flow to take us over the bar, out of the lagoon, past Old Harry and into the open sea.

V

The voyage was quite uneventful. We all fitted quite comfortably, once it was established that everyone had his own seat and that moving about was dangerous and unlawful. I appointed Gwenki as skipper and steersman under me, and he enforced his discipline with oaths and blows from his bucket. Korlam had sewn a leather bucket for each man. Gleisiad, the most stupid of the Badon boys, if there were any difference to be noted, asked on receiving his, 'What is this for?'

'Obvious, isn't it,' replied Gwenki. 'You can eat your porridge out of it, or be seasick into it, or excrete into it in any other way, or drink out of it, or wash out of it, or most important of all bail water out of the boat.'

The boat had a deck about the level of the third strake from above keel, and this we had strewn with a layer of brushwood before putting the bronze sacks on it. But there was amidships, a little before the mast, a gap in the deck looking down into the bottom of the boat where the water collected, over the sand ballast. When the weather got choppy we were to bail the water out of this by buckets full, like out of a well, passing from hand to hand. This would make sure that the buckets were washed and kept clean, although some pernickety individuals washed them out more often in the sea. The level of water was watched by Tatharn, who sat there on his millstone.

A little forward of the mast, Esau had an iron plate, and a little brazier on that to heat the cauldron and keep us well fed. Sometimes he cooked fish which he enticed aboard, and several times we had squid of varying ages, since these creatures grow a new arm for every year of their age up to the age of eight, and most of those we took were of full age. These are unlike spiders who always have eight legs.

Gwion sat in the prow, using his keen vision and his brass lungs to guide us. Part of the time, Taberon sat with him, and part of the time he sat with Gwenki to learn to steer. He asked, 'Do the savages build many ships like this?'

'No,' we told him, 'they don't build ships like this. This one was built in Britain, or perhaps in Armorica. Some Heathen stole it, and we have taken it back. These ships last, because they were properly mortised together.'

'Could we have built one,' he asked, 'instead of stealing this one from the savages?'

'Oh yes,' Keinakh told him, 'built enough in my time, at Avan at the river mouth.'

'Take long?' the lad asked.

'Not long,' the Carpenter of State told him. 'About three or four months to build, on the sands. But I'd have to have about, oh, fifteen years' notice.'

'Fifteen years' notice? What for?'

'Oh, for choosing the timber, because the ship is like a wall, you don't cut all the wood to shape, you find oak trees which are growing into the right curves for the keel and the knees and the prow and the ribs, and mark them ready. And then you cut them down, and you stack them together to dry and weather properly, and that takes about ten or twelve years if you skimp it, but fifteen years is a bit better. After you have built the hull then you sink it in the river, and leave it to soak so that all the joints clench together and when you have had it out and dried it out again she will float properly, because it is not till she is watertight that she gets her soul and has to be christened like a Christian child.'

So we sailed on, and met all the usual dangers of the sea. Nothing to make a great song about, only a whale that went by with people living on the back and cooking their dinner on a fire and giving us a pot of hot porridge which was a great act of charity. And a whole flock or herd or crowd of mermaids, which sang sweetly and tried to tempt us to jump overboard and join them, which Gleisiad was quite willing to do but Gwenki hit him with his bucket. And he asked why, and we told him that if he went he would have to live on seaweed for ever and not even boiled. So he agreed to stay, not liking laver bread nor spinach neither. And Kian watched all this and marvelled and made up songs about it in his own mind, which was a deep and murky place to make anything.

Meanwhile I talked with Oslaf, who sat with his green branch in his hand between me and Korlam where we could each put a knife in his ribs quick and easy if it were necessary. He told me a little about what he thought that Arthur had in mind for the Heathen to do instead of fighting with us, once they had taken the cities of the midlands which he had promised them without consulting their present kings. It was rather confusing and fragmentary, but at last I thought I had it. He was offering the Heathen the whole of Ireland, if only they would go there and take it, and he was going to allow them to go unhindered to the shores of Klwyd and build there enough ships to take an army across first, and all their women and children after, and so harm the Kings of Ireland that they would not come over to raid our shores. Whether the Heathen could conquer the island, or all be killed fighting there, Arthur was not concerned with, only so that they would leave our Island and let him restore unity. Which was a very good idea.

After Oslaf told us this, we looked out over the sea and saw a whole flock of angels, leaping out of the water and dropping back, so somehow we lost interest in the subject. We kept close to the shore, and most nights we were able to find a strand of good clean sand to run the ship ashore on, and light a fire and cook our oatcakes and toast our cheese for supper and make our porridge for breakfast. Only Oslaf wouldn't eat porridge at that time and insisted on having bacon grilled on the hot stones. Usually wherever we halted the people of the place would come down to us very soon and let us have milk and eggs, and we would give them a cheese or so, which they were very eager to have being so much better than they were used to, or sometimes a piece of bronze. Only when they came down to us and saw Oslaf they would not be too pleased and usually offered to take him from us, which made him cling very tightly to his branch of green holly.

They were always anxious to have news of the island from which their fathers had come. That is why they all spoke very good Cornish, almost as intelligible as a real language. They had all heard the rumour, as they called it, that Arthur was dead, and none of them believed it in the slightest. And they argued which one of us was really Arthur in disguise.

The best thing about being at sea was that we were not plagued with beetles or with spiders to spoil the food. And we sat at ease, only sometimes having to bail, for with Tatharn aboard it was no wonder that we had a good wind almost all the way and only occasionally had to work out the problems of setting and trimming and reefing the sail. So with little effort and good food and good song and conversation mostly good, except where we had to talk with Oslaf, we came around the corner of Lyonesse and south down the coast of Gaul. We came between the Beautiful Island and the shore, and past the first river and the long sands. And we came to the mouth of the second river.

Interlude 8: The Treasure

On the way south, the sun beat down ever stronger each day. Every colour new-painted, bright as an enamelled brooch, struck the woman's eye. Among the Iron Men, she had seen the cities and straight roads that Romeland once built. Now here among the Franks and Gauls, those same cities and roads, in better repair, stood under a larger sun, their shadows deeper, and their stones clearer. They plucked urgently at the eye with the bustle of a wider world.

In easy stages, along the winding river, the ship had plied its way, taking on fresh water and always welcome. Men whose skins were dark as the Shipman's stood ready and eager to bring piquant olives, sweet hairy apricots and bulging figs. Spiced meats skewered on a spit and roasted, red sausages diced with fat, cheeses ripe and runny were brought to her. At each point of embarkation, important men in a drapery of white shining cloth bowed to her and to the Shipman with deferential courtesy.

From the hold, the Shipman brought up yellow silks from bales heavy with the aroma of spice with which to drape her. She lay aside the coarse wool of the Apple Island and delighted in their caress.

At night, he lay beside her showing the star paths by which he steered, how each point and section wove in lines of light the guiding constellations. So might a man reckon his flocks and herds, she understood.

Under a brief, delightful rain, she woke to enjoy the freshness of a new day. Beneath the hull, the crabs quickened while sea anemones gave way to weeds and cresses, and the yellow flags of sweet water. Now their vessel was hailed familiarly from the riverbanks by those who welcomed home the wanderers, though she did not speak their tongue.

The Shipman hailed them back, his deep-toned voice resonant with the warmth of one returning.

Lazily, she let the sun brighten one long white side of her flesh that his hand might treasure her still.

Chapter 8

The River

I

So by the grace of God and the intercession of Tatharn and the charm of the alder pegs and by the little skill we had in seamanship we came into the mouth of the second great river of the south. I began to believe that Arthur had been wrong when he refused ever to take a priest into a ship, because Tatharn had prayed unceasingly and we had had none but favourable winds. But in the river mouth the wind fell away, and neither priests nor the alder peg having power over fresh water, we could make little headway against the flow of the river.

'There is no help for it,' Gwion called to me over the heads of our gallant crew, 'we will have to return to Armorica and come here over the land.'

And all answered, Amen.

'Nonsense. We have in the ship eight good oars, or sweeps, rather, and thole pins jointed into the upmost strake. These are enough for the gallant lads of Badon, who have suffered agonies of boredom on this journey from having too little to do, and Kian and Taberon can join them. It does not matter that they are an odd number for Oslaf will stroke and teach them at the same time.'

But in spite of this expert coaching, they did not row at all well at first, being unused to manual labour or to long and regular hours of perseverance. But with the aid of Oslaf's instruction and luck and persistence (mostly mine) and a fair amount of abuse and physical violence and a plentiful diet of fresh-caught crab, they kept us going till the sun went down and we could anchor close inshore.

Leision summed up his mates' complaints as we drank our supper. 'It's too hot to row. The heat wasn't too bad at sea, because the ship was moving and we had a nice draught.'

'Make your mind up. When we were at sea, you were always grumbling every time you got wet.'

'And if I did get wet and I wasn't who I am I might have caught my death of cold and my mam would have killed me when I got home, and you too, Morvran.'

'Then you ought to have sent your mam to sea instead, Leision. But for now, little lads, finish your suppers, drink up your nice cider, because tomorrow it's either row again or drift out to sea till we fall over the edge of the world.'

'Nice to fall off and have a bit of rest,' grumbled Gleisiad. The others called him Gleisiad the Stupid, although how they could tell I never found out. I clipped him one over the ear with his bucket, and he went to sleep and missed the third pouring of cider. Broke the bucket, though. Then I glared at the others till they all went to sleep.

While they snored, I kept watch in case any of the inhabitants might be so overcome by curiosity as to the sharpness of their knives as to come out and try them on our throats. Some time after midnight, I sensed that flesh and blood could stand no more, and so I called Tatharn, who had little enough of either, to relieve me.

At dawn we had a little wind from the northwest and caught the tide and therefore were spared rowing. In about three hours we were up to Bordigala. The lads stared in wonder at the tall houses, very dangerous, and at the stone wharf the Romans had built, being themselves too primitive to learn the art of running their ships upon a beach. I called them all to listen.

'You can see from this near to the wharf how unskilled these people are in the arts of civilisation and of comfortable living. I would not like to have you go ashore, but if I were to let you go you would find them marvellously innocent, entranced by shining baubles and apt to be persuaded, by both charm and violence to which they are equal strangers, against their better judgement and their own advantage.'

'And while you are ashore, if you are allowed ashore,' continued Esau from amidships, 'if there come to you out of dark corners and hidden alleyways, women painted to the lips and cheeks and other places I will not mention, leaving you to find out, shimmering in dyed and patterned clothes, perfumed with musk and smells unimaginable, and glittering in gold and garnets, whispering foul allurements and pressing invitations of the utmost and lepidopterous prurience such as are explicitly forbidden in great detail by Holy Writ – then follow them fast, boys, because you will find none like them in Bedwelhty.'

It was at that moment that Gwion, who was very sensitive to such things if they happened to fall close under his eye, spotted another ship at anchor nearly half an oar's length ahead. By the greatest good fortune and consummate skill on my part we were able almost to avoid ramming her by a hair's breadth. Not much damage having been done, we were able to look closely into her, with a hull empty to the bottom boards and the moss growing on them. Her timbers were shrinking in the drought and her seams beginning to start, so that the spiders who seemed to be her only crew began to look for a chance to abandon ship.

Yet those of us who had seen her in earlier years coming up to Porthskewett, heavy with sword-blades and jars of wine, shouted with joy, and I cried aloud, 'Rejoice! We have run our quarry to earth, and the Unity of the Island is safely in our hands!'

So they all cheered and began to prepare for the voyage home. But I gave orders to row for the wharf, and after some urging Taberon consented to jump ashore and make us fast by a line round a bollard. I burrowed in the bottom of the boat and found my baggage so that I could put on my best Shirt of State, all red and black hoops, over the shabby one I had on. Over that I wore the skin of a bear I had killed on Margam Mountain. Then I too went ashore.

II

Immediately I was safe on dry land I ordered my crew to row well out into the stream, and wait for me there. I did not see that they rowed hard for seven strokes till Gwion, ever watchful, noticed that Taberon had not yet untied them from the bollard, nor could he do so, the wretched lad having invented a new knot but not the method of undoing it. Rather than damage the bollard or cut the rope which was new and expensive, they went no further.

I took three steps and a man came up to me. He wore a mail coat with most of the iron rusted off the leather, and a helm with a dent in it and a socket without a feather and his hair had not been cut since the last Christmas shave he hadn't had, and a straw hung from his lower lip. He said, 'Pay up or push off.'

He spoke in a dreadful nasal accent, but I could just understand his Latin, full as it was of Gaulish and Heathen words wrongly inflected. I asked, 'Pay up what? And who are you?'

'Pay up the harbour dues!' he said. 'And it is that it is the Harbour Master and the Customs Man and the Excise Officer and the Tide Watcher and the Poll Tax Collector and the Publican and the Sinner that it is that I am. It is me that it is that they are all at once and over-worked and underpaid and under-rewarded by both sides it is that we are.'

'Only one of you?'

'Yes, it is only one of me that it is that we are. But is it not that there is the Majesty of the Law that it is behind me?'

'And is it not the power of fourteen good men and true that it is behind me? And besides I claim diplomatic exemption from all taxes and dues and freedom from search and arrest for debt on the grounds that it is a king that it is that I am.'

'If it is a king that it is that you are, then where is it that it is that you are a king of?'

'I am a King of Britain,' I told him, not thinking it worth telling him that in the social circles where I move kings are as common as sparrows on the roof.

'From Britain?' he repeated in a voice full of respect and incredulity, or perhaps just mistrust, for then he turned and shouted to the crowd which had gathered, 'From Britain it is that they are! Save yourselves and your wives and your daughters and your asses and your oxes and the strangers within your gates!'

There was a considerable hubbub of voices, and many men did indeed begin to hustle into the shelter of the houses and against their will their wives and their daughters and any other young things who had caught their fancy and seemed deserving of their protection.

I ignored this tribute to our obvious virility and manly beauty, and asked, 'Where is the Palace of the Prefect? I will pay nothing till I have talked with the Prefect of the City.'

'Up there, first left and second right. I can't take you there myself, in case another ship comes in while I'm away and unloads a cargo and takes another one on, and gets out of the river without paying me my dues.'

'Do ships come in here often, then?'

'Oh, yes, sometimes as many as two or three in the year. Very busy port, this.'

'And that one?' I indicated the empty boat.

'Oh, that is one which has not shifted since last August it is that it hasn't.'

'Any others?'

'Oh, yes, there was one that went down and out to sea about the middle of March, and a mad thing that was to do that it was, but it was coming back that it was about the third week of April. Didn't unload here, but went on upriver to Castelgai. There may have been others that I didn't see, them having come and gone in my dinner-time.'

He sat down again on his bollard and watched Theodore's old ship intently, ignoring ours although there came from beyond the bulwarks the sound of heated discussion.

I walked off with Taberon, pointing out to him the decayed and pitiful state of the town. There were many men in the place, I told him, who lived there all the year round, and having no land of their own to feed them, avoided idleness by spending their time in trifling, in making shoes or chairs or putting pieces of dirt into fires which marvellously came out as platters or cups. They presented these things to the more wealthy and industrious citizens in hope of receiving from them the means of subsistence, given out of the noble generosity of their hearts.

After a few dozen paces and still in sight of the wharf, we came to the Palace of the Prefect situated where it had always been. There was a porter asleep at the door. I was about to give him a kick to wake him up, when I remembered that I had a follower and I motioned to Taberon to fulfil the duty of a king. Which he did. But the lout was not as sound asleep as we thought, and he most unfairly rolled away so that Taberon kicked the wall and took no further part in the business for a while.

The porter looked at us stupidly, but as he had no weapon of defence but his own smell which was mainly of garlic, enough to deter anyone from close quarters, he answered me politely when I asked him what the prefect was called.

'We mostly calls him a mean-mouthed tight-arsed old skinflint, but the name he likes to go by is Julius Macrinus.'

'Then go and announce us. Tell the most honourable Prefect Julius Macrinus that his old friend, the most excellent and royal prince Morvran map Einion, Prefect of Caerwent and King of Gwent and of all the land from Skirrid to Margam and of all those who live between Wye and Neath, has deigned to come and visit him.'

'I can't go. I mustn't leave the door unguarded, and besides it's my dinner-time and the prefect's too so you can go in and disturb him at your own risk.'

So we found our own way into a little inner courtyard, where Julius Macrinus was sitting comfortably with his chins and paunch heaving rhythmically. I poked him in the ribs with the chape of my scabbard, carefully shaped by Gwenki for just such a purpose, till he awoke.

When he made an effort and zeroed his eyes, he burst out laughing. 'The last time I saw you, I told you I'd hang you as a drunken incompetent horse thief if ever I found you here again.'

'You would not hang a king, for that is what I have become.'

'Time does injustice to us all.'

'Look well on this wise and generous man,' I told Taberon loudly, 'for he is the last embodiment of Roman virtues, open hearted and open handed and benevolent and truly Christian in his eagerness to feed the hungry traveller.'

'I suppose that means that you are hoping for a meal, Morvran, but I have no food at all in the house. I am fasting to keep up my faith, and perhaps if you come after Easter I may—'

And I was thinking that he would soon damn himself in Tatharn's eyes over his calendar when a shabby man, some kind of cook's mate's assistant, came in with a folding table which he set before Julius and announced, 'Dinner is served.'

Being so caught, Julius could in honour do no less than to call for more tables and have served what we saw as an ample dinner for three but which he thought of as a mere snack for one between meals on a fast day. It was a decent enough dinner for a king on a weekday, and it gave Taberon a chance to get used to foreign food. We started with a platter of pork sausage, cold, a little dry and heavy with garlic. Then while we are still busy with that the servant brought in a pot of fowl long stewed in red wine so that the flesh melted from the bones, and a little too highly spiced for my taste, but it came free so we finished it and licked the pot. Next there was a slab of pork dipped in honey before being boiled in oil, a process necessary because their swine were too ill fed to give good dripping. And there were beans seethed in with it. And a dish of salad, lettuces and radishes and carrots and dandelions and other herbs I would not care to name or to taste at home, all made nearly palatable with a mask of oil mixed with vinegar. And all the time the man kept on bringing bread to fill the corners, but all wheat and never a taste of a decent oatcake.

There was wine which Taberon did not appreciate, it being all red and never a spot of seawater or of tar, as he was used to. On his complaining, Julius bade the man bring what he called white but which was a rich yellow, from the honey used to season it. After three cups of that Taberon gave up drinking and laid his head on his hands on the table.

Julius laughed at him, having himself been too busy of late for any conversation, polite or otherwise. 'In the afternoon when he comes to himself, he won't have a headache or even any remorse. What a wonderful thing it is to be young.'

'Oh, he's a good boy so long as you don't tell him so. He was quite good at sea when he stopped being sick.'

'So . . . but will he ever travel over the wine dark seas again?'

'Are you asking me if we are going back to the Island?'

'I am.'

'Why should you doubt it?'

'Life is uncertain. We hear rumours here, and tales, and wisps of news which may be true or false, we do not know, that Arthur has given up his dukedom, or is too ill, or is too weak from his debaucheries with Heathen women to rule with his people's consent.'

'Arthur is dead.'

'We have heard that tale, too, and many times recounting various circumstances and with contradictory details. Or rumours that he wished the world to think him dead. But in each of these rumours he has returned, or will return, to the confusion of those who acted too soon.'

'Believe what rumours you wish. Arthur is dead.'

'You were always attentive to Arthur's wishes. Well, tell me, was it Constant the new duke who killed him, or was it Mordred the Soul of Honour, the nearest relation always being the chief suspect? Some say it was the Saxons, some say the Irish . . .'

'—ineffective star worshippers who under the pretext of Christianity await the return of their great god O'Rion.'

'. . . or the great Duchess and her latest lovers.'

'She had no lovers, but sat always on her moleskin cushion and crocheted and worshipped him with her eyes. But it is true, Arthur is dead: he who killed him is dead, but who had him killed we do not know.'

'Or it is only that you wish him to be thought dead whether he is dead or not. There is no difference, not in the immediate results. What men believe is always truer in its results than the actual facts. And if Arthur is dead, or wishes to be thought dead, what is more natural but that his friends who depended on him for protection will go off on pilgrimage, as far as Rome or Bezant, to Damask and to Salem. And to each destination the road is easiest through here, and up the river.'

'Arthur is dead. I saw it, I was there. I only of the kings and bards was there. But I have come into Gaul to see something else, and I will find it, even if I have to travel to Rome and beyond to the land of silk. When I find it I will take it and hold it and carry it back for the sake of the Unity of the Island.'

'But whatever it is, and you have not yet told me, why seek it on this road?'

'I seek it from Theodore. I know that he has gone beyond here, because I have seen his ship in this river.'

'Oh, he has many ships, on many seas and rivers, but it is true that you have seen the one he always sent to Albion. He himself when he returned in the autumn went further up the river, to where he has a house upon a hill, a barren fortress of dark and mouldering stone, in the Black Hills, a debatable land which marches with the Vandals of Catalonia. To the north and west he has Franks, to the east Burgundians envy him. But no king will harm him because he holds this end of the trade road, across the inner sea to Bezant and to Damask. The kings depend on Theodore to bring them sword-blades and mail and silk and spices and dyes, which are all necessary to sovereignty. Just as they respect Bordigala as a market, and sometimes they will come through and sack it, but not very much, and the rest of the time they leave us alone to govern ourselves as we did before ever the Romans came. True, once a year he sends a ship as far as Albion, but that is for senti- ment and for old times' sake, since the voyage is long and the profit small. This year he will not send a ship.'

'No ship to Britain? None at all this year?'

'It is true he sent a vessel north this spring, but a small ship he uses to trade to Leon and to Lusitan. They passed through the port and up the river on return, not stopping to unload, or even pay port dues.'

'If Theodore lives between the Kings of the Franks and of the Burgundians, to which king do I take this case?'

'Who would dispute with Theodore? He has no army, but he controls the trade. No king would risk offending him. While he lives he brings wealth to all sides, and most of all to himself. If you want anything from him, you must row upriver and demand it from him face to face. And it may be that he will give it you, for his honour or for his amusement. But if he says no, then you can go scratch.'

'Then we will row upriver and demand it from him.'

'The Badon boys won't like that,' said Taberon, all awake on a sudden, work being mentioned.

'They'll have no time not to like it. I'll tell them there's a plague in Bordigala and we must go upstream to escape it.'

'A plague won't worry Tatharn—'

But Taberon was interrupted by the harbourmaster, who ran in shouting something that none of us could understand at all.

'This excellent citizen is called Genista,' said Julius in a prefectorial manner. 'He is a valued member of our municipality, spending his time sweeping horse dung and cabbage-leaves from the market place, and practising medicine and drawing teeth and cleaning up those who have drunk too much and arresting them and washing down the pavement after them. He needs to be soothed, and when that is done he is likely to have important and confidential news for us, which he has already imparted to the whole town.'

Genista was so agitated that it took three mugs of red wine and eight inches of cold sausage to soothe him as well as about a pound and a half of white bread which he claimed to be his due as the bearer of tidings which might make some welcome diversion in the prefect's uneventful life. When he was in a state of composure he repeated his tidings more intelligibly, although I felt that the urgency and importance of his news was such that he need not have wasted time and energy in putting it into hexameters, or in altering the meaning to match the meter.

'There are strangers in our midst,' he orated, 'causing all manner of scandal and uproar. They have drunk the town dry and thus inflamed with our good wine they have run through our streets frightening our women and insulting the horses.'

'Who are they?' asked my good friend through mouthfuls of the soft cheese which in those parts they eat raw after a proper meal as a means of cleansing the palate and the breath.

'We do not know. There is one man who claims to be a priest and he has sworn dreadfully at the Bishop. The others are upcountry men, dressed in striped shirts and talking bad Gaulish and even worse Latin.'

'How many are they?' I asked, strange suspicions stirring in my mind.

'Oh, they are in number more than the sands of the sea or the ants in a cowpat or the lice in your Majesty's hair. They outnumber us in all directions, lapping in on our flanks while we try to hold the centre against them, swamping like a flood the mightiest army we can raise. Ten or twelve by my certain count.'

'I think,' I ventured, 'that we might go down to the market place and see what is going on.'

'Oh, you northerners are so impulsive,' Julius objected. 'Stay a little and have some more wine, because there is nothing to be accomplished by haste. Meanwhile your lad may want to go to see the fun and watch while my people ring bells, hands, necks and withers. And Genista can read a proclamation.'

'Which proclamation?' asked the harbourmaster.

'Oh, any proclamation. Try the one about regulating the price of geese. We haven't read that one for two years, and it has a fine sonorous ring about it.'

We opened another jar of sweet wine, and Genista, swallowing half a pint of that, made all deliberate haste after Taberon. Julius and I were more leisurely, and finished the jar.

III

The market place was in a dreadful state with stalls overturned in all directions and a great deal of unauthorised but mutually profitable business being done in untaxed corners. Genista, having read his proc-lamation on the riverbank, stayed close to the prefect.

In the middle of the market place was a fountain, and Kian was standing in the bowl of it. He was cooling his feet while playing a harp which I was sure he had not had on board when we left the Island.

'I sang to one of the local bards,' he explained, 'an old song I learned some years ago from the Chief Bard of Ireland, Gormesor mac Tripa, and in exchange for full and exclusive rights to translation and per-formance throughout the lands of the Frank King for two hundred years this one gave me his harp. It was the tale of how Cuchullain refused for his honour's sake to blow the horn which the Great Druid had given him to summon all the hosts of Heaven and of Hell and of the voids between to help him against the host of Queen Maeve at the crossing of the river into Ulster. And so he died for his honour's sake.'

'Very touching. But where are the others?'

'Well . . . Tatharn is inside the Church. He is cursing the Bishop for Heresy, and the Bishop is excommunicating him for Schism, each with bell, book and candle, with relish and a full choir. It is a very long and eloquent curse, for Tatharn has delusions of grandeur and hopes to go down in history as one of the three great cursers of the Isle of Britain. But I am afraid that I will have to tell him that this curse will not count, being cursed outside the Island of Britain, and he would be better employed in collecting millstones from each place we visit to build a church to bear his name, it being more permanent in most cases to go down in geography than in history or in literature.'

'And Leision?'

'You may see part of him protruding from under that stall where he is holding close conversation with what I suppose must by now be one of the young matrons of this town.'

'Judging by his unsteady gait and his look of desperation and fatigue as he emerges,' remarked Julius, 'and since he is holding the small of his back with a look of pain as he turns towards us, he has now completed his argument.'

'Now, Leision, dear boy!' I hailed him. 'Is this how you uphold the honour of the Island? By rape and pillage and wholesale destruction and other civilised pleasures?'

'The destruction,' he answered with dignity, 'is more of a retail nature. It is all the fault of the people of this town.'

'Do you mean to say,' demanded Julius, 'that any rape is the fault of the ladies in question?'

'It was indeed,' said Leision. 'So if you have a complaint of rape from any maiden—'

'Ex-maiden,' Kian corrected him.

'Aye, late maiden, let us say, or recent maiden, or erstwhile maiden or retired maiden, for I am very sure that there were no active or professing maidens in the place when we came into it—'

'And none at all now,' Julius grumbled.

'Let me finish my sentence, will you now? For if any person complains that she was forced or pressed or compelled in any way, then it was entirely her own fault because if she had been more commercial and co-operative and yielding there would have been nothing but a seduction or seductions, some more rapid or enthusiastic or vocal than others, and in the majority of cases the seductions were directed against myself and my comrades, the sight of such a throng of handsome and polished and well-set-up young men being so unfamiliar to the ladies of Bordigala, whether maidens or not, that they promptly fell upon us with strange and unmentionable and irresistible lusts as you will understand from the sight of poor Taberon now being led into that alley with a garland of young girls about his neck, and perhaps I ought to offer to go and—'

'Stay where you are!' I shouted at him, for we risked having his speech turn into a life sentence. 'What about these broken and empty wine jars and overturned stalls and bloody noses?'

'Why, that was all the fault of the market people for if in the first instance they had let us have all the wine we asked for in exchange for such trifles as we offered them like pins of gold set with garnets and carnelians, and in the second instance if they had not offered to resist we would not have fought with them, and in the third instance—'

'Somebody throw a bucket of water over him,' I ordered, fearful as to what we might hear when he got to the eighth instance. 'No, no, Genista, not over that end, over his *head*. Keep hold of the bucket. That horrible bundle of rags down there must be Gwion. Water over him, too.'

'No, no, not water,' Gwion objected from where he lay. 'Make it wine and I'll come quietly. It is no fun having the sharpest eyes in Christendom if everything you see is halved in quality and it was of very low quality to start with.'

'Tell me this,' I demanded. 'Did you leave our ship unguarded and unprotected and unmanned for any robber or looter or pirate to take her and steal her and carry her off?'

'Let no one talk of being unmanned who was not here with us on this dreadful day,' Gwion answered. 'That awful man Oslaf is still aboard, clutching his green branch as if that would do him any good here, but looking so fierce and envious that none of these yokels will come near him. He would not come ashore with us, being grumpy and ill-tempered and gloomy. I'll tell you what is wrong with that man, Morvran. I'll tell you what I have worked out, he's just like all the other Heathen, only don't let anybody else know I told you.' Gwion was letting us have all this at the top of his voice. 'He's not an intellectual, Morvran, not like you and me who will stand up and drink pint for pint with any man. Not even like Kian and that Holy Man whose voice I can hear now, good lads they are, they will drink and argue with anybody who will buy the mead.'

'Go, Gwion, find that Holy Man and urge him towards the river. Kian and Leision, since you both seem to be reasonably coherent, and even unreasonably longwinded, find your companions and urge them with boot and bucket and boathook into our ship. It is my intention to sail as soon as the great and good and generous prefect has supplied us with sufficient meat and fresh bread and wine and dried grapes and cheese and honey for our voyage to the head of the river. For if we do not have enough food and drink and general sustenance we cannot possibly set out on the waters or say farewell to the maidens and the matrons and the merchants of this town.'

'I now perceive,' remarked Julius, 'what excellent and polite and God-fearing people were the Goths and the Franks and even the Vandals who were so fond of beauty in all its forms that they left us not a jewel nor a statue nor a vase when they passed through our streets, and what is more they do not count everything by threes which is a catching habit. Morvran, I will set in train a popular and entirely voluntary subscription to supply you immediately. Genista, as victualling agent, will administer it and take the legal ten per cent.'

IV

So for seven days and nights we proceeded up the river. Wide it was and very windy about and about, but nothing like as pleasant as the Severn. The fields were green enough, but on the whole the place was very colourless, the vegetation lacking all the different shades we have at home. There were fields with grapes trained in long straight lines, and other orchards as it seemed but only of twisted dark bluey-green trees, very old and played-out with nothing on them worth eating. There was early wheat well up, but no oats. Much of the time we rowed, or rather some people rowed, but thanks to Tatharn's constant praying we had a favourable wind a good deal of the way.

All the waking time, Kian played to us on his new harp and sang almost all of the classical repertoire as well as some original compositions of varying quality. The wine we'd got from Bordigala was fairly good, especially the white with the honey in it, but there was alas no cider. The food was plentiful and varied, although the sausages were a trifle over-garlicky. There were several jars of what we thought were black cherries preserved in oil but they were nothing of the kind: when we tasted them we found them bitter. We threw most of them into the river, hoping that they might attract fish to the lines we trailed behind us, or at least poison a few, but we were unlucky.

We passed many places where the fields came down to the river edge, and men were working in them. Several times we saw high rocks looming over the river as high as Dumbarton or Eiddin, with on the tops sometimes a single ruined tower, sometimes a chief's dun and sometimes a town with walls round it and a church tower within. And at these places we heard the bells ringing and saw nobody to talk to.

In other places we were able to pull in and talk with the people, who spoke a very bad Latin mixed up with scraps of Gaulish which is rather like Cornish. And sometimes there were men who spoke with Oslaf in the common language of the Heathen which they speak from Rhine-mouth to the Tiber and which he thought none of us understood. They told him what Julius had told me but I had kept a secret from him, that in Tolosa the Frank King had dethroned the prefect and put in his place his own man, named Agaric, who had the title of Count.

One day in the pale dawn we knew from the rubbish in the water and from the smells that we were near to Tolosa. We therefore moored and spent the day silent, hidden under a willow.

When it was quite dark we set off, hoping to get beyond the town unseen. But when we had passed the first ring of walls, boats came at us out of the darkness. Before we knew what was happening well-armed barbarians had us in tow to the quay where they moored us without asking whether we wanted to go there or not.

When they had us alongside, they asked us who was the Chief.

'That's me,' I said, in Latin, but Tatharn said the same thing, also in Latin, and Oslaf in his own tongue loudly claimed primacy. Gwion had the sense to stuff the piece of an old shirt in Leision's mouth and hold it there, and he also kept his own trap shut. Before we three had time to regret having spoken, we were hauled out of the boat and made to run through the streets which were paved and lined with high walls reminding me a little of Caerwent. This cheered me, but not a great deal.

When we were rushed into the Count's Hall, just at his dinner-time, I thought at first that he was no Heathen, because at the bottom of the lowest table, there were four priests placed. Or at least three priests and a bishop. Not even sitting now, but standing to sing Grace. When this was done, Agaric looked at me sternly, being in the middle, and asked us who we were and why we were sliding past the town by night.

I answered in Latin as politely as I could manage and told him that we were a party of poor pilgrims from Demed bound in piety for Bezant and Salem to see the Tomb of Moses and the bones of the Virgin before we died. And if it was in the dark that we were going by Tolosa, why that was merely to spare the place the terrible devastation that the men of Bordigala had provoked us to.

While I was still priding myself on my oratory, Agaric ordered, in Latin so that I could understand, 'After supper, beat them to death with clubs slowly, here, so that we can all have some fun. And after that the other twelve. We knew that enemies of the state were coming because Julius sent a messenger by land to warn me.'

I could not blame Julius, because after all he had to live in his town after we had gone, but I did blame his messenger who turned out to be the Bishop of Bordigala. And I felt more desperate than ever before in my life, even worse than at Second Caledon when the left wing broke and Arthur was not to be seen. And what was worse was that the deaths of the others, especially the Badon boys, who had no idea what all this was about but had come only for the mead and because Bedwyr sent them, would be due to me.

Immediately Tatharn began a fine curse on the Count and on the Prefect, which was likely to take full effect, him being such a Holy Man, but a bit late. I also would have explained myself more fully, only one of the guards clapped his hand over my mouth and held it there although I bit it till my teeth met. Nasty, he tasted.

When the noise was over, Tatharn being silenced too in the same way, Oslaf said clearly in the common tongue of the Heathen, 'Will you lay hands on me, that am Odin-born?'

There was a silence. Then Agaric ordered, 'Send out the priests!'

So the Bishop and the three priests were hustled out, and Tatharn with them. He was singing very loudly a hymn of rejoicing that he was to be martyred, calling on us to remember the fate of Saint Madvalh, who was gnawed to death by newts. Disappointed he said he was, later: very.

Agaric asked Oslaf very mildly, as one might speak to the Devil met by chance on the road, 'This is a grave thing to say. Can you show it?'

Oslaf said nothing. He took off his shirts one by one, because he was wearing three, and turned his back on the Count. As he stood naked to the waist but for his gold neck-chains, seven of them, the Franks were greatly amazed by the way his hair grew, sparsely but perceptibly, down his back from nape to coccyx and red in colour, in a ridge like a horse's mane. Now this is not unusual among those of us great-grandsons of Cunedha and other descendants of Buddug the Bitch who ruled Eiddin with a rod of iron, and of her husband of a night, Votan, from who we are called the Votadini. I or Tatharn or even Taberon, being all of us cousins in some degree or other, could have showed the same ridge of hair, although we did not think it respectable to go round half naked as the savages do, even on sunny days. When Oslaf turned himself round to show himself to the Franks in this disgusting condition, they left their seats and knelt humbly before him.

Agaric asked him with great reverence, 'Lord, whence do you come?'

'I am Oslaf, Cueldgil's son. We go to Odin by way of Wecta. And we hold Lindsey against Christ and the Welshmen.'

'Our king,' said Agaric nervously, 'goes to Votan by way of Cutha, and he would welcome you as a brother were he here.' Catching a gleam in Oslaf's eye, he added, 'As an elder brother, of course.'

'Then you must entertain me in his place,' Oslaf ordered.

Agaric moved along the bench and Oslaf took his seat on the heaped cushions of the bench of honour, on Agaric's left hand. Then he pointed to me, and announced in their language which he thought I did not understand, 'This is one of my people who brought me here with skill, and indeed among the Welsh men he is a king or what passes for a king among them, being a man of birth and breeding and by their standards handsome. We are brothers by dangers passed and by sweat, although not yet by blood.'

That is all you know, I thought. Not yet, but soon, I will have Lindsey back from you, and blood with it. But I was surprised that Oslaf must have given me his real name, by which he would pass in this company. Oslaf had me sit at his right hand, so Agaric had to move another place down the table. His Countess, the famous Amanita, by repute as deadly as her husband, poured wine for us.

Oslaf ordered, 'Let the priests return. They are harmless.'

They came back and very humbly took their places at the bottom of the table where they took no part in the conversation, being nothing like so holy or so argumentative as the Saints of the Island or of Ireland.

'Is my ship safe?' Oslaf demanded. 'And my crew?'

I did not question his proprietary manner, seeing that he had standing here and I had not.

'Yes, Lord, till I say otherwise.'

'Send them food and drink fit for a king, and then more drink. And then, women.'

Agaric snapped his fingers and his servants ran to do his bidding, for in those days a king's word was law, and it seemed that Oslaf was a king of some importance. Oslaf took from round his neck one of the gold chains he had been concealing from us and hung it round Agaric's neck. Agaric then had no option but to take off the best of the chains he was unwisely wearing in full view and put it on Oslaf. Now it was not generally known but I was wearing under my shirt half the treasury of the Kingdom of Gwent. I therefore took from under my shirt the lightest of the chains I had and presented it to Agaric. There was then nothing he could do but give to me the thinnest of the chains he was wearing, which was at least twice the weight of the one I had given him: on such lightning calculations are empires founded.

Tatharn now advanced up the Hall with an expression of benevolence which had Agaric nervously fingering the lightest of the chains he had left. However, the Saint meant no material gesture. He merely wished, warm-hearted creature that he was, to remove from Agaric the curse he had earlier put on him. I explained this in Latin, but I did not think it prudent to point out that this release was conditional on our safe return home, and that in any case it did not apply to Julius Macrinus who remained under the ban. Tatharn had, he told me later, a most interesting professional conversation with the Bishop, and that although they differed on minor points such as the Person of Christ and Predestination, yet on essentials such as the date of Easter and the length of the lace on the alb they were in perfect agreement.

Meanwhile, Agaric, being reassured, was most interested to learn that we intended to visit Theodore. 'I hope that you enjoy your cakes,' he told us, but did not elaborate further on the point. 'Look out for the Burgundians. They claim Catalonia, which lies astride the mountains and is held at present by the Vandals, although properly the domain of the Ravenn Emperor, which we Franks have undertaken to govern for him. But there are some disloyal men in that province who take their disputes to the King of the Burgundians and not to me as my King Clothair has ordered.' And he threw back his cloak so that we could see that the brooch wide as a fist which secured it at the shoulder was cast as a bee, of gold with eyes of ruby or glass or garnet or something else as precious: and under my shirt I fingered the brooch I had taken from the body of the man who killed Arthur. 'And where they take their cases, there they also pay their taxes.'

'To whom,' I asked, 'does Theodore pay his taxes?'

'Theodore takes his cases to no man lower than the Bezant Emperor, and we must assume that it is there he pays his taxes. One might almost say that he is an emperor in his own right. For years his ships have been the only ones to travel the Middle Sea, and without him we would get neither sword-blades nor silk nor spices. Just think how unpalatable this meat would be without the pepper and mustard and coriander and all the other herbs he brings us from the east.'

I wondered what if anything could make the beef I was eating taste any worse, for although no more than lukewarm to the fingers, to the mouth it seemed as hot as fire.

'Will Theodore have sailed out on the Middle Sea by now?' I asked.

'Surely Julius told you all this? Theodore never sails on the sea himself. He sends his men out, for he is a great wizard and not only does he possess magic ships with which he trades with his brothers in Bezant and Damask, but also he has seamen under his spell who will go anywhere and do anything which he commands and this not for money but for the magic cakes he gives them, but sparingly.'

'Then he will be short of bronze?'

'Oh, bronze is nothing. He says he will not send out ships this year, for bronze or steel or silk or spices. The Bezant Emperor has sent one of his nobles, Belesar of Dar, to take the land of Italy from the rightful Rome-King ordained by the last Ravenn Emperor. This Rome-King is Witiges, who goes to Odin by way of Cutha, and is my own seventh cousin.'

It is always a surprise to me to find Heathens who know the stages of their descent: mostly they seem not even to know who are their own fathers.

'Will Belesar conquer?'

'It appears so. He is a magician, like Theodore, and he has brought into the cities of Italy the sneezing death to torment the land and empty all the towns. So while there is war and plague in Italy, there is no trade between Theodore and his brothers. But next year will be better. Surely you know all this. The Bezant Emperor, they say, has sent to Arthur to come over into Frankland and help him, because while he is in the field, our king will not move in strength in Italy or Spain. Therefore we are very interested in knowing if this rumour is true, that Arthur is dead, or if he is merely in hiding as so often before, and will come in war against us.'

Then many things became clear. But I saw no reason to seem to know more than Agaric did, especially since Oslaf did not say anything.

Agaric then said, 'Enough of politics. Bring on the minstrels. Are there no minstrels in your ship?'

So we sent for Kian, who arrived in a bad temper having been interrupted in an intellectual conversation with one of the yellow-haired girls of the town. Although I had to spend a great deal of time in translating his poem line by line into Latin hexameters as he chanted it, yet it was received with much applause. He chose, to avoid contention, the epic about the young man on the yellow horse who comes to Rome to serve the Emperor and is befriended by the three Praetorians. Also, although mercifully this needed no translation, his backwards leap over two benches while holding a candle burning at both ends and throwing his voice into an empty wine jar drew general approbation and a gift of three gold pieces from Agaric. Although Kian did admit that the Count's own minstrel outdid him by carving a whole roast pig, eating it, drinking a pint of wine and voiding the undigested residue while sitting at a table on a tight rope slung between two rafters, above the Bishop. Nevertheless he did very well for the honour of the Island of the Mighty.

We went back to the ship in the pale dawn. I was most disappointed to see that the high buildings which I had sensed in the dark were not as magnificent as I had hoped, for they showed none of the skill of the thatcher and the carpenter, nor of the stonefinder or even the stone-cutter, but were roofed and walled with lumps of clay burnt red in the fire. And this lack of culture I impressed on Taberon.

Interlude 9: Paradise

The woman lay naked on her satin couch, under the canopy in the inmost courtyard where no man came, save Theodore. The sun at noonday was too harsh for her white skin. The girls, her girls, clustered about her. They rubbed the skin of her body with softening oils that smelled like the opening gates of heaven.

The girls chattered together in their own languages. They spoke to her in Latin, in bad Latin, she could tell that. They tried to teach her their own common language, which they told her was sometimes called Hellenic, sometimes the Koine. She had learned enough now to answer when they called her *Kuria*.

When the evening came and the sun disappeared, but the air was still hot, she would leave off her crocheting of nets and walk about the outer courts and the gardens beyond them. The flies did not harm her: it seemed that they did not like the scents she was anointed with. She played with the little monkeys, who were always eager for crumbs of bread dipped in honey, or for fragments of the honeycomb itself, and for the strange fruits, for grapes both black and green and white, for round globes of juice as red as gold, for pomegranates full of small juicy seeds, and for the great peaches. The juice ran down her cheeks, and her girls made her gorgets of linen cloth to save the collars of her silken gowns.

The golden apple of the day gave way to the silver globe. The cicadas sang to drown the nightingales. The great beasts in their cages roared at the myriad stars, the tiger and the leopard, the big black apes and the small savage cats. In the basin in the fenced courtyard the crocodile lay close under the surface and looked for live meat, although dinner-time this month was still a few days away.

Everything, the girls told her, making her understand their Latin with some difficulty, had been brought in for her and for her alone. There had been nothing here at first on the hilltop, neither animals nor birds, no fruit trees or rose bushes or lily bulbs, no gold or silk or amber, neither glass nor statues nor beds nor curtains, only the barren walls of a stone fortress, and below it the sheds and warehouses of a merchant, here at the watershed and the midpoint of the portage between the boats that came up from the western ocean and the boats that went down to the inner sea, the centre of the world, that was a path to Rome Town and to Bezant. There had been no people save the hard-handed seamen and the carriers of bales and the muleteers. Below in the plain around the sheds lived the peasants who grew the food and the vines, who trod out the grapes to make the wine and who mixed it with the salt seawater or with turpentine, as required.

All this, and the girls themselves and all the other servants had been brought in and set in place during this one winter, and all for her. This was called a paradise of delights, they told her, and there were many such within the Bezant Empire, in Antioch and in Damask, in Alexandria and in Kandahar and in the land of the Seres. Thence had come the bales of silk that made her gowns and that she now worked with her hook into a great golden net to throw over the bed to which Theodore came sometimes but not often, for he was sick. Sick or well, he was welcome to come and to be tended and healed.

But nowhere in Romeland nor in Gaul nor anywhere in the Island was there such a place as this, raised by one man for the woman he loved, conjured up for her in the twinkling of a winter's moon, to stand as it were a daintier and a richer and a more permanent Camelot. All here could be as she willed, but she willed nothing, only to be here and at peace. For other things, this was not the place: nor the time.

Chapter 9

Montgai

I

My gallant crew was not at all content with only seeing Tolosa from the middle of the river, without being allowed to land and re-arrange its beauties as they had at Bordigala. But they had been well nourished and entertained. We even had to stop two miles upstream to allow the departure of two ladies of the town who had stowed away: or been stowed away, there was no point in asking which. It was a good thing they both swam well, entertaining us with the sight of their bare arms and other features of interest as they struck out for dear life for the shore. The ship being thus lightened, my lads rowed well after I had berated them. They always obeyed my orders faithfully, confident that if they did so I would provide them with food, drink and entertainment.

We rowed for some days up the river. Whenever we came to a fork in the stream, Oslaf told us which way to go. Agaric had explained the turnings and forks to him in some detail, but in the Heathen tongue believing that I would not understand. But I did understand, and memorised it as well, so that I was all ready to put a spear into him if he chose wrong, not fatally but accurately and palpably. The stream got shallower and shallower, and one morning when it was doubtful that we would be able to get any further, we saw a jetty by the north bank, and a small ship, about our size, moored to it.

'That is one of Theodore's,' called Gwion. 'Does that mean that we have arrived? I have never felt it right for a gentleman to travel sitting down except on a horse.'

'Almost there, if Theodore is at home.'

'And if he is not?'

'Then we walk up the stream, and down the other side of this land to the Middle Sea and go by ship to Bezant.'

'But what of our ship? Is there not a waterway down on the other side?'

'I doubt it. But it is very simple. We will carry her to the other sea: that is, she will be carried by those of us who are stronger – the Badon boys, for example.'

There was another short mutiny, put down by judicious application of the steering oar. Some of the people of the place came down to watch over our innocent amusement. When something like peace was restored, for our voyage was never entirely harmonious, I asked them, 'Where is Theodore?'

They knew that name at least, and gabbled away, pointing inland.

Remembering the name that Julius and Agaric had used, I asked them, 'Mons Gaii? Mons Gaii?'

They all nodded and pointed, and said, 'Montgai, Montgai.'

The most prominent of this group then spoke to me in tolerable but badly accented Latin, giving me to understand that it was near enough for beasts to carry sacks there in one day and then return for supper.

'Right,' I ordered, 'we'll walk. Come back for the cargo later.'

'If it's still here,' said Gleisiad. He held one of the locals by the ears; his feet, I noticed, did not now quite touch the ground. 'Here, you, we go walkee-walkee. You lookee after ship. If you not lookee after ship, I come back and bashee-bashee head.'

'Here, not that way,' objected Leision. 'Use tact.' He held up the man by his big toes, and hissed, 'Nothing personal. You not lookee-lookee after ship, I bashee-bashee *all* heads.'

'There's a better way still,' I pointed out. I told the man who spoke Latin, 'This boat Theodore's boat. You people not look after boat, Theodore come bashee-bashee all heads.'

'We know, we wait for ship,' the man replied. 'You got bronze, we take out, we got sword-blades, we put blades in, and wine, like always. No silk: silk-witch here already.'

This, I decided, must be the regular pattern of trade here. Anyway, there wasn't much I could do without leaving a few men behind to look after the boat and the cargo, and I didn't want to do that. I therefore mustered my crew on shore. We had searched the ship for more interesting stowaways and found none. Now we all got our personal gear and our weapons out, and Leision found a few horses with pack-saddles to carry the gear and the mail and Esau's cooking pot and bakestone and a bite of food for the night. And cider. Tatharn wanted to bring his millstone, and I said yes, if he could carry it himself. He left it: but he did take his staff.

In front of us to the north there loomed a great mass of mountains like the Black Mountains at home, but nothing as high as Skirrid. There were greater mountains a long way off to the south, and I reminded Taberon that beyond them there lay Africa which is a province of Spain. There were isolated foothills a few miles off, and in an hour we were close enough to see some buildings on the nearest one. And the wide and well-beaten track went that way.

I summed up to my men: 'It's all quite clear. This is Theodore's wharf and any ship that gets in here, his lackeys exchange cargoes. They load the cargo coming in on packhorses and take it up to his stronghold. Then he sees it taken down to the other sea. I heard Synager talking about a system like this that Vortigern handled in London, and they called it import-export dealing.'

'Interesting, and a work of genius,' observed Gwion, 'but what do we do about the building on the hill, which looks to me like a halfway decent stronghold? Storm it?'

'It may come to that. But seeing how near noon it is and how close we are to the walls, let us go into that shady copse and confer.'

It was a decent little grove, and on going into it with Oslaf behind me I met a Fairy. We are used enough to them at home, but it was strange to find one in foreign parts. It had been clear for some time that something was going on from the loud singing of the grasshoppers. I had pointed this out to Taberon, and reminded him of the difference between the industrious and public-spirited cricket who spends his time making music for man's delectation and the idle ant, forever scurrying aimlessly hither and yon: and with the spider who merely lies evilly in wait for what she can devour and is therefore an enemy of man. This was why I had had Tatharn walk in front, singing a hymn about having the wings of a dove and how if he'd had his way he'd have been out of there like a shot and bound for somewhere called Nebo which I understood to be up near Bala.

This Fairy was one of the larger kind, about eighteen hands tall, dressed all in green with twigs sticking out of his ears, and elaborate gold embroidery around his wrists. He bowed to us and asked, 'Is this, please, the way to the great Judgement Mound in Arberth?'

'Trust a navigator,' said another Fairy. I now realised that there were seven or eight of them of different colours and some carrying bundles. The first speaker went on, ignoring them, 'And it *is* barley sowing time, is it not?'

'Timeless wonder,' said another Fairy. I was pleased to see that discipline in this band was no better than in my ship.

I thought it better to be polite and answered, the Awen being on me and guiding my words although I could not understand them myself, 'The Judgement Mound is in the Island of the Mighty. Go about eight miles west, and you'll find a ley line transecting the river, heading a smidgeon west of north, say about three-five-five. Follow that for about eight radians and it brings you to the Standing Stones. Then the Judgement Mound is about fifteen miles north by a little west.'

'And the date?'

'It is nearer to barley reaping time than to sowing. That is in another seven months.'

'Ever see a navigator tie his shoelaces?' asked a smaller and rather impertinent-looking Fairy.

But what seemed to be, as far as one can ever tell, a relatively elderly Fairy with gold embroidery all the way up his arms stepped forward and said to me earnestly, 'At that period, and at the Stones, in the first night of the new moon, meet me there.'

He and the other Fairies got back into their ship and went off with their usual fuss and noise and smoke. At least it left a dry flat space for us to camp on.

'I was most interested,' I said to Oslaf, 'to hear that Fairy speak in the language of the Angels as we speak it in the Island.'

'What? That Troll? I myself was astonished to hear you converse in the common speech of my people. It shows the depths of your treachery, that you have heard and understood all that I and my kinsmen have been saying in our private conversations.'

So that secret was out, and I realised that each of us understood the other's language and that all the trouble we had gone to in speaking Latin was wasted effort. But neither of us thought the less of the other or complained further about the level of deceit which is normal and laudable in time of war.

II

On the open field south of the copse Esau had got a fire going and sent Gwion and Kimokh to find a homeless sheep, which did not take very long. The rest of us stood in cover on the other edge of the copse to take a good look at the stronghold which was Montgai.

It rose from the plain to high above us. The strange thickness of the air and the brightness of the light had made us think it was a much higher mountain and much further away than it really was. Or perhaps that was Theodore's magic. The hill was shaped like an upturned bucket, as is the Fortress of Traprain near Eiddin or the Judgement Mound in Arberth. Not a considerable mountain as we had been deceived into thinking, but still a strong site for a fortress.

The walls around the base of the hill were of stones grafted together to nearly three times the height of a man, and therefore by the ancient rule at least two fathoms thick at the base. Beyond them, to the top of the hill, we could see a scatter of roofs, one of them obviously over a Hall. The plain between us and the wall was dusty and still, as are all the open fields in that country, and even the yards of the houses for fear of the heat of the sun at noon. Near to the walls, nothing stirred between rows of vines.

'That is our goal,' I announced.

'Then what are we doing, just looking at it?' demanded Gwion, who had brought in a good fat sheep, enough for two days. 'Let us go up at once and storm it, before they know we are here. This is a time for courage.'

'And you the far-sighted one,' I rebuked him. 'Look at that open slope, and the height of the walls. How are we to climb them? Think what is the strength of that gate, and of the tower over it. How are we to cast fire on the thatch behind such walls? And even to do that, how are we to cross this plain? How is our mighty host to reach the walls unseen?'

'I can see a path.' Gwion was defensive. 'And there is a way a man may climb the face of the wall, using cracks and crevices.'

'One man alone may reach the wall unseen,' suggested Leision. 'From here to that first bush, left to the twisted tree with the bitter cherries, and so to the rows of vines.'

'One man, only,' I agreed. 'And that man must be me.'

'You are too valuable to be risked, my King,' objected Taberon; all the others except Oslaf mumbled agreement. 'Let me go. I am too unimportant to be noticed. If I can get near enough to a grazing stag to kill with an arrow which will not pierce at over twenty paces, then surely I can hide from these sleeping men.'

'It is I who must go,' I insisted. 'There are strong reasons. One is that I have sworn an oath and I must keep it myself and not by proxy. And a second is that I have been here before, many years ago when the fortress was nothing like as strong, and I know Theodore, and therefore I know what I am to do once I get inside.'

'All good things come in threes,' put in Kian, 'and that is why they are true. Tell us the third reason.'

'The third reason is this, that I am older and wiser and craftier and harder and altogether nastier than any of you – indeed than all of you, and therefore you will do what I say.'

'If we wait till dark' – Leision was still complaining and I marked him down as a good man and likely to be very useful in a council of war, on the enemy's side – 'we can all go together then and I cannot see what all the fuss is about.'

'This is how I shall get inside without fighting and in the daylight, and it is a stratagem possible for only one. I shall go up now in the heat when all are asleep and wait in hiding outside the gate till the dusk.

When the butler comes out to cry that the wine is in the cup and the knife is in the meat and that all who are pre-eminent in the arts may enter, then I will rush into the Hall and take the host by surprise or by the throat, whichever seems more appropriate.'

'You do not know,' said Oslaf, 'that this Lord will in fact follow what you think to be universal rules of polite behaviour although they are not known outside the Island. And in any case, he must be Theodore. What is he to you? The ally who rode with you against the Irish in your youth? Or a cheating merchant? Or an enemy in war whose Hall you must sack?'

'My bard will explain.' I dodged the question, since it was one I had myself asked and could not answer, the matter being less than plain to me and capable of resolution only by the laws of poetic logic. 'Now, we cannot wait till tomorrow evening. We have a fire here already, and to light a fire on one day is the act of a casual passer-by. But to light a fire on two days is the act of a watcher. And if we stay the night here, then it is likely that a man out hunting early or exercising his dogs or looking for a lost sheep will stumble on us. So I will go alone, and in a while, when the heat of the day is a little less, and it will not be strange to see a man walking alone.'

I ate a meal of a couple of grilled mutton chops, and some cider, with twice-baked oatcake I had brought out from Caerwent as an emergency ration, and it was so good I almost broke my back teeth. After a little belching time, I decided that the moment had come and I began to move out with caution across the broken ground as if I were stalking a stag with a javelin. And speed was not easy as I had put on my mail shirt for the first time in Gaul, and another woollen shirt over it, and my helm was on my head; I had untied the riding strings on Bees in the Summer Meadow, and I had my shield on my left arm and my pike over my right shoulder.

Making intelligent use of cover, I reached the bush in one short dash, and then in another the trees with the false cherries. As I lay there planning my next move, I heard a breath behind me. I was sorry at first I had not brought a javelin, but when I turned I saw it was Taberon's throat my pike was set at. In any case I could tell it was one of us by the smell.

'You see, my King, my uncle, you need someone to watch your back.'

I was tempted to take the skin off his back with my tongue and hang it up where he could watch it, but he was too loyal and innocent for me to see any pleasure in it. I merely grumbled at him, 'You are too close. You must follow at a distance. Remember what you must do, being overlooked from the walls if we are incautious. When you move, move quickly and not too far at a time. Do not give a watcher time to watch you move. Make short dashes from cover to cover. Do not choose the same patches of cover as I do. Once you reach cover, stay very still for a long time so that if someone has seen you out of the corner of his eye he will get tired with watching and think he was mistaken. Remember that a man is not as clever as a stag, because he is not as frightened. The waiting time you can spend planning your next move, and the move after that.'

He had been taught all that already. It is what I learned fighting the Heathen, and this skill is the root cause of our superiority. We each gained the shelter of the vines in two or three moves. Now danger of being seen was greater and we moved from row to row, Taberon two rows behind, as silent as a wounded boar. If you do not think a wounded boar can be silent, try going into a thicket after one.

When we were near to the bottom of the last few yards of path leading up to the gate, I left the cover of the vines and slipped across into the shadow of a stone pillar. I hunched up there and settled to wait for the butler to come out and call that dinner was served. I was wound up ready for the rush to the gate. I waited and waited. I felt sleepy in the heat, and to make sure that I did not wait too long or just nod off I recited interesting passages of scripture. I was in the middle of the Tables of Kindred and Affinity, always a preventer of sleep since an acute spur to the imagination, when I felt something well known to those who have been thrown down in battle or caught in the wrong bed by the lady's husband, and I have known both situations. I heard nothing and smelled nothing, but there was a sudden coldness at the base of my neck and the way it had length without breadth taught me something about the local grindstones. A gurgling cry behind me, cut short, told me that Taberon was taken, perhaps dead.

And a voice spoke to me, in a labial Latin, very quietly, 'Keep your hands by your sides and stand up very slowly!'

I had no choice. I kept my hands from my sword hilt and left my pike leaning against the pillar. A hand came round and unbuckled my belt so that Bees in the Summer Meadow fell to the ground. I was disarmed.

'Go forward up the path, Very slowly.'

I went forward, one step after another. Now, for the first time, as the path wound about, I saw the gate of Montgai clear and close, oak planking faced with leather, hinged and barred with bronze. I wondered if the bronze had come from Caerwent.

The gates did not open, the walls did not gape, but in an instant there was a postern that invited, and in silence like a ghost he stood there. And he said, 'Come forward, Morvran the Ugly, King of Gwent, and be welcomed.'

III

I came to Theodore, and we embraced as we always had done on meeting whether on the quays of Caerwent or among the ferny hills of Brecon. Then I stood back to look at him, because what I had felt in my arms disturbed me greatly.

He was not the man I had known. He had lost, I should say, a stone and a half over the winter. The bones stood out in his face that had been chubby, and the skin was transparent so that below the sallow he was pale. His thin hands that had dealt with the steering oar would not now have shaded a candle. He looked tired as if all the weight of the world had lain upon his shoulders for half a hundred years, and the man who stood behind him was there for support, and not for protection. And yet he looked into my face and laughed aloud for joy. Or laughed as if for joy.

'You and your men are keen-sighted,' I told him, 'and they move silently.' One of them went by us, carrying Taberon in his arms like a sleeping baby.

'Did you think that you could come into our country unknown when the Heathen could not cross yours without being watched by men or Fairies at every step? There has not been a pace you have taken on land, not an oarstroke on the river that has not been revealed to me. Did you think that Julius the Prefect, who depends on me for dyes and steel and silk, would talk to you only and not to me? Do you think that Agaric who takes my gold for letting my ships pass his city would not warn me of every stranger in the river? If you were not expected, you would never have got here, my old friend.'

'I had no thought to attack you, only to surprise you. I was waiting only for the butler to open the gates and call out that the meal was ready.'

'And to invite you in as pre-eminent in noise and clumsiness? Oh, my innocent king, we would never do that here, where life is hard and treachery is never far away. You have never had a night in the Island where at dinner every other man turned on his neighbour and blooded his long knife. I love you, poor unworldy King Morvran, still only a bard at heart, limping along the roads of the world in search of something but no one knows what. I will let you inside the gate, where my people have set out a table under a canopy against the sun, and will bring us wine and fruit and cheese and sweet cakes, but I will not let you into my Hall, pre-eminent in innocence though you may be.'

'Why,' I asked him, 'should I wish to enter your Hall, when I can speak with you here in the open?'

'What is it you seek?' Theodore asked. 'Why have you come to my gate all armed? What treasure has drawn you here today?'

We sat underneath the canopy, ate cheese on salted bread, drank the sweet wine, but only a little, to show willing. Taberon sat at table, but at my glance ate and drank only a sip and a morsel, and said nothing at all. He was still very frightened, but not too frightened to look around at the white stone buildings and the gardens all hedged with roses astride a gate across the path to the Hall.

'I seek a treasure indeed, which if you have it you will not, I am sure, display openly in your Hall. It is something with which I will buy the Unity of the Island.'

'Gold?' he asked. 'Gold to buy the unity of the Island, to buy kings and wine and swords, to buy the Heathen out of the land to sail against Ireland or perhaps even back to Armorig and make you, Morvran the

Ugly, the one king of a united Kingdom? Not all the gold of Cardigan will be enough for that.'

'For the Unity of the Island,' I answered, 'I will give all the gold I have or could have, even the golden blood out of my body. But as for kingship – except in Gwent, that is beyond me.'

'So every man says, till kingship is offered and is within his grasp. The golden treasure, you seek it only as the key to Empery and to domination and to glory. But look now, and see the golden prize you seek!'

The gate in the rose hedge opened. It did not swing, there was no creaking of hinges, it merely dissolved. I looked into a courtyard, a garden full of flowering trees, of lilies and violets, of flowers all out of season. Beyond the flowers, on a golden chair lonely and supreme, sat the golden Lady. So, I thought, had she so often sat in Camelot unburnt, at the head of the Hall, beyond the High Table where Arthur sat with kings. Then I remembered she had only looked golden when we saw her by the light of the candles or torches or the fire. But in the soft light of day we knew that the pale yellow was the colour of flax and that the light blue eyes were the colour of flax flowers.

So for a short while I looked at her, dressed in a gown of silk, with fine gold wires woven into the weft. The golden maids of many colours were around her, red and yellow, white and black. Even the throne on which she sat, of white shining stone with silver eagles at her shoulders, was unlike the throne of any Christian king, but it was the throne of the Heathen, and, I knew in my bones without ever having been told it, the throne of my father's family, of the House of Cunedha of Eiddin, of the Votadini.

'How then will you take your prize, Morvran?' The gates closed, the golden vision faded. Theodore gestured towards them. 'How will you enter? Can you burst these gates? Look at the leather that makes them proof against fires. It is the skin of men, men of many races. Men from Rome and from Bezant, Vandals and Goths, Nubians and Carthaginians, all came to burst these gates and take the treasures of Montgai, and all died here. They left us their skins. Those whom we defeated are our best guardians. Look at these walls which the Titans raised in the age of ages gone. Will you tumble them yourselves? The golden treasure is not yours, Morvran, it is beyond the grasp of the men of the Island of the Mighty.'

'Even if it be beyond all our powers,' I told him, I reminded myself, 'yet I must burst your gates, I must tumble your walls, it is my oath and my burden, and my gesa that I must keep or die.'

'And see all your men die around you, and you the last?'

It was that which reminded me, and hardened my heart. These were my men, and I had brought them, even Oslaf. They had not come abroad with me, they had not taken my orders, simply to be killed for nothing. They had come for the Unity of the Island. I had no living sons, but were not Taberon and Kian and Leision my sons, were not all the others my sons, even Gwion who was my elder and Keinakh who had found me when Lindsey fell and brought me out of the fire on his shoulders to be King in Gwent? All were my sons. I could not offer them up, however bright the bush burned. My sons must live.

I told Theodore, 'The oath is mine. No one else swore it. I myself, alone, I will burst your gate, I will pull down your walls, I will scatter any army you send against me, whether they be alive or dead.' The Awen was upon me. I was inspired; no magician was more powerful than I in the grip of the Muse.

Theodore saw it. He asked, 'And will you defeat my gatekeeper?'

'I will defeat him, or die myself. But my men, my sons, will take no part in this. It is not fitting that the people should die for one man. Yet if the gatekeeper fall, who will keep the gate in his place?'

'The gatekeeper will come out to fight with you, Morvran, and with you alone. Tomorrow at noon, by the copse where you have made your palace. If you die, then your men may go home unhindered, and must not seek a blood-price. They must leave what you call Gaul and we must now call Frankland for ever.'

'And if the gatekeeper fall? Must I then fight your armies man by man till I lay waste all Gaul?'

'If the gatekeeper is killed, then the gate is burst, and the palace is open to you to take and sack and ravage and bear away the treasure.'

Theodore stood back and the Awen went from me. I was nothing but a tired old king, worrying about the laws, about food, about ways of retreat, about outflanking, about treachery in the night. Theodore read my mind: what else should a king think of?

'I will send down food for you, beef and pork well cooked, and cheeses and wine, and above all I will send you some of these cakes, made with honey and oil and spices from far beyond Damask.'

But I had old knowledge of witchcraft and I shook my head. We would eat or drink nothing of Theodore's gift, nothing of his making, or of his servants' making, only what we had brought or stolen for ourselves. I found Taberon standing at my elbow, very pale but with all his limbs still attached, which he had not expected. I beckoned and we took up our arms where they had been piled; we shouldered our pikes and marched together down the hill, away from the garden of delights.

IV

We lay out that night, not quite under the stars, because the lads had built booths of branches as we use to sleep out in the summer, up at the havod watching the sheep. So we all could pretend we were young, except Oslaf who had no experience of the delights of sheep-watching up in the hills with the girls of the village. The lads agreed with me that any food here wasn't safe to eat, being bewitched. But that didn't apply to the sheep, and we finished it, almost, since we wouldn't need to keep any for the morrow. But we had little heart to eat anyway. Only I had to be merry to keep the others' spirits up.

'Perhaps we could not reach the walls for a surprise in the day, but night time is different,' urged Oslaf. I was pleased to see that he counted himself one of us; but I still did not trust him, and kept the spear ready where I could reach it – and him. 'With fifteen of us, we could overwhelm the night watch, because they will not sit up all the night even if they kept eyes on us all day.'

But we would not be fifteen, only one. I had given my word of honour. I was sure that the Heathen would not understand such a Christian concept, and I found other arguments.

'If we storm, night or day, then someone will be killed, and it is as likely to be one of us as one of them. And I cannot ask these men to come to a probable death. They are my people, my sons, and I must bring them home or suffer in my soul.' I did not mention Hell, as Oslaf was going there anyway and would not be interested in meeting me again.

'What else did they come for,' Oslaf demanded, 'but to die for their king? You are their king. Order them to follow you, and if they demur, kill them yourself. That is what I would do, or any other king among my nation. A king's pleasure is more important than his subjects' lives, and it is their duty to obey him.'

'Is that what you Heathen mean by a king?'

'It is a king's duty to see himself obeyed. The king *is* the Nation and his pleasure is the aim of the Nation.'

'Not among us,' I told him. 'Among you, a man becomes a king by no effort but simply because he is his father's eldest son, and comes from Odin by one way or another.' I had learned something about their customs since we had set out. 'Among us it is merely an advantage if a man comes from a Royal line, and since we count our descent with care there are few among us who cannot claim descent from one king or another, within four generations or so, and many even legitimately. Which Arthur could not do. So within that wide group, a settlement can choose whom they wish to be king. And the duty of a king—'

'The duty of a king,' said Gwion, lying on his side and picking the meat off a blade bone, 'is to know the laws and to be a judge in disputes or even to see them coming and prevent dissension, so that men do not come to blows. And as a price for thus keeping peace among the people, then he is given land to live on, and to build a Hall where he may sit at the great feasts. And so that the king may be able to entertain travellers, especially those of his people who may wish to call upon him, and to give and return feasts, he is given the fines for great offences where these are paid in gold or cattle. And also it is his duty, if times are grave and there is no other way, to strap on his sword and pick up his shield and shoulder his pike and call on his people to follow him to war, if they wish to come. For a man who is driven to war, even if his life is at stake, will not fight as well as the man who goes willingly with joy.'

'But if Morvran could not compel you to come, then why are you here?' asked Oslaf with the air of a man struggling with new concepts, for as we have seen he was no intellectual.

'Because I remember a day,' said Keinakh, 'when I rode in the household of my king out of Gwent as far as Morvran's first kingdom in Lindsey where he was sent by his grandfather Cunedha to hold as long as he could against the Heathen so that Elmet should not be ravished. And we brought him out in time, for we found his kingdom wasted and himself lying with his leg broken and his own Household around him, most dead and the rest wounded, and his wife Teleri and his two daughters and his infant son dead and his house burning over his head. On that field we lost also our own King Galar the son of Gorvoledh, and both his sons; yet Gwent did not mourn for Galar and his sons for they died for the Unity of the Island, and we buried them there with Teleri and her children.

'But Arthur had already bargained away the Kingdom of Lindsey to Cueldgil Cretta's son without Morvran's knowledge. When Morvran's leg was healed for him to walk, although limping, then we asked him to be our King in Gwent, for he was of a royal line, and legitimate which was useful because a bastard may not become a king and we knew nobody like him for his wisdom and his humour even when he was sick, and for his knowledge, being a chaired bard. Therefore I will follow my king whom I have chosen for good or ill, because for the safety of Gwent he gave his agility.'

'I will put that into a song some day,' said Kian, 'because to find subjects for verse it was that I came.'

'And be a bit more careful with the truth than you usually are,' I warned him.

Tatharn spoke, unasked. 'Six nights before we left Caerwent, and five nights before and four nights before, I dreamed that the Lord commanded me to go out into the world and follow a lost sheep coloured black with red stripes, and bring it home though it take me to the end of the world. So Morvran it is that I have followed here, which is certainly near the end of the world, and I will help him bring back whatever it is he has come for, and I have not asked him. I am here because it is the will of God, and I did not wish to travel, only to do right.'

Leision felt the Pagan's eyes on him, and he said, 'I am Leision the son of Gwroldeb from Glevum. I am one of King Bedwyr's Household. We young men – we have come from all parts of the island to serve Bedwyr in his Hall and to learn the arts of war and peace and of hunting which is between the two, for three years and a day or till death, whichever period is the longer. King Bedwyr told us to go with King Morvran and to serve him as we would himself till we returned and none of our business is it where we go or why. But the obligation is on our souls as it is on Tatharn's, and although we do not go where we will yet we do not go against our wills.'

And all the other Badon boys murmured agreement.

Last the Heathen's eye fell on Taberon, and he, having some time to prepare himself, said, 'I am Taberon and my father was Kynoldeb son of Ceredig and I am Morvran's sister's youngest son. When Morvran is dead and my brother Mabon is as is likely King in Gwent, for most Gwent men will follow him, then I will be Prefect of Caerwent if I cannot find a kingdom, and I will marry Tegai if she will have me. Till then I am fostered by Morvran, and I polish his mail and I sharpen his great sword Bees in the Summer Meadow and I honour her and I have cut my fingers a thousand times and I rub down his horse and dung out his stable when he has a horse which praise the Lord but he has not now, and I follow him into the oat field at the sowing and at the harvest, and I ride with him to hunt the wolf from Skirrid to Margam, and therefore I have come to sea with him which is no fate for a gentleman. And I suffer it because he is kinsman and Lord to me and kinder than my mother Creulon, and more generous than my father who is a skinflint, and faithful towards me beyond all lovers. And I come because this is the fate of younger sons.'

There was a long silence while we all tried to think about happier things. But Oslaf said,

'You intend to fight tomorrow. Do you know anything about this . . . gatekeeper? How big he is, how heavy, how handed, left or right, whether—?'

I cut him short.

'No more than I would know about any man who came against me in battle, if we stood in line against each other. If we two met there, what would we know about each other's way of fighting? We cannot pick and choose, we must take what comes.'

'Speak for yourself,' said Oslaf. 'You know nothing of me, but you, Morvran, are well known.'

I shrugged. I am not used to such flattery. Taberon, hearing a gap and anxious to fill it, came in where he could. 'I think the gatekeeper must be the man who came up behind you, my king. He was bigger than you are, and he looked horrible, all black.'

I hardly needed to be told that. I turned the conversation. 'And the one who held you, my lad, was yellow-faced. This is not uncommon among the Romans, who are often born of mixed colours, like puppies or kittens in a litter. Or even spotted or striped: flea-bitten is the most common.'

This raised a laugh. The lads asked, 'Are the black ones Jews?'

'No,' Tatharn told him, 'Jews are wholly imaginary beings like Egyptians and Hittites, being only known from Holy Writ, unlike Fairies and Mermaids which we meet every day.'

Gwion objected, 'If it's bringing you up to the fighting line I have to be in the morning, Morvran, then it's asleep it is you ought to be, not telling stories.'

So I turned over, wrapped in my cloak, and tried to prepare myself by reciting the Book of the Prophet Obadiah. And I took it next day as a good omen, that the last verse I could remember saying to myself was 'How are his hidden treasures sought up.'

V

They woke me an hour after sunrise. I went apart and knelt before Tatharn, who shrived me. Our bucklers were heaped together to build an altar. Esau had baked an oatcake, and Tatharn had a flask of the local wine. We hung our cloaks on our pikes to make a screen between us and the altar. Taberon served the Mass, Esau sang the Epistle, and Gleisiad, who could read, was the Gospeller. Tatharn preached us a sermon full of cheer, reminding us that it was the day of Saint Socrat who was martyred by the Heathen because he turned the youths from the worship of their demons: in token of his scorn he bequeathed in his will his private parts to their chief demon, Aeskleop.

I made my communion fasting, and the part of the Host given to me was marked from the bakestone, as was proper. So did all the people partake, except for Oslaf the unbaptised who stood apart in case he were bewitched, and watched the castle.

Afterwards he taunted me, 'Now you have done your magic, we must hope that you fight well for your god of peace.'

'I die for my people, but not if I can help it.' There might be no other chance for me to make a fine ringing speech, so I went on, 'These are my men, and I am their king. Where I travel they must go. Where I find death, they too will find death – or deal it. Where they deal death without just cause, where they steal or ravish or commit sacrilege, wherever there is a blood-price, a *Galanas*, held against them I will pay their *Galanas* myself, whether in money or in blood. In these matters I will die for them if necessary, although in spite of the patent iniquity inborn and well known of the men of Gwent, the sight of my offer, sword in hand, is usually sufficient to clear any such debt. But to die for the Unity of the Island is another matter, and no *Galanas*, however paid, can clear me of that debt. I die so that my men shall live, yes, but more than that, I die for the Unity of the Island.'

Now, Gwion took me, still fasting, apart to the west side of the copse, and we left the others to argue with the Heathen the concept of justice. Now I found with wonder that this was a grove of nine trees, oak and ash and pine, myrtle and fig and willow, apple and wild vine and last the mistletoe that reigned over them all, rooted in the thunder-stroke. Surely this had long been a place of power.

Brushing away the morning cobwebs, I faced to the west, whither the dead go over the sea into the Summer Isles. Korlam took my knife, and searched me thoroughly to be sure that there was no iron left on me. He carried my sword and my pike and my coat of mail well away, to the east side of the grove, to polish and sew and patch and mend and tinker. He had Taberon working hard.

Esau brought from his bag a small pot, turned with a bronze knife from a branch of yew. Here he kept a store of a precious stuff, goose-grease mixed with woad, such as we Kings of the North wear on great days, for birth or bridal, for crowning or on the battle morning, and for the day of death. We prayed now to the elder Saints, to Saint Dagda and Saint Morrigan, to Saint Taran and Saint Manannan son of Lear: these were the first Saints which Tatharn did not know, but who still walk among us, real as Fairies, collared in gold. Tatharn kept himself aloof, outside the grove, facing the east, preaching to the birds.

I sat upon an oak stump, looking west, while Leision brought a brush made from the tailings of a white mare. He painted my face with woad in the manner proper to my House: a wolf's head on each cheek and the horns of a goat on my temples, a garland of seagulls about my neck, and a snake that crawled down my nose from a sunburst crossed and hooked and blessing between my eyes. Now I was anointed with the ancient power against the chance of battle and against death and against the conceit of victory that drives men to seek their doom.

I came out of the grove and called them, and they came. Over us they flew, their wings sweeping, their pinions crackling, their voices booming like trumpets, northward flew the Wild Geese. Fifteen there were in the flock, and the last one had only half a left leg. And part of my mind looked to victory, and part of my mind looked to Christ for forgiveness. And all except Tatharn cried with the voice of triumph.

On the morning of a battle I usually look on half a biscuit and a cup of cold water as a good breakfast, and do not always get as much. But Esau had been at work and sent Taberon at the dawn, as invisible as words and woad could make him, about boys' business in hen roosts and farmhouse larders. So they served me now porridge of oats strengthened with honey and the cream of the first milking of a new-calved cow that had borne a bull-calf. And then Esau gave me a platter of bacon hot and sizzling, with flat rounds of oatcakes to sop up the yolks of new-laid eggs.

Kian sang 'The Triad of the Eggs', which goes, 'One egg before the hunt, two eggs after adultery, three eggs on the battle morn.' Thus are summed up the three chief pleasures of man.

After that, I had more flat oatcakes, still hot from the griddle, covered with honey and a compost of apples. And to remind me of our home, Taberon poured for me a cup of Iarwen's dandelion-and-elderberry mead. I brushed away the flies which came for the honey. There were never any flies in Camelot after the Lady came, nor had I been pestered by any while drinking sweet wine at the fortress gate.

And when the lads had breakfasted as well, there was nothing more left to eat in our baggage and precious little left to drink, Gwion warned, 'They are coming.'

I objected, 'No, no, you are wrong, the time we fixed was noon.'

Gwion corrected himself, 'There are two horses but only one man, and he is unarmed.'

The big black man who had stood at Theodore's side and held his knife to my throat threw down the bridle of the light horse to Taberon, and came on to me. 'My master sends you a horse. He is trained to fight.'

I handed him my wine cup, which we had hastily refilled with the last of Iarwen's mead. The black man drained it with hardly a shudder, which demonstrated his power of will. He offered my cup back to me, but I waved it aside. 'Keep it, in memory of this day.'

It was out of the great treasury of Brecon, half a pint in capacity, made from silver-gilt and set around with precious stones, emeralds and garnets and rubies and even, most costly, pieces of green glass, except here and there some evil-minded person had stolen them before we sacked the town. But of course we both knew that if I were victorious I would take back that cup and another of equal worth if Theodore had anything as valuable. The black man rode away.

Beyond the grove, Oslaf did his part according to his lights, dim though they were. He danced alone, the ox-tails flaring below his knees, beating his sword hilt on his shield, singing in a monotonous four-beat rhythm, hardly subtle enough to be called a meter, monotonous as rain on a roof.

I watched him, as I stood to face as was proper the four quarters of the winds in turn. Soon the blade would be in the flesh and the wine-red blood in the cup that might not pass from the drinkers till its filling spilled out to make rich the dry earth. It was now my task to cry to the world that I, the pre-eminent warrior, was ready for battle, and that I did.

I prayed to the sources of my being. I prayed to the Thunder and heard the Thunder answer. I prayed to the Light, and the Lightning

answered me, nine times nine times nine, a triad of triads, triple-forked.
I called on Water, and the wind drove the rain of the thundercloud
into our faces while a man might recite the Creed.

I called on Darkness. The Darkness did not come. The Darkness
waited.

Interlude 10: The Arming

The deep well of the outer courtyard was full of javelins being readied, swords being sharpened and the hurrying of servants and grooms. Bright blocks of sun and dense shadow contended together. The cacophony struck at the heart of the ordered household. The mastery of Montgai had been held by no cruelty nor barbarity. Slave and servant knew no raised hand nor voice. Under the sun, all enjoyed the bounty of the south, secure that its treasury was deeper than need could desire, for none wanted here.

Armies, invaders, raiders, all had struck yet none had conquered the fortress. Why then did its people draw closer together on this day? No mighty force encamped at their gate. Their master had parleyed and returned full of good spirits. Why then should they shudder at the pale, ugly man without?

In the door of her inner chamber, she saw he was ready accoutred, the mail shirt falling even to his wrists. He had not yet put on the helm, which crouched under his arm. At all points he was covered, like a crab, from any retaliatory blow.

The chime of the overlapping rings was a remembered sound. At Badon, the Iron Men had worn such mail over their shirts and swung such swords down upon the Great Race from the height of their iron-shod horses. The litter of the death they struck that day was measured in mounds raised over shiploads of such men. His eyes asked her if he looked well.

She paused. Under the crab-casing of his mail shirt his body seemed strong enough. His face, gaunt, grey, determined, told another tale. She nodded. All warriors bound for conflict needed the courage that only a woman's nod might give.

He knelt for the helm to be fastened on. She smoothed away one black wing of hair, warmed one last time by the nearly consumed gaze, before the faceguard was closed.

Her eyes were flax, her mouth was coral, her skin the lilies that grew in the inner court of the Bezant Emperor. She was the Empress on the throne of Votan and he her champion.

He turned away to meet his adversary.

Chapter 10

Battle

I

I tried out all the javelins we had by throwing them into a molehill and chose the three that seemed best balanced, two of mine and one of Leision's. I looked well at the horse. A stallion of fourteen hands. Chestnut, the best colour. The head was small, the forehead broad and white-starred, the knees lean, the pastern short, the hooves thin, the feet broad, the hind legs white-stockinged, the nostrils agape, the neck slender, the chest open and broad, the back short, the ribs long, the loins short before a long tail. The best of horses. I patted his neck and breathed into his nostrils, and so made him mine.

Leision said, 'There is no need to tire him.'

We took off the saddle, which was of good leather, fine-stitched and well-polished. There were stirrups which some like to ride with all the time, and I find comfortable for a long journey: but today I would need my legs free to fight. The beast stood unhobbled under the shade of a tree and cropped the grass, showing no fear of our shouts or of the mail and the spears we flashed and rattled around him. Thus I knew he would do well.

I walked past him, and through the grove again, entering from the west, the lucky side, the side of the good death. On this side there was an oak stump, a three-hundred-year-old tree struck down by lightning seven years ago for this very purpose. I sat there to be armed. Keinakh brought my mail, eased it on over two sheepskins, set fleece to fleece. Esau slid the bronze armlets over my hands to cover my wrists, while Korlam laced my collar. Again we called on the older Saints, on Esus and on Taran, on the Dagda and the Morrigan and on Saint Segamo who went first armed into battle, and above all, here in his own country, on Saint Cernunnos.

Gwenki brought my boots and drew them on for Korlam to lace. Leision unwrapped the cover from my shield, so that instead of the gay red and black of honour it showed the bitter brown of war. Kian crowned me with my stout helm of bull's hide, triple layered, and boiled to shape, stiffened with a brow ring of iron and capped with crossed bars of bronze. Only Taberon waited with four Badon boys as a guard, holding Bees in the Summer Meadow, with her riding strings tied, undrawn.

The sun was high now in the heavens, so high that it seemed it must topple and bring down the sky in fragments around us. It was as near noon as could make no difference. Leision led the horse up, saddled. He was a good beast, and well trained. I stroked his nose and fed him apples, let him taste my scent and know me for his friend.

Gwion called, 'It is true this time, he comes armed.'

While Gwion the Huntsman watched, Leision the Huntsman knelt to give me a knee to mount. Taberon brought to me Bees in the Summer Meadow, her riding strings now untied. Kian handed up to me the three javelins, new polished to fly straight, the shafts sanded smooth. I checked my stirrups were still crossed over the saddlebow, for I would ride unhampered. I looked to war, to the Castle of Montgai.

II

There were three figures coming. One man sat on a horse, the bridle in one hand. The second marched at the horse's head, balancing over his shoulder, of all things, a pike: but very long for a pike: a pike for a giant but frailer. In front, a smaller man on foot beat on a little drum hung with bells. We could hear him at a distance. We looked to Kian, because it was his business as a poet to know all the laws and customs of war and how such things ought to be managed.

But it was Gwion, remembering earlier wars, who cried, 'Shall we be out-voiced? Let's have a song, now, all of you!'

We sang loud and long, all of us except Tatharn because he was too busy praying, and Oslaf who did not know the words and would have fought us if he did. We sang the old songs, 'Three Came Back' and 'Death in the Marshes', 'Heads on the Gate' and 'The Hunting of the Black Pig'. Last of all, loudest and holiest we sang 'The Song of the Little Cauldron'.

Thus it was to the greatest music of civilisation that I went out to battle.

Before I moved off, I said to Taberon, as if confidentially but so that all might hear, 'Have them all wait here, under the trees.' After all he was a king's son and might well some day be a king himself: it was time for him to exercise some authority. 'Keep them out of the killing sun. If I fall, do not come out to bury me, not even to take home my head. Go straight back to the boat, at the run. Make sure that the men of the Island return to the Island. Especially the Badon boys who did not ask to come and have no say in the matter.'

'Kindly meant but bloody nonsense,' said Leision.

But Gwion standing at my knee whispered in his usual dulled bellow, 'I wonder who he has sent out to fight. By the size, it may be the black man who brought the message and the horse. He must expect to fight you on foot because he has brought his pike. Stay in the saddle if you can, but if you have to get down, come inside the pike's reach and take the sword to him. If he remains mounted and you are on foot he will hammer you into the ground.' All this was obvious to me, but it helped Gwion to hide his fear.

I rode forward. Kian went in front of me. He was playing a set of pipes he had brought from Bordigala: it was a thin and haunting tune that had words to it telling of a love lost and never found, of corn that ripened while locks lacked keys and girdles were not untied. That light music, the air of the hills between Avan and Ogwr, drowned out the tumult of the drum and bells and the shout of the grasshoppers. And then there was no more music.

The two horses were now about forty fathoms apart on the open field. The sun beat on us like a hammer: I've heard some good sermons on Hell in my time, but this was the best, wordless. From nowhere, a crowd of the local people had gathered. Taberon, my last companion, at the horse's head, said very quietly as if he were afraid his voice might carry, 'I can't see his face. He has mail round it. I see no way to hurt him. It is he who should be called an Iron Man, not you. His arms are mailed and yours are bare.'

'You must learn,' I told him, 'how to fight men who are better armed than yourself.'

'That lesson I am learning already, since I have neither sword nor mail of my own.'

'Then steal some. This must be a dreadful place for thieves, for even this man does not trust anyone else with his pike. See that our men get back to the ship unrobbed. On these three javelins now depends the fate of the Unity of the Island.'

III

We were alone, now, the mailed man and I. He was using his stirrups. He shaded his eyes to see me since he had me to his south. My horse was no Bucephalus: we had tried him with shadows and he shied at them. I watched the other man's gloved hands, the left on the bridle, the right holding his pike, a fathom and a half of it, with a pennant of yellow netting tied below the point. It was very thin so he meant to throw it from horseback, I assumed.

The man with the drum stood under a twisted tree by the far side of the field. My own people were all in the shade. My adversary began to edge his horse around to his right, to get the sun out of his eyes. I watched his hand on the bridle, and had my steed sidle to the right also, falling back a little to keep our distance and our angle to the sun.

I saw his forearm tense a little. Before he had finished the thought, before he had pushed his horse forward, I rode at him. I shouted my name. I challenged him and all the earth. My own people shouted. The warcries were of Gwent, of Calleva, of Caledon, of Lindsey.

The first javelin, you throw at a distance. It may do the job, provided you cast it close enough to penetrate. Throw before he throws his. Timing is a nice calculation. I cast at twenty paces, closer than I like.

It flew well. It brushed his eyelids. I was watching that sizeable pike. I waited for his cast. There would be time to ward it off with my buckler. But there was no cast. He rode at me steady, the pike level as if he were on foot. His arm did not come up. I did not believe this. He was riding right up to me. He was trying to stab me with his pike. He had both hands to it. His horse guided itself. I pulled my horse away to the left. I leaned away from the point. It missed me, or I missed it, by a skin's thickness.

That was one of the closest escapes I have ever had. It left me sweating and shivering at the same time, always a bad sign. I jabbed my heels into my horse's side and got well away from him before he could turn. Whoever before had thought of using a pike on horseback, as if you were an infantryman? It would be invincible. There must be a way to counter it. There must be a way.

But he was coming at me again. I had my feet in the stirrups now. I rode at him, fast, and watched him coming towards me. He was making a good hand gallop. I slowed to a trot. This might do it. I waited till well inside the throwing distance. We had met before right hand to right hand. Now I pulled my horse to my right so that we would pass left to left. And at two fathoms I threw, not at him but at his horse's eyes. His steed turned to the right against all his efforts, and he could not bring the pike across its neck against me.

But this was no good. All I had done was prevent him from killing me. What I needed to do was to kill him instead. I asked myself what was his main weapon. Not the pike, but what gave it power. It was speed. He was getting the power into his thrust not merely from his arm but from his horse's speed and from my horse's too as they came against each other. And he expected me to ride against him at my best speed, and let him thrust at me? A delusion. No one knows the value of position as well as does a lame man.

I looked around me, planned my route. I had one javelin left against his pike. I had a moment's respite. My adversary had pulled up his frightened horse, was soothing it, talking to it.

At last he seemed ready, and began the sequence, walk, trot, gallop. I came to the trot, not directly towards him, but toward the place I had chosen. That made him cast out wide to come at me from my front.

But I was at the trot, he was at the gallop, fast as a bird, fast as a dolphin. I came down to a walk, and not a walk the way he wanted.

I threw from five fathoms. Standing still, this was close enough to be accurate. I threw with force. A spear at his eyes shook him as much as it did his horse. I hit him, somewhere. I did not see where. I was sliding out of my saddle on the blind side away from him and pushing my horse across his path.

I was right in my guess. His horse, blocked, turned towards me. I lifted my buckler with both hands and took the pike-point deep in the linden wood. I heaved down on the shield, lifting my feet off the ground. The speed which had pushed him against me now pushed him back. He wavered in his seat, trying to recover the pike, his feet imprisoned in his stirrups. He let go too late to save his balance. As he dropped the pike he got his feet out of the stirrups. The horse was rearing and he could not steady it. He was trying to do too many things at once. He slid over the tail into the dust. I had come down lightly on my feet: he fell on his back.

Both horses were trained for war. Without riders, each stood still. I had the pike, and for a moment thought of running at him with it. But where would be the glory in that? Besides, my knee would not let me run. I simply balanced the pike in my hand and threw it away. This was no Rhon. No Saint rode it against the sun. It landed halfway to the grove. It did not even bury its point in the earth but skidded along the grass. Kimokh found it.

My adversary was on his feet now His sword was out, his buckler covered his left side. I looked for my sword. Terror would not let me run. I forced myself to think, which is often as useful as flight, but not always. I whistled. My horse came to me. I unhooked Bees in the Summer Meadow from the saddle. My buckler was gone somewhere. I would have to use the scabbard in my left hand.

I did not like this. I had made a mistake. On horseback I could tackle anybody. I had just shown that. Now on foot I would be hobbling, if I could move at all. I must stand my ground like Oslaf's uncle at Badon, the Caister man, not moving forward or back, favouring my stiff knee. My adversary had not banked on a fight like this. I had no aid but my sword. I called her name, I kissed her, I told her how beautiful she was, I asked her to work with me. I promised her a new scabbard, bronze mounted, set with jewels and glass, to replace the one that would surely now be hacked to pieces. Like a good animal, a well-schooled horse or a faithful wife, she listened to me.

I stood and he moved in against me. He too had lost his shield, or thrown it down to be more agile. It would depend on the edge of the sword alone. There would be no clash of leather facing against bronze studs, of lime planks against iron point. There would be no pushing. In this fight a light agile man would be the equal of a heavier, stronger one. The cleverer man would win. The only trouble was, I did not know which one was me.

I was ready for him. Nobody knew as much about swordsmanship as I did. I'd taught enough men – killed enough, at that. He came at me steadily, step by step. I offered him Guard Three. He knew so little of his business that he replied with Cut Nine instead of Thrust Seven and nearly had my head off. I swayed away and cut at his legs. Instead of guarding, he jumped away. To get the sun out of his eyes, he came at me from the general direction of my left buttock. How do you fight at all against someone who takes no notice of the rules laid down of old and comes at you unfairly to make you pivot on your bad leg? Heathen ways!

Three more passes and it was clear: he was the more agile, that I knew, but he was also the more skilful in this trade. I could not get past his guard, or even near to it. I could hardly keep him out as he danced around me, his blade flailing like a duck's wing. I could only hope to keep out his blows till he fell over a cowpat. I took a step backwards towards a piece of ground which had been well-fertilised: he saw that danger and came at me from the flank. But that brought the sun into his eyes again. Now I knew it: he could not think of three things at once, a fatal disability in battle, although useful for a merchant or a judge.

He had made a mistake. Was he tiring? I felt a new weakness in his blows. I heard the straining of his breath. Had he been hurt by the fall from his horse? There had not been any cry of pain when he went down, only the grunt that comes from shocked lungs and labouring muscles. Yet that first flash of frenzy in the attack had come from a man who knew that his time was short. He had hoped to make a quick killing of it. Clumsy as I was, I had denied him that.

His blows, when I parried, grated less savagely on my blade, there was less variety in his swordplay. He had avoided the dung only to catch the sun, and he was conscious of his mistake, was thinking more of that than of the present. Another fatal disability in battle. I had got back the breath I had lost, my panic was over, but he had lost the breath he had. Now to bring him panic.

I disengaged, fell back out of contact. It unsettled him, that I, who had seemed fated to stand still on my good leg, should now move at all. I had been entirely on the defensive. Now I struck at him as he followed me. My lovely Bees, trained to sting, hummed in the air.

Now I could risk a step forward again. I beat down his blade by sheer force. I struck forward inside his guard. Twice I felt the grinding of mail laid harsh and unpadded over soft flesh. Twice I had to recover before my blade dropped too far, twice I prayed that my leg would hold me.

Then forward again. The stroke that bit into softness. With the sweat in your eyes, in the unseeing lust of battle, even screaming with your own pain, you cannot mistake that feel. Strike, then, again. This is no time for softness.

He fell like a tree. The lightning mastered the oak. After the rending, there was a silence.

IV

The dust caked in my drying sweat. I shivered in my clammy mail, my soaked sheepskins. My soul returned from Christ who holds all our souls in the heat of battle lest in the moment of a good death we slip into the Abyss and are lost.

There was a crowd around me. There were the people of the land, the dwellers by the river, who came out from the holes in the ground, from the hedges and the ditches where they had hidden to watch. My own men came forward from the edge of the Grove of the Nine Trees. There were people from the fortress, red and yellow, black and white. But there was one who did not come.

Gwion clapped me on the back. 'Good lad, good! You had me frightened when you took him on foot. But you played it right.'

I took off my helm. Taberon caught it from my hand. I wanted to be sick from sheer weariness, with the pain of bruises. But this was not the moment to be weak. Korlam called me forward. I looked into the drooping eyelids of Theodore, seller of swords, bringer of wine, Master of the ways of the Inner Sea, Lord of Montgai.

'I did not know who it was,' Taberon whispered. 'I could not see for the heat and the dust, and for the mail on the face . . .'

But I knew. I knew during the night. Who but the Lord will fight for the Castle? Who but the lover will fight for a woman? For if he send another champion to do battle for her, how can he ever look her in the eyes again?

'But how many,' Kian asked, 'did Arthur ask to go to fight Lawnslot for him?'

Theodore opened his eyes, looked at me. I knelt and asked, 'Was it worth all this?'

'To have her, naked under my hands, in my bed between me and the wall? There sat the Lady, lonely and supreme. Besides, the steel is kinder than the crab.'

'I ask your pardon.'

'You have it. And my gratitude. The last months – who can bear them?' After a little he asked, 'Where is the lad?'

I beckoned Taberon to kneel by me. Theodore spoke very low, so that only we two could hear him, but that was not by his choice. 'I promised him a sword. When he came to my house. Let him take my sword. Seven times quenched. And my mail. Wear it all for the sake of God. And His Mother.'

Taberon reached out and touched the hilt of Theodore's sword that lay in the dust at his side. He answered Theodore, 'I will wield her against the Heathen. For the sake of God. And His Mother.' He had pitched his voice as if for a response in church. Then, as if still following a rite, he commanded, 'Name this sword!'

Theodore murmured, as if wandering his mind, 'Name . . . name . . . whose name . . . whose . . .' He turned his face away from us, said more distinctly, 'It is getting dark . . . In the east.'

I stood up. I turned my head away. I had called on the darkness. Now the darkness came. I could not watch him die, not the friend I had killed. I heard as if from far away, Gwenki saying to Taberon, 'That is a fine name for a sword, Darkness Comes from the East. Good steel she is too, although gapped and dinted a little by the day's work. Quenched a seventh time in the blood of an old and bitter woman, to give a taste for vengeance. Let me have her and I will grind and set the edge clear again. And Korlam will help me patch the mail.'

But the mail, all slashed and bloody, was still on Theodore's back. He sought me with his eyes. I knelt again and heard him. 'Wine ... my own wine ... marked with ... with my name ... wine for the kings.'

Tatharn now knelt by the dying man, and with him someone black-bearded, a priest by the way he moved. I heard them pray, versicle and response as is appointed, but in Greek for these two were equals in authority and in learning. Where I could I joined in, for I knew the order and sound of the liturgy, although I could not everywhere follow the meaning. I faced the east and I waited for the sound of crickets. I waited at noon for the night to come.

Presently the Greek Priest said to me, in Latin, 'You knew him best. As king to king, as to a man who rode with you in battle, you have one more duty. You delivered him from Hell, in that he did not die unshriven, nor linger on in pain to curse God and die. Will you close his eyes?'

I came to do it, and prayed to the Virgin for his soul. I took from my pouch two pieces of gold, Roman work, a full ounce each, that I had dug from a grave between Avan and Ogwr. I weighted down the eyelids of my friend with the head of Claudius Rome-King, who brought the true faith into the Island.

I went apart into the grove of the nine trees, to weep in silence. But Oslaf, who was no intellectual and had little understanding of life, followed me and threw his arms round my shoulders, shouting, 'Rejoice, rejoice, do not weep! You have killed a man. Wear your ox-tail and praise your gods – your enemy is dead!'

I pulled away from him, but not too sharply that he should not think I did it because I could not stand the smell of a lifetime of wheat bread and barley beer. Although truly I did find that intolerable.

'God forbid that I should rejoice in the death of any man, or praise Him that I had killed one of His creatures! I may yet come to face you, Oslaf, across the steel and linden planks. Even when I kill you with the ox-tails about your knees and the sacred vessels of the altar in your hands, and the blood of my cousins wet to your elbows – even then I will not rejoice in it. What profit is there in destroying what God has made? He gave that life, why should I be pleased to take it away?'

'But he was your enemy, and therefore you killed him!'

'He was my friend, and yet I killed him. He was my friend even though the laws of civilised society and the needs of the Unity of the Island demanded that we fight. Nor was there anything else he wanted more than death, death soon and swiftly.'

'Why should he want death? He had here all that a man could want in the Roman fashion, wine and gold and power. Even her, he had *her*.'

'He had all that you would want, Oslaf. But he had more. Were you to open him now, you would find his body a mass of tangled corruption. My father died thus, while I watched him, slowly. Theodore would not wait, and nor would he condemn her to watch him.'

'But if he wanted death, why then not fall on his sword and go to his god in a blaze of splendour, floating down this river in his burning ship? And if he fought only to die, why then did he try so hard to kill you?'

'God forbade us to kill ourselves. Once swords were drawn, then his honour, which comes from God, would not allow him to do anything but to fight to the death, his death or mine. It is a mark of Christian men, Oslaf, that what they do they do to the end. Theodore had to fight with all his might before he died, before the crab had struck and left him unfit to wear mail or to sit a horse. And above all before she should see him thus weakened.' And I did not say, before he could hear, that she had refused to nurse him, thus enfeebled, or even to stay with him.

I turned from the Heathen to the Saint and I asked Tatharn, 'How to bury him?'

'As a warrior, bloody and unwashed, not as a merchant in scent and flowers. The coffin was nailed and the tomb cut in the rock, for one of you, before ever we came into the river. They have stripped him of his mail and given it to Taberon. His body is wrapped in red silk from Cathay.'

'May he rest in peace.'

The Roman loomed before me, the black man, the steward. 'My master that rode out to die left a message for you. You are to be Master of the Funeral Feast, and it is to be a Feast of Thanksgiving for a good life lived in full to the end. We have already prepared it, a feast as great as any king's. And after that, he ordered, you may sack the castle, and carry away whatever you wish, or what you can carry. For after you will come the Franks.'

V

We passed through the great gate, wide open now. The Hall, the court-yards, the orchards, the groves where vines were trained up stone columns, all were at our mercy. We wandered around in twos or threes, hardly daring to touch the hangings on the walls, the curtains all worked in strange pictures, the fruit that grew on trees set in tubs.

The beasts, too, were something to talk about. The greatest marvel was a baby dragon, hardly three fathoms long. His wings had not yet sprouted, and he still had his fledgling scales of a greenish-grey, not yet red or silver. Because of the danger of fire they kept him in a pond with low railings around. There was a unicorn with his spikes, in a paddock fenced with a palisade of tree trunks, and a heavier and stouter beast than we are usually told. Gleisiad began to debate whether he was any uglier than I am, so I hit him again with a bucket. There was a leopard, spotted and patched all over and standing a horse and a half high at the shoulder, with a neck of two fathoms more. There were lions, one of the common kind, with a mane of dense hair, and two females which are striped and have no manes. And there was even a man, much taller and stouter than even a Pagan of Logres, twenty hands high and as wide, with low brows that stood out as ridges, black-skinned and covered all over with black hair. He must have been mad, because they kept him in a cage with stout bars, which he shook while he shouted at us in his own language which sounded very beastly. Our guide, the yellow man who had beaten on the drum before Theodore, told us his name was Pongo Pongo.

I asked the steward, the black man, where the wine cellars were. He took me to the other side of the walls, to the north. There he showed us some barns. In one there were great baskets of grapes, and the people of the country were bringing in others, last year's, he told me, all dried in the sun to make them sweeter. In another barn, men were sweating at a great press most marvellously worked by the turning of a machine called a screw, to squeeze out the juice into big jars of baked dirt. In another we saw rows and rows of these jars standing. Here, I understood with difficulty from the steward, the grape juice was turned into wine, red or white or in-between according to the buyer's taste.

'But where is the Greek wine?' I asked. 'The wine from Bezant?'

'No wine is brought from Bezant,' the steward told me, 'not for many years, because it is too heavy and the jars get broken. But for what Theodore brought you, what you call Bezant wine, come and see.'

This was in another barn, with many half-full jars ranged along one wall, and a familiar smell. 'Here is the turpentine, which would be mixed with the wine for Albion. Or honey. Or sometimes seawater which was brought up from the Inner Sea. Or all three together, with thyme and mint and strange oils that will never freeze, for flavour. And for bulk.'

'Theodore cheated us?' I felt very angry. 'He sold us for its weight in bronze the cheap common wine of this country, doctored to taste Greek?'

'How else,' asked the steward reasonably, 'would a merchant make a living? In any case, here are twelve jars of Theodore's own wine, marked with his name, which he ordered to be served to you at this feast, being the most precious fluid of anyone's imagining.'

I shook my head. 'We are not worthy to drink this marvellous stuff. We will take it home to feast the great Kings of the Island of the Mighty. Call together any men you command and any mules, and have all these jars marked with a T for Theodore taken down to my ship. You may clear the hold and bring back here the bronze which the people of the place were unloading. Now, sword-blades?'

There was a storehouse with many swords, some with no grips over the iron hilts but others with grips built up from horn and limewood.

The steward showed me that they were stowed separately by quenchings. None were seven times quenched. I ordered all the six times quenched which had grips to be taken down to my ship and loaded. And in the warehouse, my eye was taken by the flash of a bale of shirts, all in a royal scarlet, just come, I was told, from Rome Town. I had these packed also and taken down to the ship.

When we had seen what we wanted to see, and every mule in the place was on its way down to the ship, we passed all of us in order into the Great Hall.

I sat in the centre of the High Table, with Taberon on my right hand and Oslaf on my left, still clutching his green branch. There were a great many of the girls of the Household who fluttered around us like so many butterflies, to serve us and choose our food for us, to cut it and heap it on our plates. The platters were as usual in those parts made of baked clay, which saved washing up because we simply threw them to break on the floor.

We had each of us bathed our skins in warm and scented water, being thus persuaded in spite of our manly natures, and assisted in the baths by the multicoloured girls. They brought us new shirts of a light cloth cool to the skin and at first resembling silk, which the Seres spin from the leaves of mulberry trees, whatever they are. But this was a cloth made in a place called Kos from the excrement of caterpillars. There the people are so poor they wear nothing but what they weave from the webs of spiders, and are otherwise noted as magicians, but incompetent ones. I no longer hid my wealth beneath my shirt but wore gold around my neck and bronze and precious glass about my forearms.

Taberon, being of an idle turn of mind, had opened a kind of prison where were kept a number of Roman children, all black and hairy and having tails which I suppose drop off at the age of puberty. They were very rude and uneducated, running about the Hall and up and down on the tables, snatching our food from our very mouths and then climbing the walls to sit in the rafters to eat it and spatter us. But there were not many of them and they were soon satisfied, and in any case we had plenty of food to spare.

There was bread, but, alas, all of wheat, no oatcake at all. It was smeared with oil instead of butter: this made it very greasy and is not to be recommended as a start for a happy evening, since the oil delays the start of drunkenness till boredom sets in and thus gives a worse head in the morning. Little beef or pork was served, but a great deal of lamb. This may sound homely but it was so vilely cooked as to seem unpalatable. Some of it was cut very fine and mixed with rosemary and other strange herbs. This was served either in a piecrust or wrapped in vine leaves.

'Be careful,' I warned Taberon, 'because there is no knowing what the birds have been doing but guesses are very likely true.'

'Something wrong with the kitchen,' grumbled Esau. 'No flies there, nor any here at the table. Like that in Camelot, towards the end.' Some of the lamb was served in almost a civilised way, cut into gobbets, thrush-sized, and threaded on iron skewers to be grilled over a brazier. But they were alternated on the rod with onions and mushrooms and other vegetables I would not like to name, and it was wise to make the girls taste each kind first. I found it strange that these people were so uncivilised as not to have learned to pack the fine-cut mutton with the liver and heart and kidney sliced and a couple of handfuls of oatmeal into the sheep's stomach and boil for a day or so. And I would have given much for a good leg of nine-year-old mutton covered with honey and simmered gently in a pot of cider for a few hours.

There were honeycakes, but I did not touch these, or indeed any other dish, till I had seen Oslaf try them after the girls. The steward had shown me a bundle of what looked like grass which he said Theodore had always given to his guests to eat, or burnt before them on the brazier. I told him to burn it, indeed, but outside in the open air, not to spoil the smell of the wood smoke. I had seen Theodore's sailors with this and I had to be assured that there was none left in the storehouse before I put more wood on the Hall fire. It always seemed to me an unnatural way of getting drunk.

There was fruit of all kinds, grapes both fresh and dried, and pears and peaches and plums. Also very juicy yellow globes the size of apples, sharp to taste but of no great substance, and others with thick skins, full of seeds each surrounded by a soft flesh. The juice stained our hands and our shirts black. Not many apples, which are scarce in those parts.

The wine was on the table, in great jugs of burnt clay, red or white, mixed with turpentine or seawater or honey as we wished. Each man found in front of him a variety of cups, in burnt clay or silver or gold or even in glass. The butterfly girls poured wine for the lads, a yellow lass looking after Taberon, and a black one clinging to Oslaf. But no one poured wine for me. I was left with a triplet of jugs before me, and no cup.

But when the table had been well served and my men were filled with meat and bread and fruit, if not yet with wine, there fell a silence. The curtains at the foot of the Hall, a magnificent dark red in colour with narrow stripes of gold woven into them, parted. And the Gwenevere entered. Tall she was, and slender as a willow branch. She wore a gown of silk from Cathay, in the Heathen manner, one seamless piece swept from high collar to ankles, a pale yellow, the yellow of the sun-struck buttercup and of the well-ripened wheat. She wore in her hair a gold coronet upon her braided and circled hair, and about her neck were gold chains. Her belt was of yellow silk sewn and buckled with gold plates. Her shoes were of leather covered with gold leaf. And down the front of the gown, where the amber buttons held it close, was a scarf of a fine net of a silk warp and a gold weft.

The men stood to honour her, even those who did not know her, and the butterfly girls knelt on the floor before her. In front of her walked two of these maidens, tall girls with pale yellow hair that hung down to their waists, unbraided. And either hand she kept on their shoulders. One of these girls carried a jug of gold, as high as my forearm is long. The other carried what looked to be a small cup of silver gilt, dotted with colours, a poor tawdry thing among all this wealth.

Slowly the Gwenevere passed through the Hall from the door to the edge of the dais. For a while she stood there. She bowed to us. Immediately Kian, who had had no chance of an audience till this, stood up with his harp, the one he had borrowed in Bordigala, and began to sing his new song, the one you have all heard and may well take for the truth. But now you know it is all lies, and only to be excused by the appeal to the Awen. All the bards sing it now, that ought to know better. He sang of the death of Arthur, of how the Great Duke of Peace and War fought against Mordred, and how they killed each other, riding with their pikes as weapons, by the borders of the winter sea near the Glass Mountain. There was not a word of truth in it, except that it was Bedwyr that threw Caliburn into the Mere. My name did not come into it, for which I was grateful. I ought to have stormed at Kian and warned him that Mordred the Soul of Honour would not take it kindly, but I could not show anger with the Lady present in the Hall.

While Kian sang, she stood at my elbow, the last Great Duchess of Peace and War. When the bard had finished, and in fact this early version of the song was quite short, since later he expanded it with much additional material of doubtful validity, one of the young maidens placed a cup on the table before me. Not just any cup, or a gold cup of the house. It was my own cup, the pride of the Treasury of Gwent and Brecon, that I had given to the steward. The Lady took the jug from the maiden and poured the wine for me. And for me only.

I drained the cup. The Lady bowed low to me, only, and passed through the curtain at my back, at the head of the Hall. The two maidens remained, but I followed her.

VI

It was well on in the night. I came back from the courtyard of the Castle of Montgai. In the Hall, my own fourteen men had caroused and sung and stuffed themselves, and debauched themselves under tables and behind screens and on chests and benches. Their partners were the butterfly girls, and other women of the House, black and white and red and yellow. The women of the villages around had come in, too, willing to undergo any indignity for the sake of a full belly and a head dulled with wine, for a gaudy trifle and a wisp of cloth. Most of these, not otherwise engaged for the night, were quarrelling over the carcases of sheep and hens. In one corner, Tatharn and the Greek priest were in deep theological discussion, or in prayer, their heads flat on their hands on the table. I stood and watched awhile. I grudged none of them their pleasure, but I wanted no part of it.

When I could find him, I called Gwion from the embraces of an eastern girl as saffron as an Irishman's cloak. 'Come out to the wall!'

We climbed to where the night before we had looked into the sunset and wondered what the morrow would bring. Now we looked again over the meadow into what ought to be a distant darkness. In the west there shone a semicircle of flickering lights: not a line but a belt of irregular flames, like the star-spattered sky.

'Bonfires?' marvelled Gwion. 'But would the whole land have thus mourned their master's death? Or do they rejoice? And how did the news reach them so soon?'

'Last time,' I reminded him, 'we saw a ring of fires like that was on the night before we opened the attack at Badon. And then they were our fires. But come round to the other side, and look to the north.'

'More fires than ever before, only a little further away. Two armies out there, waiting for the dawn?'

'Are you sober enough to flee? Perhaps the lads ought to wait till they're fit enough to run.'

'I'll have them sober soon enough. Just let me get my kicking boots on.' Which he did. They came to me one by one, in the beginning of the earliest twilight. They disengaged themselves, slowly.

I gathered them together and spoke to them, sharp-tongued. 'Each of you may take away some small thing, or things, of value as booty. Not merely small enough to carry, but small enough to leave your hands free if you have to swim. Or fight. Just to say we've sacked the place. As precious as you please, so long as it leaves your hands free. We have other things to take as well. I have sent swords and wine and cloth down into the ship already. The rest, the people of the place may try to keep as much as they can under the eyes of two armies. The warriors will be here by dawn, and fighting by afternoon for the control of this junction of the two paths to the seas. This fortress holds the roads and it will not be comfortable here then.'

For the most part the lads took pieces of jewellery, rings or brooches or armlets. Gleisiad took a silver bucket. Oslaf took two silver spoons, each the length of his forearms, with bowls the size of his palms. They were marked, one Saul, the other Paul, the names of the two Saints who fought with Apollyon in the straight streets of Damask and shed the blood with which the swords of Damask are quenched. I found Taberon trying to carry off a thin brown girl whom I judged neither light nor valuable enough for our purpose, though portable all right – she said she could swim.

'Put down that unconsumed portion of the night's passion,' I told him. 'Instead, come and help me set free some of the prisoners.'

With axes, he and I broke open most of the cages and paddocks. The big cats ran free through the gates when we shouted at them, and separated to find their own food, which mooed or baaed at them in every corner. The unicorn lumbered off into a wood, and the leopard followed him to an olive grove to stoop at the tops of the trees. We looked at the hairy black man in his cage, but he shouted at us and snatched at our faces, so that we were afraid to come near. But we were able, at some risk, from outside the bars to cut through the chain about his waist and smash the lock on his gate, which thus stayed closed but would give to a hearty push. We piled there for him a great deal of food, bread and meat and fruit. We guessed that he would be out before the armies came, and would join one troop or other, passing as a Pagan without question.

Last of all, we considered the dragon. It would have been nice to have taken him home, and since he swam very well in his pond, we might have used him to pull the ship in calm weather. However, he seemed too big to carry down to the wharf, and therefore we regretfully left him behind. Taberon insisted on leaving open the gate in his fence, although I guessed that he would probably burn his way out.

For myself, I took nothing of value. I had Taberon put a sidesaddle on a horse, the one I had ridden to the fight. He guessed my purpose and asked again if he could take the brown girl. I said, 'I keep on telling you, when you've had one you've had most of them.'

He continued to grumble that this was one of the minority, but I ignored his words. I found the steward, and warned him, 'There are two armies coming.'

'Three,' he corrected me. 'The Vandals too are coming through the passes to fight against both the Franks and the Burgundians who are fighting each other. Look south.' He pointed and in the twilight I could see sparks of flame, although whether campfires, cooking breakfasts or farmsteads burning, I could not tell.

I asked, 'Will your people be safe?'

'We have known for some weeks that this would happen. We have made our preparations and will be safe, as long as you take no more horses. We will go down to the east and reach Narbon, which is in the Kingdom of Septimania, whose territory the Vandals of Catalonia are now invading. There we have ships waiting, and we will go, some to Bezant, others to Rome Town or Africa.'

'Move fast and go with God,' I said, and I embraced him.

Taberon brought the Lady out into the main courtyard. She came unquestioning, as she never questioned what was done to her or about her, almost as if we were merely doing what she had willed, which was impossible. We wrapped her in a cloak of good wool, light and warm, of saffron colour to contrast with her ashen hair. We also packed for her, since she would never have thought of doing such a thing herself, a bundle of her better clothes and jewels. I calmed the horse and persuaded her to mount. We left the courtyard.

Oslaf was at the gate, peering into the slowly breaking dawn. 'Shall we burn the rest?'

'Christian men count it a sin to destroy any work of man wantonly. The Heathen will do that soon enough. It will make them quarrel and delay them. We must get clear of the jaws of three nutcrackers.'

'Agaric warned me that this would happen. It was plain that as soon as Theodore was out of the way – not even dead but made harmless by poison or witchcraft or love – these kings would fight for the lordship. Agaric sent us on to do the job for him. He did not know that Theodore was already disabled. We have fried the egg that hatches his golden goose. As soon as we landed in Gaul, Theodore sent for the Burgundians, and I suppose for the Goths.'

'Which side will you take?'

'Who offers me more. And you?'

'Neither. I work only for the Unity of the Island.'

We led the horse slowly down the ramp from the castle into the plain.

'Count the fading stars, Gwion Sharp Eyes. There is one more tonight, and that a bright one.'

'No time for that, Morvran the Ugly, unless you hold back the day. Of course, Tatharn could do that, if he were here.'

'Tatharn!' I rushed back into the fortress, I found the Chapel. This side of the screen, the black Roman and his fellows, stewards and cooks and butterfly girls, said the responses. In the sanctuary, Tatharn read the Last Gospel of Theodore's Requiem. The Greek priest had served the Mass. It was over in a few more lines. We were full of Grace and Truth.

The people of the castle, at the Greek priest's orders, gave to Tatharn the golden chalice and paten, and the cruets. We were the last to honour the altar and the holy shrine.

Then Tatharn and I left the gates.

VII

We moved out into the mists of the dawn. As we went we heard far away a familiar sound. Savage spear butts beat on shields, slow and steady with no subtlety of rhythm, not like our people where every free man is at liberty to choose his own pace of song, thus adding to the harmony. With our ears to the ground we could hear the dancing feet. Sometimes we thought we could even hear voices.

We knew what they would be shouting, all, baptised or not: 'Hoya! Hoya! Odin aid, Thor help! Thor strike, Odin burn! Hoya! Hoya!'

The houses near the wharf were empty. There were dead men in the street. The ship, strangely, was intact. We had rigged a shelter amidships under a spare sail, and we were about to hand the Lady up into her place. Gwion shouted from where he clung halfway up the mast. The rest of us on the ground hardly needed the warning. We could not merely hear the hooves, but the horses' blowing and panting.

I asked out of politeness, although the answer was hardly important, 'How many?'

'The first wave, about thirty horsemen. But there's a big crowd, on foot, a mile behind.'

I myself turned as it is a commander's privilege to watch what goes on. The horses were coming on, at a slow trot, and it did not look as if they could actually manage that any more. I could see footmen with pikes running between them, clinging to the stirrups. A good tactic to try, I thought, the next time we have to chase the Heathen. Then I took a longer look at the horsemen, and that was not pleasant. They too were all carrying pikes, and with their feet in stirrups they would fight like Theodore. I realised for the first time how frightening we Iron Men must be in the Island when we bore down on the Heathen. If we copied this new tactic, there might be some way of countering it, but if they took it up before we did . . . A long-term investment, I reflected, is of little use in staving off imminent bankruptcy.

'Look after the Lady,' I told Taberon. 'See her into the ship.' I ought to have told him, fight for her to the end, and if it seems the Franks will take her, kill her. But looking at my sister's son and in my mind seeing him hacked like a carcase on a hook, I told him instead, 'If they come about you, then surrender with the Lady and go with her into the Heathen camp. She will protect you.'

I then drew up my battle-line, with the Badon boys in the pack plus Gwion as lock. Leision I sent to stand off, and Taberon to partner him. I took up my usual specialist position at silly long stop, close enough to control the action but far enough back to let me carry home the news of defeat.

As for Oslaf, I told him, 'Go to deep third man and lie well back in case they make a break against the head.'

'Don't know about that,' he said in the usual stubborn way of the Pagans. 'I usually go midfield, sweeper on the right.'

'Well, if you cling to your wicked ways, choose your own path to Hell. Just stand fast and sell your life dearly if you have to like the rest of us. I don't think we'll cost them very much, considering the hangovers you all have from last night. Can you hear that noise across the river? It's a different lot of them coming up, and if we have luck they'll collide before we get involved.'

'Shouldn't be too difficult,' said Gwion, coming down at last. 'Now they've stopped, the infantry are falling down with the effort of keeping up with the cavalry, and the horses are blown and sweaty. The footmen that can stand are all putting their heads between their legs to be sick. Most of the horsemen are sneezing like mad and wiping their noses with the ends of their cloaks. Probably from sleeping out of doors last night when they're not used to it.'

'Then prepare to sell your lives,' I ordered.

Gwion shouted, 'Remember the word is, "Up and Under"! Then do your duty!'

'All right to say "Up and Under",' grumbled Gleisiad, 'but what does it mean?'

'I've told you often enough. When we break you go right.'

'Which way is right?'

'Oh, for the Saints' sake! Follow me when we break.'

'Back to the ship, is it then?' Gleisiad asked with some show of interest at last. 'Because I'm getting out of this as soon as I can.'

So with my gallant men trained to a hair and thirsting to be at the enemy, I prepared for the encounter. The horsemen had stopped in fact quite near to us, but nobody there showed any eagerness to come close, either. I stepped forward and faced the threatening hooves.

'All hail, Great Agaric, humble vassal and faithless servant of the King of the Franks. I, Morvran King of Gwent and vassal to no man, welcome you to our departure feast.' I spoke in the common tongue of the Heathen. I hoped he would misunderstand or refuse our feast since we had nothing to offer so proud a man.

'You evil man, you wizard,' he screamed in reply, 'you have killed Theodore, the mountain man, our friend who brought us our swords and silken clothes. You have taken from his castle his gold and women and silk shirts and dancing girls and wine and concubines and the strange beasts that were his familiars and—'

'By no means,' I answered as calmly and slowly as I could, since it was clear from the movement at the back of the crowd that the longer we talked the smaller would be the force we faced. 'The castle is full of gold and jewels and wine and cloth, and from the smoke that rises it is clear that your comrades are already taking your shares. Surely you ought to be facing the other way, as most of your bodyguard are doing, and moving to guard the right flank of your king, unless you are hoping that those Franks and the Goths will kill each other and leave you to rule over all Gaul.'

I paused for rhetorical effect, and Oslaf leaped in, intoning in a grandiose way, 'I speak as a king, Lindsey I hold, to a mere Count—'

'Hit him!' I ordered, but Esau had already done so and sat on his head, Gwion being otherwise engaged on a house-top and able to see many things which he could not very well tell us. While this disturbance occupied our attention, Tatharn stepped forward. I remembered the proverb about the devil you don't know being better than the Saint next door. For he was intent on confirming the curse he had put on Agaric and I settled down to listen for a good half-hour as I expected.

But Agaric immediately began to scream, 'Greek! Image worshipper! Arian! Heretic! Pelagian!' Which last two in my country are rather compliments than otherwise. His men, what were left of them, joined in with strained voices, calling on Saint Loki and Saint Freya, these being strangers to me in that guise. When I could I tried to return to my original train of speech.

'It is true that I killed Theodore who was my friend, but it was in battle and therefore no sin and as he wished, and we gave him a proper funeral and a fine wake. And none of us has taken anything except that each of us has brought away the cup from which he drank and the plate from which he ate and the napkin of the feast to tie up his chin at death.'

'That death will be soon!' shouted Agaric, and both his remaining followers squeaked their agreement. They were having difficulty in controlling their horses, and I saw why. Out of the nearest clump of trees came the dragon, poor little bewildered morsel, and he ran straight at us. I felt Bees in the Summer Meadow stir out of jealousy, for only Caliburn was eight times quenched having been heated in a dragon's breath and then cooled in his blood. But it seemed that Agaric's horse did not like the smell of dragons because he reared and screamed and toppled over into the roadway. The dragon in passing saved the Count the trouble of disengaging his feet from the stirrups and seized him by the leg. He dragged Agaric down towards the river and into it, where both disappeared under the water. My men were very worried in case the poor dragon had drowned, but I was able to discourage Gleisiad and Kimokh in my usual fashion from going to dive to rescue it.

Gwion came down from the house roof, and ran to me with the news of the battle which was opening a couple of miles to the north. But we had no time to listen. Oslaf had got up from the ground where

Esau had been holding him. He ran over and seized the bridle of Agaric's horse, which was now on his feet. While we watched he swung himself into the saddle but from the wrong side which almost had him off again.

'Farewell to you all,' he said, 'and I wish you a smooth voyage home for the Lady's sake. For myself, I will go and join in the fun. It is not fitting that one Odin-born should wait the convenience of a mere king, or even of three kings. I think that the Frank King will win this battle only if I will help him, and from that I will gain gold and favour and come home to face you all across the steel and the linden wood.'

Taberon, always mindful of the needs of justice, handed up Oslaf's bundle with his sword and the two silver spoons tied up in it. We did not want that with us in case there was a curse on it that Tatharn had not put there. Oslaf did not put on his mail. Instead he peeled off his silk shirt, so that all could see the ridge of hair down his back which to them proclaimed his royalty. I remembered how the Heathen in the Island would go absolutely berserk and come at us half naked, and I pitied the Burgundians and the Vandals.

Oslaf rode off towards the noise of battle. We got ourselves into the ship and settled the Lady beneath her canopy. When we were all in our places I took the steering oar myself and cast off into the stream.

The Badon boys objected strongly when I told them that we had enough food to reach Armorica and there we would stop first. I pointed out that after what we had done in Bordigala we would not be as welcome there as before and that Tolosa was no great shakes. I quelled the mutiny in my normal fashion having no difficulty after pointing out that Genista would certainly want one-tenth of what we were carrying as harbour dues.

'But I wanted to see Bezant,' Taberon complained.

'So did I, and all the rest of us. But there is no pressing need to go there now, or even to Ravenn. We have what we came for. We have learned that there is trouble enough near home without going far afield for it, and I at least have learned a great deal about my friends and my enemies. And we all have learned that the weather in Gaul is horrible, sun, sun, sun, nothing but sun and never a day of rain. Now, Taberon, you want to learn to be a king. Take the steering oar, and bring us down the river. I will, for a time, take my ease beneath the canopy and talk with the Lady.'

VIII

So we went out to the salt sea. By the prayers of Tatharn and the aid of Saint Dylan Son of the Wave who was martyred by being forced to drink nothing but fresh water, we had a wind from the southwest and a placid sea and blue skies. It was all too like the horrid weather of Gaul where there was not a day of cloud when we all yearned for it.

When we were far enough to the northward to sight the beautiful Island and to pass between it and the land, I took the steering oar myself and turned to starboard.

'Yonder,' I announced, 'is the land of Esmeralda, which is the best part of Armorica. Here I know of a long beach of sand, as splendid as the beach between Avan and Margam. We can run up ashore there to scrape our bottom, and rest from our labours for a few days.'

Tatharn became very angry. 'I cannot waste my precious time sitting on a beach in this frightful sun. I am needed in the Island: I can feel it in my bones, having little blood for the purpose. Get out my millstone.'

It took a great deal of unpacking and restowing to find it, so that at one point Tatharn accused the Badon boys of stealing it to sell for the favours of a baker's wife in Bordigala. But with much straining we had it out and balanced on the upper strake amidships where Tatharn wanted it, and the ship heeled dangerously to port so that everyone moved over to the starboard side without being told. Tatharn also found his oak staff, that fathom of oak with a bronze ferrule.

The Saint then recited several Psalms, chosen as far as we could tell at random from those he remembered. Then he heaved the millstone out into the water and stood on it where it floated. He hung his bag of belongings around his neck, including the golden vessels from the castle, and with the staff in his right hand and never a word of farewell he paddled away to the north as fast as a porpoise. We were about a day's sail from land.

We that were left felt lighter and more comfortable for the lack of such a stern sermonising Saint. We turned to starboard and in the early evening ran the ship high up on a beach and got our goods out of her. We built bowers of branches for ourselves as we would do in a havod up in the summer hills.

Next day the people of the place came down to us, speaking not a Heathen language or even Gaulish which is not much better but a debased version of our own language, like Cornish. They brought us not only wine but the more welcome cider, pleasant as honeycakes, and they brought honeycakes as well, and fat pork, both farmed and wild, and fowls and eggs and salt butter and oatcakes and all the other delicacies of civilised life which we had missed so badly. In return for our gracious acceptance of these gifts so natural to our status and dignity we allowed the lads of the village to lift all the cargo out of the vessel while we gave what entertainment we could to the girls of the place.

Later, other personages from all over Armorica, kings and lords and their great ladies, came to us, and went, finding we had little they could rob us of, and even that little never left unguarded. Stealing one sword is easy, but getting away with a bundle of twenty tied together and greased and wrapped in sacking is another matter. There also came a variety of bards, chaired or not. Kian spent the first few days walking on the seashore completing his verses on the Death of Arthur, all lies of course, but inspired lies and in proper meter. When he was finished, he let me be the first to hear it.

I objected, 'But Arthur did not die in battle, and we all know it. He did not fight with Mordred. Mordred is the Soul of Honour, the perfect King of Justice and Honesty, and everyone knows that too. None of this is true!'

'What has poetry to do with the truth?' Kian asked me. 'When you use one word rather than another because it fits better the meter and the rhyme and the alliteration, you give up the petty details of the truth, but you exalt the spirit of poetry. The first aim of man demanded by God is not, as Tatharn and the priests will preach, to tell the truth, but to make poetry which alone will be immortal. The bards of Armorica shall come and we will hold a session. You may sit with us in your chair, if we can borrow one for the occasion.'

'But you swore and all the bards of the world have sworn, to uphold the Truth against the World,' I reminded him.

'Which is more important? The Truth, or the Unity of the Island? Who will fight for the memory of a pig stealer? It is necessary that Arthur should have died in battle for that Unity, to bring others to secure it. The greater the shame of the fact, the greater must be the glory of the fiction.'

So the bards did come, great names like Syrth and Sothakh and Tail, true descendants in spirit of the first great Archdruid Ysbwriel and I walked on the beach, afraid of witchcraft. My absence was noticed.

Kian did sing his song of the Death of Arthur, and was much acclaimed. Only now did some of the bards acknowledge that Arthur was indeed dead, although others insisted that he was only gone into hiding and might return at any moment. Nevertheless, they voted Kian a chair and he was settled into the one they had brought for me.

Kian was very pleased and as soon as the session was over he got drunk and told me, now speaking as an equal since we were both admitted bards, 'Whether I sing the truth or not it is my song that will be remembered for ever and not your facts or your service or your lost kingdom.'

It is a mark of my royal dignity that I did not kill him there and then, but I was not as drunk as he was.

While we thus quarrelled about the meaning of truth, Gwion and Leision and the Badon boys went out hunting in a marsh that is in that country called Gwerant, where the people make salt. They took deer and duck, which is natural. But in the sandhills behind the beach they found a strange kind of hare, rather small and with longer ears, which live in holes in the ground and not in nests on the surface. They went very well roasted with a bit of pork. They might do well at Margam.

Small boys and even grown men, fishermen and the like, came to look at our ship which seemed to them like something out of a legend, and to learn about her by helping to make her fit to go to sea again. Among the most eager of these were the local youths who thus did not see my own people making fast friends of the girls of the country. So we got the bottom scraped and the cargo restowed and the ship back into the water again on the cheap.

As for myself, I had a bower built where the Lady might lie at her ease on the great coverlet she had crocheted from golden silk to bring away with her, and watch the porpoises out at sea and the gulls and the butterflies which were caught when the little spiders spun their webs. And I sat with her, and we shared conversation and jokes, nonsense and mutual attentions as the poet says. Both by day and by night.

Interlude 11: The Weaving

The ship's canopy was pitched upon a green bank overlooking the beach. The woman sat under it, in her bower bright with hangings from the deep storehouse of Theodore. They hung together, the golden silks of Bezant, the striped linens from Alexandria with the homespun shawls of Armorica, so that the sun should not spoil her whiteness.

Her fingers were busy upon her cushion as the sailors and the Armorican youths completed their scouring of the ship's hull. Husks of barnacles and sea-wrack were borne away by the black-haired chattering girls, to be dumped upon the shore. Fresh water was hauled in leather buckets from sweet wells to refresh the voyage home.

And at every point, the cloven-faced man with the limp, directing the toil, telling each party what was expected of them. Like the leaders of her own people, he did not disdain to move among his men with courtesy, wit and command. Such a man would have made a good steward, except this one had the scars of a warrior upon his body and had known war as a king. She knew that beneath his shirt, he bore the proof that he went to Votan by way of Buddog the Bitch, by the bristle of the red crest that she had caressed from the nape of his neck to the end of his spine.

He caught the arm of one of the Armorican girls to fill his cup, with a quip that caused the girl to giggle. The cup poised to drink, he caught her eye, unafraid now these many nights to hold her gaze. With two hands about the silver cup, as she had once seen Melvas uphold the sacred vessel upon the Island of Saints, he brought her water. Sun-glints netted the surface. She laid her hands over his as she drank, catching a stray drop with the tip of her tongue. He drank after her, emptying the cup.

Her ears were accustomed now to the sound of his language. She understood the cheerful sailors, eager for their homes. She acknowledged his coming overseas to find her.

As he limped back to directing the toil, around his shoulders, clear to her eyes, the mantle of the elder lineage hung. It was a weaving such as many a woman had made down the generations. To her hands it had come, to make the peace-weaving.

Eager hands pushed the ship down the silver sands into the waters. The giggling girls of Arrmorica drew down the canopy, exclaiming over the strange smoothness of the silks, undoing the knots that held their shawls and the foreign coverings together.

Then he came limping back to escort her to the ship, helping her climb the rope ladder, his hand behind her legs until she was handed up aloft.

The sun shone clear upon the dark blue waters. The coast of the Island of the Mighty was so near, maybe half a day's sailing. Only a line of clouds demarked its shores.

It could not now be long before the completion of the weaving.

Chapter 11

Northward

I

I had climbed with Constant up the Ring of Chancton. There were more kings with us than had come to the Funeral. I had no other companion. Taberon had gone off to Emlyn in Cardi country where Tegai's father was building a new castle to hold that hub of the universe and centre of all activity. He had taken to her the two pieces of booty he had brought from the Castle of Montgai: a cloak of silk in a soft grey colour, and a ring made of lodestone with a crystal of adamant set in it the size of his thumbnail. These wonders were much admired, and people came to see them from *yards* around.

It was Tatharn who had called the kings together, landing before us since he had gone direct back to the lagoon and walked on from there. We had caught a bad wind and come past the back end of Cornwall before we could turn to starboard and up the Channel.

Constant had asked me, 'I suppose you have been to the land of strange meats and ate there food cooked by angels?'

'If it is the food you are thinking of then I would not recommend you to go to Gaul, since there is not a bit of salted butter in the place, not even to spread on oatcake under the honey. Better go to Ireland. How is Igerna? We still have a jar of the dandelion-and-elderflower left for her.'

'A widower it is I am now, didn't you know? Igerna was eaten by a wolf on the Feast of the Assumption.'

'A wolf? In August?'

'You think it was easy to arrange? And the amount I had to pay to Dubrig the Bishop who was passing! Let me tell you that it may be young that he is but so holy that you could smell him a mile off and I think that it was him the wolf would have preferred. But there, considering what my last wife's relatives did to my predecessor, any sacrifice is justified in the interests of the Unity of the Island.'

'And what did they do?'

'Why, it was the Irish who killed Arthur.'

And in the Table when everybody had settled down and come to order, which took some time since not everybody realised that it was Constant who thought that he was the head of the Table, and such doubt would not have occurred if Arthur had been there, he repeated, 'It was the Irish who killed Arthur.'

I insisted, 'There is no more truth in that than there is in Kian's song which you all listened to after the dinner last night, and a good thing it was that Mordred has not come. In any case, I know who killed Arthur.'

'Does it matter who killed Arthur?' asked Bedwyr. 'Is that not all over and done with?'

'Yes,' I told him. 'It does matter as long as we worship the Truth against the World, as long as we believe that the Word Was God. Let us review what we have learned. Arthur was plotting what any of you would call treason to the Unity of the Island. There was no place for the duke while there was no war. But he was still mad with the love of power, of Empery for its own sake. He could be duke in this Island, but never king, being a bastard. There was a rightful emperor in Bezant. But there was Ireland, which was never Roman. He was always having the bards sing his favourite tale, how Macsen Wledig took all the young men of the Island from Segont, and went into Gaul to fight the Ravenn Emperor and conquer him. He would do the same thing, he would go into Ireland. The Kings of the Island would not go, not on his terms, he knew that before asking. So he would take the Heathen.'

'No, surely not the Heathen,' objected Lot.

'Yes, the Heathen. They were constantly sending messengers to arrange terms, to see how they should take Deva from us, and take Segont from my family, so that they could cross the seas to Ireland unhindered. Two came to him in Caerwent, when we last gathered there, and my people caught them under the walls and killed them. So, we may ask, who was the most likely to kill Arthur? Yes, I admit the Irish had cause, but had they the wit? There were others, with more cunning. Who engaged the axe thrower to do his deadly work? Who was afraid that Arthur would raise an army among the Heathen and take it elsewhere, not to Ireland? Into Gaul, maybe? The Heathen would never notice the difference, both countries being quite unciv-ilised, only Gaul is weaker and has more booty. The Kings of Cornwall consider all Gaul to be their private property which at the moment they do not control. Was it the Corns? Was it you, Gormant?'

'Me? No, why should it be me?'

'Gormant, who came up through the woods unchallenged that night, and could have spoken to anyone, bought anyone. Who was eager to have Arthur dead and the new Duke someone out of your own pocket? Was it you, Gormant? There were others. The Franks would not like to see an army out of the Island come into Gaul where everyone knows about Arthur, about his power and skill in war. Or the Kings of Armorig. Or was it the Bezant Emperor who is even now reconquering the Ravenn Empire and Gaul? They all had reason to distrust Arthur or to see him dead.'

'You can talk as you like,' said Bedwyr, 'but we have no evidence against anyone. We are all judges, we can see that.'

'We have evidence against all of them,' I rounded on him. 'On the body of the axe thrower, I found jewels. He wore the armbands of a prince of Armorig, a gold ring with the eagle badge of the Bezant Emperor, a brooch of precious bronze in the shape of the bees of the King of the Franks. Any of those could have been the reward for this deed. I may say that they are all now in the treasury of Caerwent. Were these jewels the price of blood, or the badges of high officers in some Household? Somebody paid the axe thrower, at any rate, and someone had authority over him.'

In the tone of someone who *knew* and could not be persuaded otherwise, Constant ruled, 'It was the Irish.'

'Arthur was killed,' I told them, 'at that time and at that place, for those jewels, so that someone could have another jewel, the greatest jewel of Arthur's treasury, of his life. While he lived no other man could touch it. The author of this crime had heard of this jewel, had come to see it for himself. Without heed for the final consequences, he had loaded his creature with gold and gems, which he was so bold as to wear openly in my own Hall on the night before, enchanted with magic cakes and strange smoke, he went out to kill the Duke in the middle of his own Household. No sane man, unbewitched, would have done that. But the prime mover, the thief, was safe away, we all saw him go. At his leisure he could send his servants to fetch away *his* jewel, now unguarded.'

'And now you have brought back the jewel from the toad's head,' said Gareth. 'And have you brought back the poison with it? Kian's verses will tell us what such a jewel can do in setting brother against brother. Have you returned, Morvran, a toad now yourself?'

'Kian has betrayed the whole spirit of poetry,' I objected, 'and therefore what he says is unreliable and need not be brought into the discussion. All he says is lies, we now know well. Arthur was not killed for reasons of high policy, although many policies were altered by his death. Arthur was killed where he was killed and when, simply because Theodore wanted the woman for his last few months, when she knew he had only those few months to live. And he had no concern whatever with the Unity of the Island.'

'The evidence?' asked Bedwyr. 'Simply that you found the woman in Theodore's castle, brought, you think, in Theodore's ship? And that the killer also happened to have come in Theodore's ship? Simply coincidence.'

'No, there is nothing here.' Constant tried to sum up as Arthur used to do. 'Nothing implicates the Irish. No one knows the Irish as I do. The lack of connection is clear proof that the Irish planned it all. We must sail to invade Ireland.'

'I agree with the Great Duke,' said Bedwyr.

'What?' I demanded. 'Do you accept *him* as Great Duke, Bedwyr? You, of all people? You accept something as true simply because you want it to be true, because you want to curry favour with someone else who wants it to be true, against the weight of all the evidence?'

'Oh, Morvran, Morvran,' said Bedwyr, 'Morvran the Ugly, Morvran the Bard, Morvran the Wanderer. There have been many changes in this island since you went gallivanting off across the seas for your pleasure. We must have a Great Duke or the Island cannot survive. Constant has had no truck with the Heathen, so we can accept him as the Great Duke, no matter how stupid he may seem. We kings all accept him, except for your family, Morvran, and they are all waiting for your agreement. And if you do not agree, they will cast you off.'

'The Votadini,' I reminded him, '*and* Mordred.'

'It was very convenient for Mordred and for other people to have Arthur dead at this time,' said Bedwyr coldly.

I could understand now that whoever might be accepted as the Great Duke, yet the power would remain in Bedwyr's hands.

'And this new verse of Kian's, once it gets sung round the market places by the lesser bards – why, in a few years' time there will be no one who remembers that Arthur died as you say he died. By then Mordred too will be discredited as Arthur never will be. But even if the kings accept Constant as Great Duke and follow him, yet their men will not follow them to fight under Constant if they believe that the last Great Duke was killed stealing a pig. They must believe that a Great Duke is always a man of honour, of glory. No Great Duke can be killed except in battle, no Great Duke can be killed by a foreign enemy, but only by the treachery of his nearest kin. It is part of the definition of a Great Duke – any properly trained bard will tell you that, will he not, King Morvran the Bard?'

'Mordred,' I mused, 'was always the very Soul of Honour. He could betray no one.'

'The House of the Votadini, Morvran – they are waiting for you to lead them, or to abandon them. Join us, and establish the Unity of the Island, or you are lost.'

I had a moment to reflect that if this had been Mordred arguing, then I would have agreed. But this was only Bedwyr. And Constant. I recovered myself, and told them, 'Yet the Unity of the Island – not only the unity of the Christians but the unity of the Heathens with them as well – to that I have brought back the key. I tell you this: Oslaf has gone to tell all the Kingdoms of the Heathen. There will be no war in the Island. I have brought back the woman, the hostage, the Gwenevere, from whom the Bretwalda will be born to rule all the Island.'

I clapped my hands.

They had been waiting below the crest and now came up through the banks of the Ring. Leision walked before her, sword unsheathed. Kian and Taberon came close behind her. Taberon was still a little out of breath. It must be only this morning that he had got back from Emlyn's new castle. He wore a new Cardi shirt double-hooped in gold on black. Kian wore his usual green and yellow, and Leision had on his new scarlet shirt out of the ship.

But she was clothed as we all remembered her, in a gown from neck to ankles in one piece of golden silk, with gold at her head and gold at her feet and a golden girdle. She came as a cloud, floating. All the kings rose at the sight.

Only Constant did not rise. He continued as if there had never been any interruption in his argument, as indeed there had been none in his train of thought which was impervious to any outside influence. 'We merely have to decide who will marry her now, from the eligible bachelors and widowers in our midst. And therefore who will be the father of the Bretwalda. I myself am no longer married and I put myself at the disposal—'

But Lot of Norroway was jumping up and down in fury and screaming, 'We'll have none of that nonsense. She brought the curse of Bladulf on us, and we will have no peace while she lives, the slayer of Arthur. If we do not kill her ourselves, than we ought to send her back to the Heathen and let them sacrifice her to their idols.'

'If we send her back to her own people,' argued Gormant, and it was a change to hear any sense out of that mouth, 'they will have a son from her by God knows who and combine against us, claiming the Treaty, and for all we know, some of our kings will join them. Mordred may well do that. Keep her safe here, in a fortress, and they will have to worry about her sons when we have grown strong enough to claim our own again. Let them have no peace of mind. Keep her safe here.'

'Dead is safest,' and this was Selgi, who had a kingdom in that place of beauty, Bagilht. He still held to the school of the oyster shells.

Dunwal of Eiddin hissed behind him, 'This woman sent for her paramour to kill Arthur, and then she fled to him. It was brave of Morvran to go to bring her back, but we would be better off if she were still there in the south.'

'She did not—'

But I was shouted down by a chorus of lesser kings, 'Kill her! Kill ... her! Kill ... her! Killkillkill—!

The noise continued for some time. While it was going on, the Gwenevere motioned to Kian to help her from the horse. As had been usual in Camelot, Leision threw down his russet cloak before her feet so that she need not touch the soil. She stood on it, and then motioned again. Taberon took down a bundle which was tied behind her saddle. She undid the knot and shook out on the centre of the Table before herself a great scarlet coverlet of crocheted silken net. And she stepped forward on to it, to face the kings in their anger.

But Melvas rose. He had been silent till now, sitting on his throne with a Saint of the Isle of Glass at either hand, one carrying the golden chalice and one the paten which Tatharn had brought back to him from Gaul as a gift for the Church in the Mere. Melvas stopped all the shouting with one sweep of his staff that had all the little kings ducking in case they were beheaded, and the taller they were the lower they ducked; it was good to see.

But before he could speak into the silence which he had ordained, it was the Gwenevere who said, 'I am With Child.'

There was a sound like the passing of a wind overhead, a mixture of *Ah!* and *Ha!* and *Aha?* of interrogation and disbelief and dissatisfaction. This was the first time that many of the kings had heard her voice, for she never spoke in the Hall of Camelot at dinner, and had no business in the disputes of politics or at the Tables. Besides, Arthur was proud of her, his booty under the Treaty, and did not like it that she should talk to other men whatever their rank. It was therefore enough to bring a note of wonder that she was a light soprano, with not too much force behind the words, but yet a carrying voice. She said no more.

I thought at first, it is too soon, she cannot know yet, there is not enough time since the beach opposite the Beautiful Island or the funeral night in Gaul. But then I knew, sadly, no, no, no, it is someone else.

I said low into the silence the words that created silence, 'The child will be Bretwalda, heir to the whole Island, heir to Arthur, heir to

Bladulf. The child, whoever the father may be, is Count of Britain, Lord of all the Island in its unity under the Bezant Emperor.'

Surprisingly it was Dunwal who saw the necessity, and asked the Table, 'Should we, then, kill the Bretwalda?'

There was a long silence. There were many who thought in their hearts that indeed we ought at once to kill the Bretwalda, and her who bore him, so that the Heathen should have no say within their kingdoms, and that no mere Gwletic should be sovereign over their persons. But they were ashamed to say it aloud, to propose that we should in fact now kill this woman who stood alone on her web coverlet before the kings and abbots and prefects of cities, who were met to debate the Unity of the Island.

At last Melvas offered, not so much in earnest but in case we should be kept there past his dinner-time, and so simply to move the debate along quickly to the point where he knew it would come in the end, 'Let me take her. I will keep her safe till the child is born.'

'As you did before,' Constant jeered.

'That was different. Then she was a person of no value, a mere relict that nobody wanted to have in their charge. I kept her then in the Abbey out of mere charity that she should not starve to death or wander home, mad and appealing to her own people who might come to avenge her. But this is more important than charity, it is a matter of politics, of statecraft, of the Unity of the Island.'

'Back again then to the Glass Island in the Apple Land?' asked Bedwyr. Then of course, her care would be a concern of his, and probably the cost also, since I could see none of the other kings offering to pay for it. I could keep calm only as long as I looked at this as a judge, as if it were brought to me as a case for decision, the care of a posthumous child, whose parentage was known only by common repute since the mother refused to speak. As this mother would refuse to speak on the matter, would never name whoever it might be was the father, whether it was Theodore or one of his men or someone she had picked up by the way, Agaric or some other Pagan. I only knew it could not be Arthur, or myself, nor any of the men from my ship.

I was trying to remember the complete table of precedents which I had once learned, and all the amendments I had been forced to make under the pressure of facts. Would the mother, if unmarried, or the child be entitled to all the father's possessions? If the father was dead, and the woman had before or since been married to someone else, which of these men's possessions would be the subject of the litigation? Would the sequence of the deaths in time be relevant? Could she claim both the possessions of her husband on her own account, and the possessions of the other man on the child's? Could the child inherit from his real father's sisters as if he were legitimate? Or from the sisters of his mother's husband?

I knew I was not the only man thinking like this. Each of the kings here was used to judging in such cases, or at least in expressing them clearly so that the arguments to follow should keep to the point. What else did the people keep a king to do? And worse was yet to come. Could the child sue us, in person or through a nearest relation, for the restitution of his father's property, or for the restitution of his mother's late husband's property, or for both? Would Bedwyr and I alone, or all the kings who had been present at the funeral, be liable for the vast wealth of Camelot, which we had destroyed? Would I alone be liable to the unborn child for the wealth of the Castle of Montgai which I had not stayed to defend but left to the Franks and the Burgundians?

Nothing could come of this but trouble. I felt tempted to deny now the death of Arthur and to proclaim that he was yet alive and in hiding somewhere. Now I really missed him: it had been our custom as judges when we had a case too difficult for us to ask him for his opinion, out of courtesy, as it were, and then to act on it. There was no obligation on us, but it did make life simpler to have a higher authority to blame mistakes on. I could not think of taking the case to Constant: nobody would accept his judgements.

But Melvas was still speaking. 'Once I depended on the Kings of the Island to keep her safe. It was not wise to maintain her so near the sea. There is beyond Glevum a house of Holy Women, who might be Saints were their work not so demanding of cleanliness and order, for they are the persons who copy out Bibles and Missals and other works of piety. They are not allowed to know how to read, only how to form letters, for if they know what it is they are writing out they may be tempted to alter it, and that is the way to ruin. They live in an old house of the

Romans, and I have people there who till the ground and feed them more lavishly than we eat in the Glass Island. There she would be more contented, and her taste for living on soups and slops and custards satisfied. Since these sisters guard themselves closely to maintain their own holiness and virginity there would be little chance of sea rovers coming so far inland from Ireland or from Gaul or wherever you may expect it and taking her away, and less temptation to her to go.'

'Why women for this task?' asked Kai.

'Cheaper,' answered Melvas. 'Cost a little but not too much. Men copyists are ruinous.'

'And who would pay for all this?' asked Bedwyr.

'Holy Church would pay, if nobody else has a penny to spare,' answered Melvas. 'Has anyone a better plan?'

There was no answer, the school of oyster shells feeling themselves outvoted, although they still had a lingering feeling that on the grounds of economy their scheme was preferable although politically out of favour. Melvas offered to put his arm around the Gwenevere's shoulders.

'*I* will help her down the slope,' said Leision, 'as *I* helped her up. I will return to my home in Glevum and from there I will guard her.'

And then he sneezed. All the kings there knew who he was, and knew his reputation and what was his virtue. And everybody laughed. That broke the tension, there was no argument, the woman would be left to Melvas, and other uses could be found for oyster shells.

II

Some of the lesser kings stood up as if to leave. I called out, 'Wait! We have not finished. I have been far into Gaul, and I have brought back things which we need. I have brought back a shipload of wine, even though it is only Gaulish stuff, as I now know, yet it is just what Theodore always brought us. Who of you has ever done that just by sailing out of the Island? It is a pity that no one else will be able to do it, because soon after we got the ship back to Porthskewett and grounded her, she broke her back, simply splitting in half in the middle as we unloaded her forward half. But we got almost everything out.

'There are six jars of very fine wine, guaranteed from Bezant, which Theodore had kept for his own, and which we shall drink together, all the kings, tonight. There are, as far as I can count, sword-blades to give three to every king who has come here, and ten extra to each of those who sent bronze. And to each of my companions who were not of my household, the Badon boys, I have given a bale of scarlet shirts, to distribute among their friends in their own cities, all fresh from Bezant. And to each of the Badon boys I have given a sword, six times quenched, well hilted in ivory and scabbarded, and a coat of mail. So in Corin and in Ratae, in Viricon and in London, the bravest of the brave will strut in the armour of the Empire, and their friends will follow all scarlet-shirted.

'More! I have seen a new way of fighting on horseback. The Heathen do it. They no longer ride up to the enemy and throw javelins at them to break the line before the infantry move in. Their cavalry—'

'What cavalry?' demanded Kai. 'The Heathen have no cavalry. They are afraid of horses; only Christian men ride on horses to war.'

'In Gaul the Heathen ride horses, and fight in this new way, and I can tell you it is most terrifying—'

'To a lame man,' someone shouted.

I ignored him. 'They do not throw javelins. They use stirrups—'

'Like women!' and there was some disorder.

'They use stirrups which lets them carry their pikes on horseback and they use them to thrust with. Their cavalry ride right up to the infantry and thrust them down. I have faced a man thus armed, in the Gothic manner. No men on foot can stand against those horsemen armed with long pikes without the aid of God and the Saints, which we can depend on. Let each of you go home and practise riding while holding your pikes, and thrusting with them while keeping your feet in stirrups. Train all your Households. Then when we meet the Heathen as we must in the spring—'

Constant interrupted me, 'The problem is not how to scatter the Heathen when we met them, but to bring them to battle. They come at us in small bands, burn farms and flee again with what they can steal. We must tempt them to come out in a great army in battle array, as they did at Badon, so that we can have them all together on a killing ground. You have been away a long time, Morvran, enjoying yourself all the summer, while we have been hard at work planning this.'

'Where do you mean to fight? Where will you concentrate? Where have you been bringing together the food for an army? How many days, how many men? And remounts – have you seen to gathering the new horses?'

'Oh, be your age, Morvran. All that nonsense – Arthur never bothered about it, he just collected his men and rode at the enemy and cut them down. And they fled before him.'

'If you have too few men, and those hungry, then you will flee before them.'

'And there is no need for all this nonsense about collecting horses, and making pikes. It is a fact of nature that the Heathen are worse than we are, man for man, and cannot stand against us. Everybody knows that. So we will not go to war with all the kings and their Households on horses as before. We will go into battle on foot and face them with the steel over our shields. All this winter we will call the young men from the farms into the cities and train them to fight the Heathen with their swords and axes and beat them into submission. We will have our men in Badon, Glevum, Ratae, London, Carliol, Corin. By the spring we will have a great army and take the Island again. If you are afraid to come with us, then stay at home till we find a better King for Gwent. War is a game for young men, Morvran the Ugly, Morvran the Old. But we will keep Theodore's finest wine for our victory feast.'

'That is folly,' I protested. 'At least teach them the new tactic of Up and Under.'

But all the kings were walking away, down the slope. Only Bedwyr murmured as he passed by, 'Aunty Flossie died in July. Of measles. The third time. Be careful, Morvran boy.'

III

The Table was all empty, the kings had gone. I asked Taberon, 'What will you do this winter? Will you stay in Caerwent with Mabon and train the young men how to fight like Heathen, on horses with stirrups and pike or even on foot with sword and shield and the new tactics?

Or will you go into the Cardi country and live in Emlyn's Hall to court Tegai? Or will you come up to Skirrid with me? You are a grown man now, with sword and mail fairly won. You can choose what you will do. Do not ask me for advice, certainly not for a decision.'

I hoped that he would choose to come with me, but he answered, 'I choose. If we are to fight like Heathen, we must live like the Heathen, we must think like the Heathen, we must *be* Heathen. We may even have to learn their language to talk it to each other. Some choose that. I choose for myself. I will take my sword and my mail, my helm and my pike, I will put my saddle with the stirrups on the back of a horse if I can steal one, and I will go beyond Glevum.'

'With her?'

'What else would you have me do? Would you let her go alone? Who else would you send to guard her? Bedwyr?'

'Alone?'

'Kian will be with me.'

Interlude 12: The Golden Valley

The Lady, the Gwenevere, walked in the aisles and cloisters of the old Roman house in the Golden Valley, east of Glevum. She walked among the Writing Sisters as they copied the words they could not understand.

The Lady looked over their shoulders. She could read what they had written. She could read well enough, both in the runes of her own people and in the Roman letters. The writers did not know that she could read. There were many things that she could do that she had told no one.

Among the letters the Writers drew the long sea beasts, the sea serpents, coiling around the letters so that it was impossible to tell which tail belonged to which head. The serpents, both land and sea, feared the spiders. The Writers thought that she liked to see the sea serpents and the land dragons. But she was planning downfall.

The Writers fed her well, as she liked. They brought her custards, cream and honey. They brought her soups made from dripping steaks, and soups of fat mutton with the stars of fat floating on the top. All this she ate to make the child strong and cunning. So her mother had carried her.

In the short days she worked with her needle and her hook, with her bobbins and her threads, and during the long nights she recited what she knew so that the child might hear it. And she waited for the child.

When the days were getting longer, the child came.

And the Iron Men came.

Chapter 12

The Last Table

I

I spent another winter in the hills above Raglan. We folded the sheep and killed the beasts we could not feed. We salted the meat and also the pork. With that and the game of the winter we ate well. We would not have to feed Arthur and his Household in the coming year. Constant we would not feed, however much he ranted.

I was there because the Brecon men were not entirely settled, and we watched for sheep-stealers from the north. It was known that I stayed there and therefore we kept all our sheep that winter, the Brecon men finding it easier pickings among the Cardi farmers. If they stole from me it was no profit: if they stole in other kingdoms, then I claimed my share. Better than dandelions.

When the days were markedly longer than the nights and we were expecting to begin lambing soon, Taberon came to me over the hills from Glevum, through the snows which were half melted and which were therefore harder to ride over. No careful man would travel during the thaw. He came to me in the sheepfold, after we had brought in the first lamb of the year.

He said, instead of greeting, 'It is not only sheep.'

I looked at him, a man now, to be treated as one, to speak few words with and those all serious. I asked, 'Already?'

'She is in labour. Early. She is afraid. She told me to bring you, and anyone who will ride with you.'

'Kian?'

'He is waiting there. He must be planning to shave, because he spends his time honing Butter in a Lordly Dish, that was Hennin's sword.'

'I have ordered fresh horses.'

'We are going to Glevum?'

'I am going to Glevum. I will go the quickest way, not by Caerwent. You are going first to Avan across the mountains. Call on my Principal Officers of State, to bring all the young men they have, armed to fight on horseback and each one with a spare horse. Bring them to Caerwent, and call on Mabon with the same message. Until you meet Mabon, you will act for me, tell Gwenki and Gwion that any orders you give must be treated as mine. Meet me at Glevum. If I have moved on, then follow me. My path will be obvious.'

II

He went west. I rode east over the hills to the Wye, and then through the wolf woods to the Severn and north of east again along the bank to Glevum. It was a long journey and a lonely one. I never saw even a shepherd, but I did not expect one at that time of year, or a wolf, for wolves were as wise as I.

I came to the gates of the city in a midmorning. The mist had already risen from the river. The leaves of the gate were hanging open. I stood outside a while, and then I shouted for the porter.

There was no answer, only a half-hearted echo off the walls as if stones had more life than people. There was no noise at all, no hubbub in the town, no smoke of fires, no pigs outside, no chickens. This empty town was not what Constant had promised. He claimed that he could order all the kings to lead their people to winter inside the cities. Plainly here the people were wiser than the Great Duke, as I had been. There might be a family or two inside the walls. I entered.

Just inside the gate my horse shied. There was a dead man in the gutter, a rusted knife. He had been there some time in the winter rain:

animals had been at his face. No one could ever tell who he had been except by his clothes. I knew that shirt, it was one I had brought myself from Theodore's cellar. Was this Leision, clutching at what he could save with no thought of its value? Leision had brought a knife from Theodore's castle.

I rode on through the streets. I looked into a house here and there, where my horses, one pack, one saddle, cropped the grass that sprouted up between the slabs of the street. The dead lay in them where they had fallen or lain down to die. They were hunched over tables, a few in doorways or on the street. Most were in beds or curled up by cold fireplaces. They were gnawed or eaten a little, by rats or birds or mice, but otherwise dried by the cold of the winter. The thaw was only just beginning: the stench was not yet overpowering. It was still not worth the wolves' while to venture inside to scavenge.

I crossed the city and saw no one, not alive. Not men nor women nor children, and no horses or dogs or pigs. Only an occasional cat. My own horses were as nervous as I was. I came out of the town to the Theatre. Smoke curled up from behind the ramparts. I stood outside and shouted.

It was a long time before anyone answered, long enough to recite the four Psalms for the Help of God. I hoped to be safe from the arrow by night or the pestilence that flieth in the noonday. When someone did come, I thought it was a very old man till I recognised him. He had once been on guard over Oslaf's tent in Camlann: my age or a little younger. He walked stiffly towards me, as if he were half dead with the cold.

'Go away, King Morvran,' he shouted. At least, he tried to shout but although we were near enough to hold a conversation I could hardly hear him. 'You brought it here.'

'Brought what?'

'It is the White Death, the sneezing death. It is this that killed one man in two in the towns the year before Hengist came and left the country empty for the Pagans. Now it has come again – not the small plague we had in our youth and we thought that serious enough, when it killed not more than one man in ten and most of us had it lightly, a mere kiss, and then recovered. But it came last winter when Constant had filled the city and it was like the breath of a devil, stopping our mouths with foulness. Hardly any are left alive, only those who had the small plague in our youth.'

'It is the same plague. In those days it would come into a family in a winter house, or to shepherds in a havod in the hills in the summer. All would fall ill, but few died, and nobody had it twice. Like apoplexy.'

'This time not one in ten lived, and the rest died. The first to die were those who wore the scarlet shirts that you brought them. Curse you for that, King Morvran.'

'I did not know. I have been all the winter in a farm up in the hills and have seen no strangers. Do not blame me for what has happened in the cities. Blame Constant who brought you all into the towns. In the hills we were safe.'

'We are destroyed,' the man said, and turned his back on me, went again into the Theatre. As I rode on, I could hear his voice in my mind: 'We are destroyed, utterly destroyed.' And in the language of the hills: 'Divetha . . . divetha . . .'

III

I knew the road to the Golden Valley, a lovely place sheltered from the winds. I turned towards the House of the Writers. I remembered one night we had bivouacked there, in the year before Badon, but now there was no danger from the Pagans so far west. The plague had not been here, Taberon would have mentioned it. And clearly he had not gone into Glevum as he rode to warn me. The farms by the way were deserted, the people had all gone into Glevum for the winter and perished. It was dusk when I came to the turn in the path.

The gate was open, the rickyard and stables and byre were empty. I looked into the tan house where the calf skins still hung, waiting to be scraped into vellum. In the cloister the lines of working ledgers were still there where they caught the light, but the pen boxes, the bundles of quills and the knives for trimming them or for cutting the vellum, the wooden straight edges, were gone. The floor was swept clean of scraps of discarded leather. The stools were toppled, the copyists were gone.

The Holy Women, the Writers, had left in a fair hurry, but not in terror. They had taken the leaves they were working on, and the Bibles and Missals they were copying. They had taken their inks and colours, especially the precious fragments of lapis lazuli and of cinnamon. They had taken their bedding, their cups and platters, their pots and all the kitchen gear. They had driven off their cattle and their pigs. They probably had another house, or a farm somewhere in the deep woods, and there they could stay safe till the troubles were over. But where was Kian? Where were the Lady and the child? Without a huntsman, without Gwion, say, or even Leision if he were still alive, I could do little to find them.

I went into the stables. There was a place where bales of hay were stacked to make a small shelter, a room almost. There were a couple of pieces of wooden ware, and I found a string which I thought was from a harp. This was where Taberon and Kian must have slept, and eaten what the Writing Sisters gave them. Still, there was nothing left. Taberon had, I knew, gathered up all his belongings, his campaigning outfit, into a bundle and had it with him when he came to me. If Kian had done the same then he had not been carried off by force. There was nothing in any room in the house which seemed to have been left by a mother and child seized and carried away.

So someone had come to the House and persuaded the Gwenevere to come away with them, and had warned the Holy Women, the Writers, to hide where they could return easily. Bedwyr would not have taken them away, for this was in what Bedwyr claimed as his country, since it had once been Lawnslot's. He would have come here with his Household, as he had come down into the Heath to meet me, and they would have stayed here. Who then could have taken away the Gwenevere and her child and her bard? There had been no fighting, Butter in a Lordly Dish was not here. Kian had left armed.

It might have been the Pagans. If Oslaf had come, somebody that Kian knew and to some extent trusted, and somebody that the Gwenevere would welcome as a king, and if Oslaf had been able to restrain his own men, which I had no doubt he could, being a man of a short temper and a terrifying appearance, then it might just be the Pagans.

I went outside the gates again. The ground was cut up by hooves, half hidden by cattle tracks which had at first deceived me. Horses meant Christians. I tracked a little way till the pattern became clear. Perhaps half a dozen horsemen had come to the gate, with a few light horses. A little way off, a score more, perhaps, had waited for them. They had come away again, and four of the spare horses now kept together in pairs, one pair behind the other. So they had come mounted, and gone away again with the Gwenevere in a horse-litter, and perhaps the baby. And they had gone northwest. Then the Writers had left, with their cows. This might mean anybody, anyone at all, but not Bedwyr.

I left the house and I went after them. The tracks were clear through the woods, but then they reached an old paved road, Roman work, and here it was difficult to follow them. But there were a few clues, like some horse droppings each way, and those to the north seemed fresher than those to the south. So I headed north, into the dusk.

After another mile, when it was dark, I saw a light. There was a small thatched house, with a barn on the road itself. The stone paving made a good base for a farmyard.

An old woman outside the house door was cooking something on a wood fire. Hearing me, she called out loudly.

An old man came out of the house, carrying a rusted pike. 'I know you, King Morvran. I was at Badon.'

'With the same spear, I should think. Is there no one younger to carry it?'

'Not any more. Do you want to stay the night?'

'If there is enough food, enough fodder.'

'Oh, there is food enough,' the old man told me. 'But no one to eat it or to milk the cows which is why we work on into the dark. Salt beef and bacon and cheese for forty people through the winter and only two left alive to eat it.'

'It was the sneezing death,' the old woman went on as she bustled to get food ready for the three of us. She poured me cider while the old man took my horses to the barn, leaving my bundle with my mail inside the house. 'What will become of us? We went into Glevum, but the young died, and only the old remain. There are no young men left to carry spears, or girls for them to marry. Who will plough this year? And if we plough and grow the oats, who will keep it from the Pagans?'

There was no answer to this. I asked, 'Have you seen anyone pass on this road?'

'No one,' said the old man, but his wife corrected him.

'You saw no one because you were in the woods, trying to bring in the cows, but I saw them pass, two days ago.'

'Were there many of them?'

'Oh, many, very many, beyond counting, like the stars in the sky.'

'I counted tracks of twenty horses. Were there as many as that?'

'Oh, yes, twelve or twenty or more than that even. With javelins and helmets and swords and armour. All looking as fierce as maggots, and I was afraid, but they went by, riding as hard as their horses would go, so they did not see me.'

'Only horsemen?'

'Yes, but they had one of those big box things slung between four horses, the kind that great ladies ride in.'

'A horse-litter?'

'Is that what they are called?'

'So they are properly called. Did you see anything else?'

'I think one man was a king, a great king. They carried a dragon on a pole behind him. You don't see many of those in a lifetime. And another man was riding close to the litter, and he was a bard. He carried a harp, that's why I think he was a bard. But he had a sword as well, so perhaps he wasn't.'

'They did not say who they were?'

'I told you, they did not see me, I hid. They said nothing to me.'

'But their colours? What colours did they wear? What colours on their scarves on their shirts?'

'No colours, no colour at all.'

And that was all I could get from her. She was sorry about it, but she could not remember any more. She had not taken much interest. I did not bully her, there was no need for that. She was one of my own nation, she wanted to tell me what she knew, and she knew very little. She was too honest to deceive me, even for my own comfort. She had done what she could for the Unity of the Island. I honoured her age.

When I left in the morning, I asked them again, was there anything else they had seen. And this time, the old man said, 'Nothing, not seen. But I heard things.'

'Heard?'

'You never asked what we'd heard,' the old woman defended him.

He went on, 'It were the night before last, the night after those horsemen went by. In the middle of the night, we heard more horses, a lot more, and a clashing noise of mail and spears and spurs. And about dawn, a noise of shouting. From a great way away.'

I did not ask how far, for a man like this a mile was a long distance. They knelt for a king's blessing. I pondered as I went. The case was not desperate. A large party with a woman and a child in a litter could not travel fast. If Kian was riding with her, still armed, then she was safe. And the second party, riding to join them, and shouting greetings when they met, it might be anybody. But . . . no colours?

The paved road would fork three ways at the salt pools. One branch would go due north to Bannae, another northeast to Ratae. But they would not go northwest, that would bring them to Viricon, where Mordred barred their way.

A little short of the forks, I found them. I smelled them first, before my horses did, even. There was a change in the air, and the stench of burnt-out fires, dead ashes, spoilt food, horse droppings, man droppings, the smell of an encampment, the smell of a campaign. And I smelled worse. I dismounted and went softly off the road into the bushes. It was scrubland with stunted trees.

I saw a wolf. He looked at me, took little notice, went on tearing at what he was scavenging. It was one corpse among many, a whole heap of bodies, cut and hacked with swords, stripped of their mail and even of their clothes. This had been a desperate defence, and a doomed one. I struck at the wolf with my pike. He moved away grudgingly, but not too far. There was plenty for him, scattered around.

I heard a voice calling, 'Morvran! King Morvran!'

He lay in the bushes, hunched across another body. Both were naked but for shredded rags.

'Kian! Who has done this? Was it the Pagans from the Island, or were they Franks brought in? Not Irish – it must have been Oslaf's doing.'

When he had drunk my cider, he answered,

'It was our people. Christians, Kings of the Island.'

'Christians took the Lady, the Gwenevere? And then the Pagans attacked you?'

'No. There were no Pagans. They were all Christians.'

'Christians killing Christians? And within the Island? That is impossible. Not in the Unity of the Island. And to hurt a bard – that is impossible. The Bard in his Awen is not to be harmed. It is the law.'

'Worse,' Kian told me. 'I kept the crows from his eyes.'

I gently moved him from the body beneath. It was a wiry man, my age. His head was horribly mutilated. Men had hacked it with axes, broken it apart. No one would ever venerate that head. The eyes still stared. But I knew the scars on that body, I knew where each one was gained, always for the Unity of the Island. Now the Unity of the Island was gone.

The rags on the body were black. The riders wore no colours. Black is not a colour.

'Oh, Mordred,' I lamented formally, calling his praise titles as was proper, 'oh, magnanimous King of Radnor, Prefect of Viricon, Lord of the Deva, last of the Tribunes of Britain, noblest of the Romans, Soul of Honour, heir to Vortigern the Proud, the Generous, the Unfortunate. Kian! Who has done this?'

'They wore the colours of half the Kings of Britain: Badon, Calleva, Orkney, Norroway, Cornwall . . . No boys, all grown men, over thirty. They came at us out of the mists at dawn. I had no time even to break my riding strings. Someone swung at me with an axe. When I recovered my sight, I was as you see me now. They took from me my sword, Butter in a Lordly Dish, undrawn, unblooded.'

'The first thing to do,' I said, 'is to tie up this leg. The second time you have bled for the Lady. Mourning is never useful.'

But he grumbled on, 'They smashed my harp.'

His skin was hot to the touch on hands and face. I wondered if he would ever stand to use a harp again. I tied up the worst wounds with my scarf. Then I had to get him across the horse's back, to lift the sounder leg over so that he could ride after a fashion, but painfully.

'Mordred,' he protested, 'Mordred, not the wolves for a king. And somewhere there is Lawnslot.'

'I will send to bury them,' I consoled Kian. 'But where is the Lady? And where is her son, the Gwletic? The Bretwalda that is to be, the heir to the United Island?'

'The Gwletic? The Bretwalda?' And he laughed through his pain like a ghost in the thatch in November. 'The child is a girl. All wasted. All to begin again.'

'A girl?' I could not think.

As we rode, Kian told me the story in short sentences, very low on the bardic virtues which do not withstand pain. 'The baby was born a week ago. The next day, Mordred came, and his Household. They must have been waiting close by. I think the Holy Women sent to tell them. The House of Vortigern, not the House of Uther. Bedwyr did not know that they favoured the elder line. Mordred said she would not be safe, not with a girl. I understood. We had to agree. He would not have struck a bard. We put the Lady in a horse-litter. We were riding for Viricon. We were attacked. You have seen it all.

'When we found a house, we had the people of the place wash out the wounds with hot water and with cider, and bind them with linen, and splint the limbs. I did what Korlam had taught me, and found maggots to sew into the wounds to clean them.'

Yes, they told me, the two old men and the five old women, they had seen the other horsemen with all their gay colours go by with the horse-litter. Where? This road led to Ratae, where else would they be going? They let me have food and cider, brewed or grown by young men now dead for others, now dead, to eat. All these farms were dead. There was ploughing now to finish and the oats and barley to be sown and no one to do it. There was no one to ride on with me, no one to ride back with a message, no one to bury the Royal dead. The old people only asked me to keep the Pagans away, to send Arthur soon. That I could not do.

IV

In the red morning I rode towards Ratae, to find bard-killers, king-killers, men without scruples. By dusk I was standing before the

Theatre at Ratae, outside the walls. The old town was long abandoned. At Glevum, grass grew in the streets: at Ratae, it was oak trees.

At the Theatre gate, there was a cluster of huts, mere bothies of leafless branches, thatched with damped hay. I guessed two hundred men at least outside the Theatre, perhaps half as many more inside. The men who came running to meet me wore the colours of half the Kings of Britain, but mostly of the House of Uther and a few hangers-on. Then they fell back to let Hennin through with half a dozen followers, wearing Cornish colours. Hennin was wearing his old mail stripped from Kian, and much improved by the services of Korlam, a first-rate saddler, while we were in Gaul, and Butter in a Lordly Dish was hanging at his side, the riding strings untied.

'Croak, croak, flycatcher,' I taunted him. 'Hop along and take me to your governor.'

'You may wait here at the gate,' he told me, 'while I find out if the Great Duke of War and Peace, Supreme Governor of the Island, incomparable in battle, will think you worthy of his attention, or whether he will tell you to go away and not waste his time.'

'I'll not wait on a bloodstained upstart,' I shouted, and dismounting began to stride toward the gate, which was too low to ride through. But Hennin whistled and I felt myself held by hands which were not loving. There was no disrespect, no violence or jeering, because after all, you never know. But they were firm and their hands were hard and bruising. These men had already killed the wisest and most honourable of all the Kings of Britain; they would not scruple to do the same to me.

The place was in disorder with heaps of rubbish all about. There were fires lit wherever a man wished, and cooking going on, some pots boiling over and others just starting. Men were drinking and gambling, some dressed for riding and others for war. In one corner there was a fight starting between two Orkney men and a couple of toughs from Badon. I have seen good armies in my time and bad armies, and this by all standards was a bad army, would be hard to spread out, hard to control in anything more complicated than a single line, impossible to handle and keep together in a retreat. This army could perhaps attack once, and run away once, and then dissolve. And I could only think, it would not be like this if only Arthur were here.

Hennin took his time. He strolled back from the Hall, whistling.

'The Great Duke, out of his magnanimity and kindness, says that you may attend him in the Great Hall of Camlann, and watch himself and the other Great Kings of the Island dine in state. And I among them. But first . . .'

He had a long thong of bull's hide, not a whip, but as good as a lash to the soul. He tied down Bees in the Summer Meadow by her hilt in the scabbard.

'This will spare you the humiliation, as Constant the Great Duke says, and who am I to criticise his foolish whims, of coming into his gracious presence without a sword. But you will not be able to draw it without much trouble and plenty of warning. A sword is now a mere ornament for you, old man.'

I was released although the two ruffians kept close to me, close enough for me to smell the beer on their breaths. I walked into the Theatre. Camlann was pitched within the walls, among a scatter of houses, and the tents of the other kings left little clear ground. I did not trouble myself to read all the banners as I walked. There was a large wooden Hall, an old one, built long ago, and not used lately, with the thatch ragged and the walls gappy to let in the wind and the rain. But the weather had not kept out the spiders who had almost made a ceiling of webs beneath the thatch and who brushed my face as I came through the door. Thus trailing behind a loon, a lout, a windbag, a murderer, I came into the presence of the self-proclaimed Great Duke Constant, wife-killer. Ah well, like man, like master.

Constant was seated at his ease at the head of several tables pushed together to make a square, a round table not being possible. It was covered by an immense coverlet of crocheted net, black in colour. I knew then that she was there.

There were other kings with him. Lot and Gareth I had expected, and some others of no real importance, but all of the House of Uther. No king was there from the House of Vortigern, nor any of my own House of the Votadini, nor Beli of Man, nor Dunwal. Gormant, as I expected, sat at Constant's right hand, and Bedwyr to my surprise sat to the right of him again. I do not remember who was at Constant's left hand, but I have a feeling it was Selgi of Bagilht, who was a sword pointed at the heart of the land, equally threatening Deva and Elmet and Viricon and Segont. It was a very large table, and not so many sitting at it.

Lacking direction, I sat down at the foot, where there was a big empty space, at least two swords' lengths between me and my neighbours. I kept my hands beneath the table and did my best with the bull-thong. There is a trick to such a knot: alas, I did not know it.

They had eaten and drunk well, that was obvious, and Constant had the boar's right thigh, the hero's portion. They offered me nothing, not bread nor salt which I would have refused, nor cider, which I could have done with. They deprived me of the dignity of refusal. They knew me too well. Nor did they give me a chance to speak first.

As soon as I sat down, Bedwyr said, 'Sit still, Morvran the Ugly, the Old, the Weak, and hear what the Great Duke has to say to you.' I could tell from his tone that Bedwyr saw himself as having the real power, and giving the orders to the Great Duke, and that Constant did not altogether agree that he was a mere figurehead. 'Do what he tells you, and then you have a chance that we may leave you alive to moulder away in Raglan while a real man holds Caerwent and the coasts of the Severn Sea on both sides.'

'Constant can no more be a Great Duke than I can be a cocklewoman, and that is more than I can say for you, Bedwyr.'

'So, in other words, said Mordred. And where is Mordred now?'

The kings at the Table, and Hennin in their midst, all laughed as if they were hiding from me some triumph they were sharing.

I answered, 'I have seen Mordred and I know that now he is happier in his blood and honour than any of you can be. This was a thing never known in the island that a king should be killed by a Christian in Christian lands and left unburied for the wolves and the crows. Or left unavenged.'

Hennin sniggered, but the others sat still and blank-faced. I knew how to take the bubbles out of their cider.

I went on, 'There were others dead, too. I saw Lawnslot's body in the mud. You battered all their heads so that we could not venerate them to go into the west before us. Where these great and good men have gone alone, who are we to refuse to go? And Lawnslot – he ruled the Apple Land. Was that land worth killing him for, Bedwyr? And kill one king, then kill five, a dozen, kill us all? Will you kill all, then, Constant? Will you kill Gormant the last – or the first?'

They sat glum and silent.

Then Lot argued, with little conviction in his voice, 'Have you not killed enough, Morvran?' He felt he had a right to get his words in; he was near to his own stronghold. 'You brought the plague to us in the scarlet shirts, and it went through all the cities where the young men were preparing for war. It killed all the young men and the young women, and all the children too. The Island is a land of old men. Only in the hills and the wild places are there any young men left to bear arms.'

'Will you blame me for one bad winter in Glevum?'

'And in Calleva, and in Corin, in Carliol and in London. We have only one hope, Morvran, the birth of a new Bretwalda whom the Pagans will accept. This child does not matter, if it live or die. The next time, she will throw a boy. That is why we have taken the woman. We could not let Mordred become the father of the Bretwalda.'

'There is hope,' I argued. 'When Belesar has taken back Italy for the Bezant Emperor and rages through Gaul, then he will send armies to help us.'

'Dubrig the Saint has returned from Rome,' said Selgi. 'He went there to be made a bishop in some holy place. Belesar is shut up by siege in Rome Town. The sneezing death rages like an army through all the towns of Italy and in Bezant itself. The Emperor will never come. We must look after ourselves.'

'It cannot be,' I protested. If there was no hope, how could I live?

'It is true,' said Bedwyr, and him I must believe. 'There is no choice for us but to make the best use we can of the men we have and prepare for the last defence.'

'The last defence? Of Ratae? Of Cornwall? Of Camlann, wherever it may be? There is no call for defence. The Island is large and our people are scattered, we can mass at any point. We must defend the Island as Arthur did. We must form a force of mounted men with stirrups to their saddles and carrying their pikes on horseback, Iron Men, to raid here and there rapidly, to harass the Heathen and terrify them and bewilder them and bring them at last to seek peace.'

'We must consider what we must defend.' Constant had not spoken for some time, but was patient, as if he were a teacher with a stupid class. 'There are limits to our strength, and therefore limits to the land we can hold. There is no hope of recovering the land we have lost. We must abandon the rest of the Island, all Logres, we must leave London—'

'London? No!' I shouted it. 'We must hold London, the flower of cities, the heart of our realm!'

'London must go, and Calleva too. We can hold only a small group of cities, Carliol, Glevum, Durovern, Badon. We can defend the rest of the country from that line of fortresses. Ratae is the key to that line, the centre, that is why we have come here. We have already brought the Heathen to battle, all of them in the north and the east. They are coming against us here, a mighty army. We will fight on foot and scatter them. We can defend the land to the west, and threaten the east. We can call back all the Christians in the cities which will then be empty in Logres.'

'The people will not come.'

'Oh, they will come. We will compel them to come in,' Constant went on. He had almost the authority of a Duke. If I had not known him for an evil man and a schemer I might even have obeyed him. I looked straight at him, and then at each of the others. They stared back.

Only Bedwyr dropped his eyes and would not meet mine. Constant shivered. The goose had walked over his grave. He and Bedwyr were wondering, who next for death? If I could argue well enough each would be wondering, which of themselves was next for death? Constant would not stand too long for Bedwyr's bullying.

To cover this, Constant called, 'Wine! Let the kings drink!'

She entered. She was as stately as she always had been, in Camelot or in the castle of Montgai. She glowed in the torchlight like a wax candle: she was as splendid as a walrus' tooth. She brought with her into the silence the sound of the waterfalls under Plynlimmon or the grasshoppers of the night in Gaul. She brought with her the scent of the lily and the broom and the meadowsweet. I bowed my head before her beauty and thought, how long since the night of the funeral, since the feast at

Montgai. I saw the other kings, even Hennin, look at her with the eyes of desire, the difference with them being only that each now thought that desire might be slaked.

She carried a bronze jug, and there were two servants, Hennin's men, with a jar to fill it. Constant waved his arms at her and shouted as to a stupid scullion, 'Not that stuff, you fool. Where is that good wine, that you brought from Theodore's cellars, so good that you even had Mordred bring it with you? Men, bring the jars with the green T mark. Now is the time to open it. We have a new king!'

They brought the marked jars and Constant poured out the first jug on the floor, the wine as costly as the vessel. It was refilled, and all the cups were filled from it. Then Constant stood up and shouted, 'Hail Hennin, King of Gwent!'

Ah, I thought, but who will recognise Hennin? Not my kindred, the Votadini of Segont, not Emlyn of the Cardis, not Gilloman and Gilmour, not even the scamps of Brecon, who obey me only because I thrashed them.

I sneered at Constant, 'Welcome him in the spoils I brought?'

'To the victor, the spoils.'

'And what else is the Lady – is she among the spoils?'

'What else? My spoils, to give away as I please, or to keep for my own use and pleasure.'

'Poor Igerna. And the Gwenevere's son? Booty too?'

'When she has a son. What if she only spawned a daughter? There are years of breeding in her yet. When she is ready to breed again, I will have her in my bed for my pleasure, although they say these blonde pieces are little fun, don't know how to move. Then my son will rule over all the Heathen of Logres and all the Kings of the Island. So it does not matter if we give up Logres for a little while.'

'And after that? What of her?'

'Oh, there are other kings who deserve a swig of the good wine, well cooled, once uncorked.'

Hennin sniggered. She had now poured for all. First for Constant, then for Hennin, and after that for all the kings, not heeding the talk, although I knew she understood it. I knew what languages she was skilled in; no one else did. She passed me by, filled no cup for me, although I smelled the turpentine: and another smell.

After the toast, Constant made a face. 'Not as sweet as I expected. Never mind, I know now we are better served than the Emperor. Take the rest of this jar, and the other jars, and share it out among the brave lads outside in the citadel. Let every man drink as kings drink and take heart before we ride to London to bring in the young men.'

'You will bring all the people out of London?' I asked.

'No, only the young men capable of fighting.'

'And the others? The women and the children and the men too old to fight or march? Will you leave them to the mercy of the Heathen?'

'It will probably be necessary. The exigencies of the military situation demand an apparent lack of sympathy with individuals, so that later we may enjoy the Unity of the Island and the memory of those we loved, in one faith under one Duke. And in better wine than you brought us.'

He's been working at it, I thought, he's been trying to learn to talk like a commander, like a politician, if there is any difference. He has already learned that there is no morality as effective as hypocrisy, no motive as pure as greed and ambition, no one will condemn you for those since they are faults in all men.

But then Bedwyr broke in, 'My feet are cold, boy, too cold.'

'Then stamp and get them warm!' Constant told him more roughly than Arthur would ever have spoken to a scullion.

Bedwyr in protest only said, 'Cold, damn cold.'

'Well, so are mine,' said Constant. 'Have some more wine, bring more wine, warm up the wine.'

But nobody came to pour him his wine. She, the Gwenevere, the great Lady of Camelot, of Montgai, stood near me, not moving. I heard her breathing, short and light. Constant reached forward towards her, clumsily, seeming almost unable to hold out his cup. I looked around the table. The other kings, Gormant, Kai, Kaw, Selgi, all of them, sat there on the bench, putting their weight forward on their elbows, or leaning back clutching at their stomachs. They looked at Constant, at each other, in ignorant concern, in inability to stir. Then Hennin fell forward, his face in his dish, and did not move.

'What's happening?' asked Lot. 'What's up with you all?' Then, 'We are betrayed, betrayed, undone by magic . . .'

He put his palms on the table, tried to push himself upright. He could not manage it. Then he fell backwards off the bench.

I stood and told those who could still hear, 'You drank the Imperial wine, Constant. The Bezant Emperor sent it to Theodore, who did not drink, but left it to me and my men. We did not drink, but brought it home for the common good. The Heathen are known for their treachery at table, as Vortigern found, and beyond the seas it is a common fault. The Greeks are famous for their gifts.'

The cocks can chant their requiem, I thought, and the crows can close their eyes. Why should any of them have better burial than Mordred? Who was this man who would give orders to the Kings of Britain, who would treat free men as if they were his slaves? Let the hemlock be his drink, and the foxglove his food and the bitter poppy his potion. Let him lie. This would never have happened if Arthur had been here.

V

I went out of Camlann into the courtyard of the Theatre. There were dead men lying around everywhere in and out of the tents and at the gates. Now a horseman rode in over them. I fumbled with the knots in the bull thong. Then I heard a voice and knew it.

I replied, 'You are not too late, Taberon. Are you alone?'

'No, my King. I have a few men with me, Gwion and Korlam and others.'

'Not Esau?'

'I left him to guard the kingdom. But Keinakh is with me.'

'Where is Mabon?'

'He is dead. All the young men who came into Caerwent for the winter, the young men I spent the summer with in the havods, all, all are dead. I found a few shepherds from the hill farms to come with me, raw lads, not trained to arms. Gwenki went into Caerwent to do what he could in healing and burying. There was no healing. Tatharn absolved many and then died. Gwenki brought him out of the city and buried him in his Lhan with his pewter chalice and his paten on his breast. Then Gwenki went back into the city and shut the gates behind him to keep in the plague. All are now dead. They were not buried.'

Taberon did not weep. A king has no time to weep and he would soon be a king in Gwent, a young man still alive to lead the young lads to come.

I could lament. 'So it is true. The great race of the Island is gone.'

'Not all gone, Morvran. We few are left. But will there not be war now, when the Heathen learn how few we are?'

'We who did not die by the plague owe a death to those who suffered, a death by the axe or the sword. Let us not grudge it if it is necessary. Keinakh, you will find swords in the Hall, and many here in the courtyard. Strip the dead, have no pity, we need the weapons. One sword is Kian's, you will find it on Hennin – Butter in a Lordly Dish; he has bought her twice with blood shed for the Lady.'

'We can gather an army,' said Gwion. 'Not a great host, but an army of sorts, and we can give them mail and pikes and the high saddles with stirrups. Where shall we meet?'

'We must hold Calleva if we are to save London. There we can face the Heathen if they come out of Thameshead or up the Solent out of Vecta.'

'Watch Thameshead,' Gwion argued. 'There is a tale that Oslaf has been seen there, riding a great horse, the only one of his nation with the courage to do that. We will have to fight him sometime and the sooner the better. Do not go as far as Calleva.'

'Scatter,' I told my people. 'Find the men. See if there is anyone left who loves God and Honour more than life. We must fight even if we cannot hope to win. It is the gesa that birth and God and the Saints lay on us. Let us meet then somewhere near Corin a week after the next full moon.'

The Lady came to us out of the Hall. She walked as a ship swims on calm water, slowly and in majesty. She passed by me and went to Taberon where he sat his horse. She reached up one hand to him and he looked dumbly at what she gave him. It was his carved spoon of yew wood. She reached up to him again with both her hands. She gave him the bundle that had been at her breast. She stepped back again and bowed to him, both head and knee. She went back from us again into the web-hung Hall of Camlann: she passed from us into the dark.

Keinakh called from the ramparts, 'Gwion ought to come and see this. There are campfires in the north, from one end of the heavens to the other. This is a bigger army than the Burgundians brought. It will not be comfortable here in the morning.'

'Ratae is lost whether Constant holds it or not,' I reflected. Arthur had promised it away, and now the Heathen were coming to claim it.

Taberon asked me, 'Where now?' He held the baby clumsily in the crook of his arm.

I ordered him, 'Flee and take her somewhere safe. There is now a greater gesa laid on you than any debt to king or House or army. Go into the mountains and leave her there with someone you can trust. Guard that child all your life, for in her veins runs the blood that shall rule the whole Island in ages to come. Go by Viricon and by Deva to carry the news. Stop at farms, where the women will find milk some-where. Send all the men of Radnor out of their sheepfolds to fight with me. Come back yourself if you think it politic. I, your Uncle and your King, command you.'

He said, 'I will take her to Tegai and leave her there.' A good start to a family, I thought, to take home a baby to be reared. Then he asked, 'What is her name?'

I answered, 'She is the beginning of the House of Theodore.'

He repeated it in our own more civilised language: 'Tudor. Tudor.'

Two or three of our men rode after him. Gwion asked again, 'Have you decided where the army is to meet? You have given two or three different places already.'

'Meet me at the Judgement Mound in Arberth, near to the Standing Stones.'

Interlude 13: The Web

The woman listened to the horses go. She turned again to the table. She took the empty seat at the bottom. There was the fresh cup the ugly man had not used. She poured herself wine. She sipped slowly, lazily. She drank now as she chose, she stood or sat as she pleased, at her own choice. This was a strange experience. Never in her life till now had she done as she wished with no thought of court ceremonial, the ceremonial of the Franks, the ceremonial of Bladulf's court, the ceremonial of Camelot, all derived from the ceremonial of Bezant. Up to now she had done all at the whim of others, who passed her from hand to hand, from place to place.

Her task was over. All she had been sent to do was done. She had woven her webs, she had burrowed like a mole, she had cast her spells, and all was accomplished. With her naked mind her only tool, she had settled the Unity of the Island. On her terms, for her people.

Into her web she had called Arthur. And Arthur was dead. Into her web she had called Theodore the Shipman, the Greek. Now Theodore was dead. There would be no more trade for the Welshmen, no more wine or swords. Into her web she had called the ugly man, to bring her back into the Island. Into her web she had called all the Kings of the Island. Now the kings were dead. They had died in conflict. Their unity, the unity of those who still lived, was destroyed for ever. The cities were emptied, there would be no great assaults, her people could move quietly and peacefully into the part of the land they had not held. In time her children would rule the land, all the Island, in unity.

Soon her people, her own family, would come for her. But her task was over, there was nothing left for her to do. She drank.

She was still there when the torches came sweeping over the Theatre wall into the citadel. But that was in the first daylight.

Chapter 13

Departure

Close to the Stones, by the Judgement Mound in Arberth, at dusk I met the Fairy again, the chief one, the old one.

I nodded politely as I passed, and he ordered me, 'Stop! Wait here! And watch!'

His ship lay hove to, a hundred paces away, and about a fathom and a half off the ground. I had not seen it till that moment. A golden staircase led into it, that shimmered in the starlight as if it too partook of the nature of the stars and so was no more substantial than they. My horse seemed content: he cropped grass as we waited. Suddenly he lifted his head, and sniffed the air: then, reassured, he fell again to grazing. They came from the woods by the old way of the gods. They walked the earth now in visible form as they so often walked in our dreams. They had come down from their peaks and out of their caves, from their strongholds and from their prisons. I took off my helm and would have knelt to do them reverence but my companion forbade me.

Without sound or speech he said, 'You are of their nature and of their spirit and of their blood.'

The holy ones, the true children of God, the beloved of the Virgin, passed us by. I knew them each by name and by the symbols they carried.

Saint Taran carried the wheel on which the heavens turn. The lightning flickered in our eyes as he passed, the thunder was in our ears and nowhere else, my horse took no notice. Saint Esus came, all dripping with black water, the noose about his neck and his face looking three ways at once. For he shows us thus that there is truth and there is untruth and there is that which is neither true nor false and such is the nature of the Island. Saint Camul wore the horns of the Bull, and Saint Cernunnos the antlers of the stag, many branching, thousand-pointed. Saint Palug purred from his cat face. Saint Leucad held the hand of Saint Nemeton in his own, and each carried a caduceus of serpents twined round a shaft of yew from the churchyard of Mydhvai. Saint Coccid many-caped carried pike and shield: he would no longer lead us in triumphant war. Saint Lenus led the goose that spreads her wings over booty. I wept, for the days of victory and good living were over: the days of poverty and failure were upon us.

The Holy Ladies, rich-bloused, many-skirted, came too, passing us and going up the golden staircase into the ship. Saint Gwen the triple breasted walked with Saint Epona who wore her saddle on her back and her bridle on her face: and my horse sniffed the empty air as she passed him. Saint Arianrhod showed, point down, her spear of silver, and Saint Blodeuwen moved in the fragrance of her flowers. Behind them, Saint Rhiannon, owl-faced, was almost hidden by her throng of birds.

Last of this host was Saint Nod, the giver of sleep. There was none of them but was shaven from ear to ear and forward, gold-collared and gold-belted, gold-shod that we might know their holiness as they moved among us in our daily tasks: and in their daily tasks which are beyond our understanding. And there was not one of them that did not carry in the hand or wear around the neck or on the brow a sprig of the mightiest plant, thunder-sown, the golden bough, the Mistletoe.

I asked the Fairy, 'When will they return? You are gathering together all the Holy Ones that have held the Island against the Heathen. Without them we are defenceless. Even with them we are hard-pressed. When will they return?'

The Fairy answered, 'Logres and Elmet and Caledon you will lose, and you, the native race of the language of the Angels and of the poetry of God, you will hold only the high hills, and the cliffs of Armorig. But we do not leave you comfortless. The next Holy One is here already, far in Demed. He will yoke you to the plough and drive you like cattle. He will give you pure water to drink and the harsh leeks of affliction to eat and the yellow weeds of the earth for your eyes to build beauty upon. Yet you shall love him and follow him, and worship him when he is gone.'

'How will we know him?'

'By the staff in his hand and by the dove on his shoulder. And by his name that is the name of the sky and of the weather and of the storm. His name is Dewi.'

I wept for the hardships to come. I asked again, 'When will they return? Will they ever return? Will you never bring them back?'

'When your children reach out to travel to the stars, then we will return. And when your children's children have voyaged the stars to seek them, and have found nothing, and no longer dream of leaving earth to find us because we are not where they seek us, or when they seek us – then we will bring again the Holy Ones.'

'But what of us, who need them?'

'Need is not an argument in the logic of the Universe, or in the Gaussian curves of time, twisting this way and that, forward and back. You, Morvran the Ugly, Morvran the Steadfast, will never see them in these summer woods again. You will join them and be of them, and that soon, by a road of anguish. But neither you nor the Kings of the Island will ever ride upon these smooth hills again.'

Now came the kings in holy guise, gold-collared. Caractacus came in his iron chains, and after him Coel, potbellied and cheerful, and Boadicea of the Iceni, driving her chariot without reins or whip. All these wore the Mistletoe. Then without the Mistletoe came Uther Pendragon, arm in arm with Vortigern the Proud, the Generous, the Unfortunate. Behind him came Mordred, all in black, the Soul of Honour, too proud and yet too humble even to claim honour, and Lawnslot carried the train of his garment that it might not be torn or smirched.

Last of all to pass from the earth, gold-spurred, gold-belted, in a gold collar of richness beyond imagining, marched Arthur, alone, Great Duke of War and Peace, pre-eminent of all men in honour and valour and skill.

The Fairy bowed to me, and followed him into the ship. The golden staircase melted into the hull.

The earth flickered, and the dawnlight trembled. There came steady light of roaring brilliance and a great shower of music in a gathering storm, and the Fairies and the Holy Ones passed for ever from my sight.

Now, I knew, all was over. The Unity of the Island is destroyed, and one by one the kingdoms of the great race that remain in Logres will go down before the Heathen. The House of Uther will come to an end as has already the House of Vortigern the Magnanimous, the Unfortunate, the Betrayed. Only we of the House of the Votadini, sons of Cunedha, will remain. We will hold to the mountains and to the Faith of the Saints and to the meters of the bards and to the Language of the Angels. And even we will dwindle in the end to be no more than the house of Theodore.

Before that, I must ride down into the plains about Thameshead. Somewhere out there is Oslaf, who holds my lands of Lindsey against Christ and against me. Him first I must meet across the steel and the linden planks, I must bring him down or die, and thus pay my last *Galanas* to Arthur.

THE END

Glossary

Dramatis Personae

THE NOBLES, KINGS AND THEIR WEAPONS, KNIGHTS, OFFICERS AND MEN

Arthur: the Great Duke of War and Peace, leader of the British forces against the Heathen.

Bells Beneath the Sea is Arthur's axe.

Caliburn, Hard is my Judgement, is Arthur's sword.

Pridwen, Costly is my Smile, is Arthur's battle-shield.

Rhon is Arthur's spear.

Gwynebwrthukhel, Face Against the Heights, is Arthur's shield of state.

Bedwyr: now King of Badon; his sword is Frost in the Morning.

Bees in the Summer Meadow: Morvran's sword, six times quenched.

Bors of Ciren.

Branydh Crowstail.

Butter in a Lordly Dish: Hennin's sword, four times quenched.

Cherries in May: Constant's sword, five times quenched.

Constant: son of Gormant; his sword is Cherries in May.

Crowfeaster: a sword.

Cunedha: son of Morvran's youngest sister Creulon.

Darkness Comes from the East: Theodore's sword, later Taberon's sword, seven times quenched.

Dawn Before Harvest: a sword.

Esau Penpledren: Cook of State.

Frost in the Morning: Bedwyr's sword.

Galar, King: the son of Gorvoledh.

Gildas: the Pre-eminent Chief Bard of the Island.

Gleisiad the Stupid: Morvran's man.

Gleisiad: known as the Salmon from Karliol.

Gormant: co-King of Cornwall with Kador.

Gwenki: Morvran's Smith Royal.

Gwion Lhygadgath: Huntsman at Court and Porter of the Kingdom.

Gwroldeb of Glevum: father of Leision.

Hennin: son of Broga of Cornwall; Gormant's gofer. Also known as Hennin of the Speckled Skin. His sword is Butter in a Lordly Dish.

Kador: the other King of Cornwall; Arthur's half-brother.

Kai: a Knight.

Kaw the Senile of Leodis.

Keinakh: son of Diweirdeb, Carpenter of State, from Kwmtwrkh Ukha.

Kian: son of Gormodiaeth, an apprentice bard.

Kimokh: known as the Lobster from Glevum.

Korlam: son of Kroen, Saddler of Ceremony.

Krank: known as the Crab from Calleva.

Landwaster: Oslaf's sword, seven times quenched.

Lawnslot of Glevum.

Leision: son of Gwroldeb of Glevum, Bedwyr's Huntsman.

Lhyswen: known as the Eel from Ratae.

Mabon: son of Modron, Morvran's eldest sister's son and his heir.

Medyr: a huntsman to Bedwyr Twppo, a courtier.

Melvas: King-Abbot of the Glass Island.

Mordred: King of Radnor, the last of Vortigern's line, Arthur's scout.

Morvran ap Einion: King of Gwent, once King of Lindsey, Lord of Glevissig, Prefect of Kaerwent, whose sword is Bees in the Summer Meadow. He was fostered in Cardigan.

Saer: Arthur's saddler.

Selgi of Bagilht.

Sgilti: Tinker to Arthur.

Synager: Prefect of London.

Taberon: son of Kynoildeb, son of Ceredig who came back from Cattraeth.

Tatharn: a Saint whose Lhan is neaer Kaerwent.

Theodore: son of Ariston the Greek.

Ysbwrial: Archdruid.

THE OUTLANDER KINGS

Beli: King of Man.

Dunwal of Eiddin.

Gareth of Orkney.

Gilloman of the Irish in Menevia.

Gilmour of the Irish in Lheyn.

Leoline of Eryri.

Lot: King of Norroway and Elmet.

Urien of Moray.

THE GWENEVERES

Gwenevere, the First: Ceridwen of the Cauldron, from beyond Solva.

Gwenevere, the Second: Blodeuwen, the Flower Maiden, of Vortigern's line, from Dee.

Gwenevere, the Third: Mair, of the Altar, the Weaver of the North, the stay of Dun Eiddin, sister of Dunwal of Eiddyn, of the Gododdin.

Gwenevere, the Fourth: of the Flaxen Head, or Mam Gwe, Mother of Gossamer: an unnamed Anglian enchantress.

THE WOMEN AND THEIR ATTENDANTS

Creulon: Morvran's sister. Mother of Taberon.

Iarwen: wife of Gwion.

Igerna: wife of Constant.

Keiswyn: Nonna's apprentice.

Nonna the Witch: of Solva.

Tegai: daughter of Emlyn.

THE KINGS, LORDS, EMPERORS OVERSEAS AND THEIR MEN

Agaric: Count of Toulouse.

Almasunth: an Alemanni commander.

Amanita: Agaric's sister.

Belesar of Dar: Belasarius, commander of Justinian of Byzantium.

Bezant Emperor: the Emperor of the Eastern or Byzantine Empire at Constantinople.

Clothair: King of the Franks.

Dietrikh of Beron: Dietrich von Bern (Verona), King of the Goths.

Genista: factotum of Bordigala.

Julius Macrinus: Prefect of Bordigala.

Loucas: Theodore's skipper.

Ravenn Emperor: Emperor of the West or Roman Empire at Ravenna.

Witiges: King of Rome.

THE HEATHEN

Cueldgil: son of Cretta, father of Oslaf.

Oslaf: son of Cueldgil, brother of the Fourth Gwenevere, Envoy.

Sebbald of Northumbria: Envoy.

LEGENDARY CHARACTERS, THE DEAD AND TO COME

Bladulf: the Fourth Gwenevere's father, leader of the Angles, sacker of York.

Boadicea: Boudicca, Queen of the Iceni.

Brutus: the legendary Trojan who took Britain after landing at Totnes.

Buddog the Bitch: Lady of Caledon, Morvran's foremother, who appears in *Votan*.

Caractacus, King: Catevelaunian leader of the British against the Claudian invasion by Rome.

Coel, King: legendary ancestor from Hen Ogledd, or the Old North.

Corunn: unidentified.

Cuchullain: the Hero of Ulster.

Cuedgil: Cretta's Son, father of Oswy, an Angle.

Cunedda: Cunedda ap Edyrn or Cunedda Wledig, ancestral leader who led the Votadini forces and who settled in Gwynedd, North Wales.

Dewi: St David.

Dubrig: Dubricius of Llancarvan, Bishop of Llandaff.

Gwydhno Garanhir: Gwyddno Crane's Legs, ancestral ruler of Cantre'r Gwaelod who is associated with the inundation of lands in Cardigan Bay.

Hengist and Horsa: leaders of the Heathen bridgehead into Britain: also known as 'the Holy Stallion and Mare'.

Maeve: Queen Medbh of Connacht whose bull was stolen by the Ulstermen.

Macsen Wledig: the late fourth-century usurping Emperor, Magnus Maximus, ancestor of Vortigern's children via Severa, his daughter.

Pelagius: the Latin name of Morgan, the early British fifth-century theologian whose views on free will were popular in Britain but regarded as heretical by Orthodox and Roman Christians.

Saint Arianrhod: legendary Welsh divinity of the wheel.

Saint Blodeuwen: legendary Welsh divinity Blodeuwedd, who was turned into an owl.

Saint Camul: legendary Pan-Celtic divinity of war.

Saint Cernunnos, also known as Saint Cernin or Saint Cerun: legendary Pan-Celtic divinity Cernunnos, lord of the animals.

Saint Coccid: legendary Romano-Celtic divinity of war and the woodlands.

Saint Dagda: legendary Irish divinity and a king of the Tuatha de Danaan.

Saint Dylan: legendary Welsh divinity who took to the sea as a baby.

Saint Enodoc: saint who lived as a hermit on the north coast of Cornwall.

Saint Epona: legendary Pan-Celtic divinity of horses.

Saint Esus: legendary Gaulish divinity, to whom human sacrifices were hanged.

Saint Freya: legendary Norse divinity, goddess of magic.

Saint Gwen the triple-breasted: fictitious saint invented by John James to stand for the sainted triple Gwenevere.

Saint Illtud: Arthur's kinsman and saint of Llantwit Major in Glamorganshire.

Saint Lenus: legendary East Gaulish divinity of healing.

Saint Leucad: unidentified.

Saint Loki: legendary Norse divinity, mischief-maker.

Saint Madvalh: St Neot. Madfal is Welsh for newt!

Saint Manannan son of Lear: legendary Pan-Celtic divinity, god of the sea and blessed islands.

Saint Morrigan: legendary Irish divinity of sovereignty and battle.

Saint Nemeton: fictitious saint invented by John James. A nemeton is a Celtic holy place, usually a grove within a wood.

Saint Nod: legendary divinity, Nydd, the giver of sleep.

Saint Palug: legendary monstrous cat that was overcome by Kai.

Saint Rhiannon: legendary Welsh divinity of horses, mistress of the otherworld.

Saint Segamo: legendary Gaulish divinity of war.

Saint Taran: legendary Pan-Celtic divinity of thunder.

Seithenin: steward of the embankment at Cardigan Bay under whose watch the land was inundated.

Teleri: wife of Morvran, killed by the Angles.

Tudor: the dynasty that came to the British throne in 1485, whose name is derived from 'Theodore'.

Uther: Arthur's father, also known as Uther Pendragon.

Vergilius: the Roman poet Virgil, who was believed in the early Middle Ages to be a magician and wonder-worker.

Vortigern: the ruler of Britain who invited in Saxon federate troops to defend Britain in the wake of the Roman withdrawal.

Votadini: also known as Gododdin, the people and region between the Hadrian and Antonine Walls whose capital is Eiddyn, or Edinburgh. In James' book *Votan*, the hero Photinus sleeps with Buddog and sires the rulers of the Votadini lineage.

Votadinus/Votan: Odin, also called Photinus, the main character of John James' book *Votan*.

Ysbwriel map Lhwkh: first of the Pre-eminent Bards.

REFERENCES TO CONCEPTS, EVENTS, PEOPLES AND SONGS

Awen: inspiration that comes upon a poet.

Bretwalda: the Saxons' title for Overlord or Supreme King of Britain.

Cauldron Hymn/Song of the Little Cauldron: 'Sospan Fach' or 'The Little Saucepan', a rugby song.

Ehangwen: Arthur's great tent Hall.

Friesians: people from the Netherlands.

Galanas: the honour-price payable for a death.

Gesa: the Irish term Geis (s.)/Geasa (pl.) is an obligation set upon someone or upon oneself which one is honour-bound to fulfil.

Great Race: the term used by the Saxons, Angles, Jutes &c. to describe their common ancestry and kindred.

Havod: a summer pasturing place where workers live while beasts are grazing.

Hendre: a winter residence.

Hero's Portion: the best cut of the meat, traditionally apportioned to the bravest warrior and a cause of much dissension at feasts.

Hunting of the Black Pig: a song of the quest for the monstrous pig Twrch Trwyth, from 'Culhwch and Olwen' in the *Mabinogion*.

Hwicce: one of the Heathen peoples who finally settled around modern Gloucestershire.

Iron Men, the: the Saxon name for the British warriors in their mail shirts.

Language of the Angels, the: the British tongue of the Cymru, now called 'Welsh' by the English, derived from the Saxon word 'Wealhas' or foreigner.

Lhan: the ecclesiastical enclosure of a saint.

Night of the Long Knives, the: the occasion of the underhand killing of the British nobility by the Saxons at a supposed truce, at which Vortigern alone survived.

Roaming of Gereint, the: a tale better known as 'Gereint and Enid' in the *Mabinogion*, or as Chrétien de Troyes' 'Erec and Enide'.

Saints: holy men and women, whether the blessed dead or the dedicated living.

Three Came Back and Three Hundred in the Wood of Cattraeth: the tale better known as 'The Gododdin' by Aneurin, relating the death of three hundred warriors gathered by the Votadini against the Anglian incursions into what is now Catterick.

The Wedding Hunt of Khilwkh: better known as Culhwch and Olwen.

Wends: barbarian peoples from the Baltic Sea.

White Death, the: viral influenza.

PLACES

Apple Island: Avalon.

Arberth: Narberth, Pembrokeshire, Wales.

Archan: river in Argyll and Bute.

Ardudwy: area of Gwynedd, North Wales.

Armorig: Brittany.

Avan: Afan in Aberavon, Neath, Port Talbot, Glamorgan.

Badon: Badon has been located in a variety of places from Bath in Avon to Badbury Hill Fort in Dorset.

Bamburgh: stronghold city on the Northumbrian coast.

Bannae: Banna or Birdoswald in Cumbria.

Bewelhti: Bedwellty in Monmouthshire.

Bezant: Byzantium.

Bordigala: Bordeaux.

Breze: Breizh, Brittany.

Bro Erekh: Bro Erec, southern Brittany.

Caerwent: also Kaerwent, a town in Gwent, Monmouthshire. The Romans called it Venta Silurum.

Caledon: the Caledonian Forest.

Calleva: Silchester, Hampshire.

Camelot: King Arthur's moveable tent-city.

Camlaan: near Gloucester, Constant's attempt at replicating Camelot.

Cantware: Canterbury.

Carliol: Carlisle, Cumbria.

Castlegai: Castelgaillard, Haute Garonne, France.

Chancton: Chanctonbury Ring, Sussex.

Ciren: Cirencester, Gloucestershire.

Coritan: area of Leicestershire, Nottinghamshire, Lincolnshire and part of South Yorkshire.

Damask: Dalmacia, on the Adriatic Sea.

Demed: Demetia.

Denby of the Fishes: Tenby, Pembrokeshire

Deva: Chester, Cheshire.

Durovern: Durnovaria or Dorchester, Dorset.

Eagle's Nest: Eryri, Snowdon.

Eidal, Yr: Italy.

Elmet: Kingdom covering West Yorkshire.

Esmeralda: Emerald Coast, north Brittany.

Gavenni: Abergavenny.

Glevum: Gloucester, Gloucestershire.

Golden Valley: valley of the River Dore, Herefordshire.

Gwaen-Kae-Gurwen: Gwaunn-cae-Gurwen in Neath, Glamorgan.

Gwent: southeast region of Wales.

Hamwih: Hamwich or Southampton, Hampshire.

Helen's Roads: Sarnau Elen. The roads built by Elen, wife of Macsen Wledig

Hy Brasil: Legendary otherworld in the Western Atlantic.

Island of the Mighty: Britain.

Kaerleon: Caerleon, Newport, Gwent.

Kaerwent: see Caerwent.

Klwyd: Clwyd, northeast Wales.

Kwmtwrk Ukha: Cwntwrc, a valley north of Swansea.

Lagoon, the: Poole Harbour, Dorset

Land of the Blue Stones: the Brecon Beacons.

Lead Mountains/Hills, the: the Brecon Beacons.

Leodis: Leeds, West Yorkshire.

Lhangors: Llangors, Brecon.

Lindsey: the area of Lincolnshire.

Logres: the southern part of Britain in this book; now the name used by the Welsh for England.

Lusitania: Portugal.

Margam: near Port Talbot, Glamorgan.

Marsh/Meer: the Somerset Levels.

Menevia: St Davids, Pembrokeshire.

Merlin's Town: Caermathen.

Mona: Anglesey.

Montgai: Montgailleard-Lauragais, Haute Garonne, France.

Mydhvai: Myddfai in Carmarthenshire.

Narbon: Narbonne, Languedoc-Rousillon, France.

Ogwr: near Bridgend, Mid-Glamorgan.

Old Harry: rocks at Studland, Poole, Dorset.

Penklawth: Penclawdd, Gower, Glamorgan.

Porthskewett: village in Monmouthshire.

Ratae: Leicester.

Ross: Ross-on-Wye.

Salem: Jerusalem.

Scania: Sweden.

Segont: Segontium or Caernarvon, Gwynedd.

Septimania: Western region of Gallia Narbonensis that came under
    Visigothic rule, corresponding to modern Languedoc-Roussillon.

Seres: the silk lands of the East.

Skirid: Ysgyryd Fawr, the holy mountain in the Black Mountains,
    Monmouthshire.

Solva: the north Pembrokeshire coast, St Bride's Bay.

Summer Country, the: Somerset.

Tolosa: Toulouse, Haute-Garonne, France.

Trapran: Traprain Law, 6 kilometres east of Haddington, East Lothian,
    Scotland.

Usk: the river Usk in Monmouthshire.

Vale of Klydakh: Clydach, Swansea, Glam.

Viricon: Vironium, Wroxeter, Shropshire.

Ynys Witrin: Island of Glass, Glastonbury.

Acknowledgements

Our thanks and appreciation to Penny Billington, for following the trail to the lost manuscript; to Helen Jones and David James for allowing us to complete their father's work; and to Neil Gaiman, Jo Fletcher and Peter Buckman for their encouragement and belief in the whole project.

Caitlín and John Matthews
Oxford, 2014

Turn over for your bonus content!

The Magical Making of Swords

The following note on the magical crafting of swords was among the papers found after John James' death. It is so much a part of the way he saw the ancient world that it feels appropriate to add it here.

J & C Matthews, 2014

A great sword is forged from iron of the weight of the sword heated white in charcoal and hammered into a bar twice the length of the sword, this then doubled, heated white again, twisted and hammered in charcoal to weld it together. And again and again, depending on patience, till the final sword is made from up to 128 strands. It is then tempered by being immersed in a box of charcoal buried in a pyre of burning wood for days and nights on end. After each heating, the iron is quenched to cool it suddenly (this is to prevent crystallisation in the slowly cooling metal but the mediaeval makers didn't know that, nor that the continued hammering in charcoal was to dissolve carbon in the iron to make steel.)

It is quenched first in the blood of birds, to give it lightness (preferably of wrens which fly the highest and are so light that an eagle will not notice that it is carrying one on its back). Next it is quenched in the blood of hares, to give it speed, then in the blood of serpents, to give it subtlety. (For a fishhook the blood of eels may be substituted here.) This is enough for an arrowhead or a spearhead, and in the best swords it is usual to work in an arrowhead that has killed a target. Then it is quenched in the blood of an ox to give it strength, then in the blood of a horse that has just been ridden for a day and a night and a day again, to give it endurance. Then the blood of a lion if available, otherwise of a wild cat, to give it fierceness. And last, which is why swords cannot be forged by Christian men, in the blood of a very old woman, to give it long memory of what it must do.

Caledbarn/Caliburn/Excalibur was heated and quenched an eighth time, in the breath of a Dragon, and then in its heart's blood.

John James

Morvran and the Survivors of Camlan

by Caitlín Matthews

In *The Fourth Gwenevere,* John James makes its narrator, Morvran, a descendant of Photinus, the hero of *Votan and Not for All the Gold in Ireland,* his earlier novels. In these stories that are linked through time, Morvran is descended from this Greek adventurer who slept with Buddog the Bitch, the queen of the Votadini people, to repeople the generations to come. Morfran's fictional character has been woven into the hinterland of British myth with expert cunning, as we shall see.

John James conned his Welsh myths so thoroughly that he was able to interweave many useful threads into his narrative, but one that stands hanging at the end of the book is the fate of Morvran and those who live on after the death of Arthur. Anyone who has studied the Arthurian legend in all its variety will know that the mediaeval myths mark Arthur's passing at the Battle of Camlann and that is about that for the Matter of Britain. But the Welsh traditions speak of some men who survive.

To the Welsh poets, Camlann was considered the byword in messy and unnecessary battles. Unlike the earlier battles of Arthur that were fought against the invading Saxons, Angles and Jutes, Camlann was a civil strife between Arthur's faction and another faction, later said to be Mordred's. The poets even made up an adjective out of the battle, *cadgamlan,* meaning 'messed-up'. (Even in James' novel, 'Camlaan' becomes Constant's attempt to replicate the tent-city of Arthur's fabled Camelot – a place that relocates as the tents are reset, so that no one location can claim it.) This very confusion of half-seen, half-understood deeds is what makes the central premise of James' novel so piquant: a squabble over the purloining of a pig, which results in the wreck of Britain.

Morvran himself comes with a mythic pedigree that connects him with the figure of Morfran ap Tegid, the ugliest man in the world. This mythic character is born of the powerful enchantress Ceridwen who, on seeing her baby's misshapen ugliness, calls him 'Great Crow' (Morfran) and determines to compensate him with the gift of great wisdom. Like the lady in Llanelli's rugby song, Sosban Fach (little saucepan), Ceridwen, over the course of a year, fills a cauldron with all the herbs and properties of each season, and when done, the brew will have distilled into the essentialisation of all wisdom – in just three little drops. It would all have turned out well, except that the little boy set to tend the fire, Gwion Bach, was too enthusiastic with the firewood, and on the very eve of the brew's alchemical transformation, the contents of the cauldron bubbled up and those precious drops fell on the servant boy's hand, and when he thrust his hand into his mouth to cool the burning liquor, *he* became the wisest person alive. And so Morvran was left just ugly, and the main narrator of the Arthurian myth is instead the poet Taliesin – who, as a little boy, was known as Gwion Bach.

In the Welsh texts, the survivors of the Battle of Camlann are like the Good, the Bad and the Ugly: each of them avoids death due to their distinctive character or appearance. This is how they appear in the eleventh-century tale of 'Culhwch and Olwen', one of the tales of the *Mabinogion*:

> 'Morfran, son of Tegid (no one struck him in the battle of Camlann by reason of his ugliness: all thought he was an auxiliary devil. Hair had he upon him like the hair of a stag).
>
> Sandde Bryd Angel (no one touched him with a spear in the battle of Camlann because of his beauty; all thought he was a ministering angel).
>
> And Kynwyl Sant (the third man that escaped from the battle of Camlann, and he was the last who parted from Arthur on Hengroen his horse).

Neither Sandde Bryd Angel nor St Kynwyl appear in *The Fourth Gwenevere*, since Morfran himself takes up the cudgels for all three of them in his defence of Britain.

A somewhat later Welsh tradition rounds up eight survivors, rather than three:

> 'Here are the names of the men who escaped from the battle of Camlann: Sandde Bryd Angel (Angel's form) because of his beauty, Morfran ap Tegid, because of his ugliness, St Cynfelyn from the speed of his horse, St Cedwyn from the world's blessing, St Pedrog from the strength of his spear, Derfel Gadarn (the Strong) from his strength, Geneid the tall from his speed. The year of Christ when the battle of Camlann took place was 542.'

From the *Fourth Gwenevere*, we can easily recognise the kinds of saints these last reverend gentlemen might be: the ones who rise up in the last chapter to utter a mighty oath, drink a noble cup of mead and play merry hell with anyone caught messing with the sacred island of Britain.

The poets could not leave this theme alone. William Blake himself was inspired by the Arthurian legend. He saw a close resonance between Albion, the ancient land of Britain, and the myths of Arthur: 'The Acts of Arthur are the deeds of Albion applied to a Prince of the fifth century who conquered Europe and held the empire of the world in the dark age, which the Romans never again recovered . . . All the fables of Arthur and his round table; of the warlike naked Britons; of Merlin; of Arthur's conquest of the whole world; of his death or sleep, and promise to return again . . . All these things are written in Eden.'

Taking this story of the survivors of Camlann, Blake subsumed it into his own archetypal, poetic mythos: 'In the last battle of King Arthur, only three Britons escaped, these were the Strongest man (the human sublime), the Beautifullest Man (the human pathetic) which was in the wars of Eden divided into male and female . . . and the ugliest Man (the human reason) these three marched through the field unsubdued, as Gods and the Sun of Britain set, but shall arise again with tenfold splendor when Arthur shall awake from sleep, and resume his dominion over earth and ocean . . . They were originally one man, who was fourfold, he was self-divided and his real humanity slain on the stems of generation and the form of the fourth (Los) was like the Son of God.'

In *The Fourth Gwenevere*, the high-living kings and nobles certainly comprise all these characteristics and more, in their devious loyalties, their unwavering self-interest and their unquenchable justification in all things British. Only Morfran stands clear, unreliable narrator as he is, with the skills and honour that set him among these fabled survivors as the hero of this novel.

ADDITIONAL READING

Morris Eaves and S. Foster Damon, *A Blake Dictionary*, Brown University Press, 1988

D. Gwenallt Jones ed., *Yr Areuthiau Pros*, Cardiff, University of Wales Press, 1934

Sioned Davies ed., *The Mabinogion*, Oxford University Press, 2008

Caitlín Matthews, *King Arthur and the Goddess of the Land*, Inner Traditions, 1996

John Matthews, *Taliesin: The Last Celtic Shaman*, Inner Traditions, 2002